THEODORE ROETHKE

Jay Parini

THEODORE ROETHKE

An American Romantic

University of Massachusetts Press   Amherst, 1979

For my mother and father, with love

CONTENTS

Since the publication of *Open House* in 1941,
critics have been at work on Theodore Roethke,
trying to come to terms with a poet of major
standing in American literature. Among the
earliest critics were W. H. Auden, Stanley Kunitz, and Kenneth Burke, and their pioneering
essays are still useful. But it is only since the
poet's death in 1963 that we have had Roethke's
work before us, making it possible to find the
larger patterns in his work. A clutch of intro-
ductory surveys and specialized studies has already appeared, and no doubt this is only the
beginning. For no single reading of any good
poet is final. Just as each new generation of
poets modifies the view of the previous one, so
critics participate in an ongoing critical act. The
individual critic's eye may be thought of as a
lens that colors a particular text; of course, the
better the critic, the lighter the tint, but absolute transparency remains a hypothetical ideal.
Criticism is, at its practical best, collaborative;
we are lucky in this regard, for a critical milieu
has materialized around Roethke. I have used
this situation to my advantage in this study,
making clear my innumerable debts throughout.
This is not simply an introduction to Roethke's
Collected Poems. It is an attempt to isolate major
patterns in the work, to discover the poet's mythos, and to relate his body of writing to the
Romantic tradition, its proper context. Roethke
was a remarkably self-conscious artist, fully
aware of his predecessors and his relation to
them. This relationship is complex, for Roethke
was not merely an imitator of other poets; he
carried on what amounts to an elaborate dia-

logue with his Romantic predecessors, and the exact nature of this dialogue is studied. In particular, Emerson is singled out throughout as a
major influence, and one rarely discussed before this.

The study begins with an overview of Roethke's poetry in the context
of American Romanticism, traced back to its source in Emerson. It defines the personal mythos and nature of Roethke's personal symbol system, suggesting that the autobiographical myth of the greenhouse Eden
is this poet's subject, the central image in his work from beginning to
end. This fact is easily blurred by the radical stylistic changes which
occur at various stages in his career. These changes remain, it appears,
superficial; the poet merely extends or refines his chosen subject. The
second chapter focuses on the apprentice years, the decade preceding
Open House, when Roethke discovered a poetics, a Romantic poetics, and
learned about poetry-as-collaboration. He learned the art of creative imitation from his mentors, Rolfe Humphries, Louise Bogan, and Stanley
Kunitz; this attitude would allow him throughout his career to be
strongly influenced, but not overpowered, by other poets. The brief third
chapter offers an abstract of Romanticism as Roethke himself saw it.
This chapter is referred to throughout the study, which moves from it
to a detailed reading of Roethke's poetry as the most important contribution to the literature of American Romanticism since Wallace Stevens.
The text proceeds chronologically through the *Collected Poems*, a method
dictated by the organic shape of Roethke's work, which unfolds with
uncanny integrity as if inheriting its single possible form.

I have drawn heavily throughout on unpublished material from the
Roethke Collection in possession of the University of Washington's Suz-
zallo Library, a cornucopia of manuscript drafts of poems, notebooks,
letters, and teaching materials. I am grateful to Beatrice Roethke Lush-
ington for permission to roam freely through this Roethkean harvest.
While doing this primary research I benefited from discussion with
three poets whom I wish especially to thank: David Wagoner, Richard
Hugo, and Richard Blessing. Various eyes have passed over this book
in its many drafts, but special thanks are due to the following friends for
their sympathy and intelligent guidance: A. H. Ashe and A. F. Falconer
of the University of St. Andrews, Philip Hobsbaum of Glasgow University, Thomas Vance, James A. W. Heffernan, David Wykes, and
Philip Holland of Dartmouth College, Gordon Williams of Yale University, Richard Ellmann of Oxford University and Ralph J. Mills, Jr.,
of the University of Illinois. Portions of this book have appeared, in

earlier form, in the following: *Antaeus, The Texas Quarterly, The Ball State University Forum*, and *Blake and the Moderns*, ed. Robert Bertholf and Annette Levitt (Kent State University Press). I am grateful to Doubleday and Company for permission to quote from *The Collected Poems of Theodore Roethke* (copyright © 1966 by Beatrice Roethke), and to Devon Jersild for help in preparation of the index.

J. P.—*Hanover, New Hampshire*

PART ONE

THE MAKING OF A POET

CHAPTER ONE

AMERICAN ROMANTIC

There is at the back of every artist's mind something like a pattern or type of architecture. The original quality in any man of imagination is imagery. It is a thing like the landscape of his dreams; the sort of world he would like to make or in which he would wish to wander; the strange flora and fauna of his own secret planet, the sort of thing he likes to think about. This general atmosphere, and pattern or structure of growth, governs all his creations, however varied.

G. K. Chesterton

This book offers, in effect, a map of Theodore Roethke's secret planet; it is an attempt to reconstruct his mental world, to discern the pattern at the back of his mind as it is revealed by his poems. Roethke was a great poet, the successor to Frost and Stevens in modern American poetry, and it is the measure of his greatness that his work repays detailed examination. Roethke saw himself as working within a great tradition, modifying and extending it after his own fashion. Specifically, Roethke was a Romantic. His work abounds in references to Blake, Wordsworth, and Yeats, especially, but my stress is upon the American quality of his Romanticism with Emerson and Whitman as primary ancestors, with Stevens as a strong contemporary influence. Without impugning his originality, one can read all Roethke's work as a continuing conversation with his precursors; he was a poetic ventriloquist of sorts, able to speak through masks of those whom he called "the great dead." Still, there is a voice at his core which is unmistakably his own. He has his special province, a landscape so personal and distinct that no amount of imitation or writing-like-somebody-else, as he called it, disturbs the integrity of his voice. His poetic world is self-contained and secure.

As my epigraph suggests, the genius behind any imaginative work has something to do with imagery. Roethke's verse from *Open House* (1941) to the posthumous *The Far Field* (1964) displays a consistent and vivid imagery found only in the greatest writing. His images derive from the dream world of his Michigan childhood, and one soon finds that a few key symbols operate throughout his work, most important the Father (who is alternately the poet's biological father, Otto Roethke, or God), the greenhouse, and the open field (where illuminations generally occur). There are minor symbols in this cluster, too—the wind (spirit), the stone (associated with transcendental experiences) and the tree (selfhood). The image of Woman as mother, lover, or sister is present from the beginning, taking on greater significance in the middle and later periods. The central figure in all the poems is Roethke in his mythic projection as the "lost son." Indeed, the "Lost Son" sequence, published between 1948 and 1953, represents this poet's most permanent contribution to modern poetry. The later part of the sequence, called *Praise to the End!*, takes its title from Wordsworth's consummate autobiographical poem, *The Prelude*; it was no doubt a conscious effort on Roethke's part to identify himself with this primary Romantic mode. I explore these connections fully later in this study, for Roethke is a poet of the egotistical sublime (to use Keats's description of Wordsworth). He appropriates for himself those parts of the world that make up the imagery or world picture at the back of his mind. These images became the signposts of his secret planet, and we can know Roethke best by knowing his entire work, by following his personal development from unrealized potential to self-discovery and, ultimately, self-transcendence.

Roethke's poetry will never be properly understood unless read within the context of Romanticism in its American manifestation. The work of recent critics has been invaluable in showing the breadth and continuity of the Romantic movement from its origins in eighteenth-century Germany to the present.[1] What seems constant in this nearly intractable movement is the recognition that every man is cut off from nature; given this state of affairs, art becomes indispensable in the process of reconciliation between self and nature (subject and object). Every man has either to make his peace with nature or wage his own "war between the mind and sky" (as Stevens called it).

If the European man of feeling considered himself alienated from nature, the American found his isolation all the more intense. Emerson, Thoreau, Whitman, Melville, and Hawthorne felt cut off from the old world culture; they were isolated men, forced to depend on their personal resources for inspiration and fulfillment. Even more so than English Romantics, the American Transcendentalists were dependent upon German idealism. As Emerson said: "What is properly called Transcendentalism among us: is Idealism; Idealism as it appears in 1842. As thinkers, mankind has ever divided into two sects, Materialists and Idealists; the first class founding on experience, the second on consciousness; the first class beginning to think from the data of the sense, the second perceive that the senses are not final, and say, The senses give us representations of things, but what are the things themselves, they cannot tell."[2] Emerson's far-reaching influence on some later American poets has been demonstrated, but not for Roethke,[3] although his tendency toward idealism in the later poetry can be traced directly back to Emerson's essays. Nevertheless, Roethke's attraction to the world of objects was undiminished by his belief, which he took from Emerson, that nature was the symbol of the spirit. Indeed, few poets have evoked the physical world in such concrete terms. In this, Roethke seems closer to Thoreau than Emerson, for Thoreau's nature was at once sensuously concrete *and* spiritual. One critic of Thoreau has said: "As a man studies the details of nature he discovers himself; he learns the spiritual and natural laws that operate in him and give him hope and being. Thoreau was as assiduous as Jonathan Edwards in seeking out these correspondences, these images and shadows of human things. . . . His exhaustive and obsessive effort in his journals to catalogue botanical facts as they appeared in the course of the seasons was based on the premise that he might thereby discover natural, seasonal rhythms in the human unconscious."[4] Similar claims can be made for Roethke.

Romantic poets share the concept of "nature as a living whole," an organic unity that somehow points to a spiritual realm and relates to man.[5] One can see how the doctrine of correspondences follows naturally from this conception. In *The Prelude* the growth of the poet's mind parallels his increasing awareness of nature's divine presence. The child, according to Wordsworth, has a special relationship with nature; its world suffers no radical division. Only with adulthood does the sense of isolation intervene; so the task for poetry becomes the process of recapturing lost time through the exploitation of memory. Both Yeats and Stevens in this century have seen the poet's task in similar terms, Yeats in his lifelong quest for Unity of Being (in which the soul recovers what he called "radical innocence") and Stevens in his search for "the supreme fiction" (after Baudelaire's *la plus haute fiction*). Roethke was devoted to both Yeats and Stevens, acknowledging his debt to them many times. His quest for the greenhouse Eden, as Louis L. Martz called Roethke's childhood dream world, imitates the quest patterns of the other great Romantics, although the greenhouse has more in common historically with Blake's Beulah (where nature is threatened by chaos and darkness) than Yeats's Byzantium or Stevens's wholly fictive realm, where nature is left behind.[6]

To long for a purity not available *within* nature or the natural processes is a common Romantic urge, and Roethke does not escape its pull. One critic[7] points to the poem called "Snake," where Roethke notices a young snake drawing away and says:

> I felt my slow blood warm.
> I longed to be that thing,
> The pure, sensuous form.
>
> And I may be, some time.[8]

It would seem contradictory that this form could be both "pure" and "sensuous," but Roethke wants to relinquish nothing. Like Stevens, he believes that "the greatest poverty is not to live / In a physical world. . . ."[9] He seeks out "that anguish of concreteness"—a total immersion *within* nature. In the early poem "Epidermal Macabre," Roethke, again, wishes the body away, but the spirit he longs for remains carnal:

> And willingly would I dispense
> With false accouterments of sense,
> To sleep immodestly, a most
> Incarnadine and carnal ghost.
> (CP, p. 19)

Yeats makes a similar wish in *The Tower*, and Roethke is as much a Platonist as his Irish master. His one pure expression of the body-spirit dichotomy occurs in the late poem "Infirmity" where the gradual separation of these previously integrated elements is acknowledged: "How body from spirit slowly does unwind / Until we are pure spirit in the end" (CP, p. 244). But this unwinding comes only after the body ceases to provide joy, in either old age or sickness. For the most part, Roethke accepts his physical state as something worthy of celebration. The body is the source of all energy. It is part of the natural world and, in the highest state of consciousness, self and other intermingle. Self-possession becomes world possession, as in "The Long Waters":

> I lose and find myself in the long water;
> I am gathered together once more;
> I embrace the world.
> (CP, p. 198)

Like Wordsworth, Whitman, and Yeats, Roethke was writing the poetry of autobiography, working with the materials of his own life and shaping them into a personal myth or mythos in Northrop.Frye's sense of the term as a general organizing principle of literary form. Coming well *after* the discovery of psychoanalysis, Roethke had available a vocabulary and technique for invading the unconscious dimension. When he became interested in psychoanalysis through Kenneth Burke, his colleague at Bennington in 1942, his poetry moved into the arena of greatness. But *Open House* did not suggest the beginning of a major career. With the advantage of hindsight, one can go back and find in it themes that flow into Roethke's later vein, but at the time no one knew what was coming. Roethke himself was pessimistic about his talents. He later wrote: "It took me ten years to complete one little book, and now some of the things in it seem to creak. Still, I like about ten pieces in it."[10] *Open House* will be examined later, for it serves as a prelude to Roethke's career, and the contrast between this apprentice volume and *The Lost Son* (1948) is startling. The question is what happened to the poet in the early and mid-forties to effect his transformation from minor versifier to major poet? How did the discovery of psychoanalysis work in the poet to release his imaginative energies?

The answer involves Roethke's relationship to the Romantic movement as it developed in America. An important clue is offered by Norman O. Brown in *Life Against Death*:

> If psychoanalysis must say that instincts, which at the level of animality are in a harmonious unity, are separated at the level of humanity and set into conflict with each other, and that mankind will not rest content until it is able to abolish these conflicts and restore harmony, but at the higher level of consciousness, then once again it appears that psychoanalysis completes the romantic movement and is understood only if interpreted in that light. *It is one of the great romantic visions.*[11]

Indeed, what Roethke discovered in this crucial period of his career was exactly what Wordsworth seems to have realized at Alfoxden: the use of memory. Roethke nearly always kept a journal after 1929, first as a graduate student at Michigan and then at Harvard. In the thirties, these journals are really working notebooks; they contain rough drafts of poems, odd lines that came into his head which might possibly be useful for a poem one day—but nothing personal apart from the record of a few dreams. Not until he met Kenneth Burke and began to take psychoanalysis seriously did the journals come alive. Suddenly, the reader of these mostly unpublished pages finds a poet searching his memory, working his way back in time, confronting in a most brutal and direct fashion the primal imagery at the source of his deepest conflicts. Roethke explained: "To write about one's past is not to escape but to understand the present." And again: "I go back because I want to go forward."[12] Or in this beautiful line from another journal of the period: "All the present has fallen: I am only what I remember."[13] One cannot understand the original method of Roethke's poems after 1948 without seeing how he adapted the techniques of analysis in a special way, relating them to Romantic poetics, to extend if not complete (as Brown suggests) the historical movement called Romanticism.

One central source of conflict for Roethke was his father's death when he was fifteen. He returns to this painful experience of loss throughout his career, always seeking that final atonement where conflicts are abolished and harmony is restored. I doubt whether he attained this goal, but perhaps he didn't really want to; this conflict proved a wealthy source of poetry. From this single life-crisis, Roethke generated his mythos, a world of luminous personal symbols. Otto, the father, lords over this dream world; he is the "garden master" (as Rosemary Sullivan has called Roethke himself in an excellent book).[14] Otto metamorphoses into God in the later poems, but this God is curiously like Otto: loving and terrible at once, a symbol of immense power and wrath, more like the Jehovah who punished Job than the gentler Elohim who visited Adam and Eve in the garden. Otto Roethke's father had come from Prussia in 1870 to Saginaw, Michigan, and started the greenhouses which caught the poet's imagination. Roethke says: "It was a wonderful place for a child to grow up in and around. There were not only twenty-five acres in the town, mostly under glass and intensely cultivated, but farther out in the country the last stand of virgin timber in the Saginaw Valley and, elsewhere, a wild area of cut-over second-growth timber, which my father and uncle made into a small game preserve" (SP, p. 8).

The greenhouse as a symbol was obviously rich in possibilities. In the journals, Roethke explores its full meaning: "What was this greenhouse? It was a jungle, and it was paradise; it was order and disorder. Was it an escape? No, for it was a reality harder than the various suspensions of terror."[15] There is an ambivalence here; this "greenhouse Eden" is not William Blake's Eden, wherein all the natural processes are completed, the contraries resolved. Again, it seems closer to Blake's lower paradise, Beulah, that "married land" sung of by the prophet Isaiah. Far from the transcendental state of resolution, the greenhouse stands for process, for generation. It is paradisiacal in its lushness, its proliferation of beautiful sights and smells, and its perfectly controlled atmosphere, protected from the wilderness outside its walls. But this paradise remains unnatural, artificial. Only the massive effort of the florist-father keeps it going through winter. It is analogous with the family itself, that hothouse where a child matures in the constant temperature of parental protection. The poem "Forcing House" comes to mind:

> Vines tougher than wrists
> And rubbery shoots,
> Scums, mildews, smuts along stems,
> Great cannas or delicate cyclamen tips,—
> All pulse with the knocking pipes
> That drip and sweat,
> Sweat and drip,
> Swelling the roots with steam and stench,
> Shooting up lime and dung and ground bones,—
> Fifty summers in motion at once,
> As the live heat billows from pipes and pots.
> (*CP.* p. 38)

The jungle aspect of Roethke's paradise cannot be avoided; the rubbery shoots that dangle and droop, the vines that reach out for something to wind around: these terrify the child. To press the analogy one step further, family affection threatens the child's tender ego with extinction; the father-son struggle witnessed in Roethke becomes part of the son's efforts to establish identity. Because Otto died at a crucial stage in young Theodore's development, the son never had the chance to complete this primal warfare.

What fascinates me is Roethke's willful plunge into the unconscious to find the symbols that would ground his poetry in a reality that is at the same time particular and mythic, autobiographically true and metaphorically resonant. We may gain insight into how Roethke achieved this balance by looking into Emerson's important essay, "The Poet." He writes: "The poet . . . puts eyes and a tongue into every dumb and inanimate object. He perceives the independence of the thought on the symbol, the stability of the thought, the accidency and fugacity of the symbol. As the eyes of Lyncaeus were said to see through the earth, so the poet turns the world to glass, and shows us all things in their right series and procession."[16] If Roethke's greenhouse was nothing more than a personal detail of one man's life, it would cease to interest us; instead, he has turned the greenhouse world into a symbol for all that is miraculous, lovely, and threatening about the life cycle. Blessing rephrases the Emersonian notion of perceiving "the thought on the symbol" when he says "the relationships among the concrete figures of a poem may be analogous to the relationships among a potentially infinite number of abstract ideas, and that as the relationships in the literary work shift and develop, so, too, do the ideas they may represent shift and develop.

Roethke, by using as few abstractions as possible and by insisting that, for the most part, both tenor and vehicle of his metaphors will be rooted in the physical world, has left the range of interpretation almost as wide as did the original greenhouse in which he grew up."[17] In other words, Roethke has allowed each symbol to stand naked in all its "anguish of concreteness," and this allows the reader a special burden of interpretation. It was Ezra Pound who warned the apprentice poet never to say "dim lands of peace"; "dim lands" must suffice, if the poet knows how to write. Roethke did know how, of course; his greenhouse poems, especially, are among the most concrete (and symbolically charged) that have been written in this century.

One can read the "Lost Son" sequence on many levels. Karl Malkoff really laid the groundwork for interpretation in his seminal commentary on the sequence; he singles out the movement of the protagonist through early adolescence into sexual maturity, and this literal plot should never get too far out of sight.[18] But these poems have a symbolic richness exceeding the basic plot; the generalizing energy of myth takes control from the beginning of the sequence; the tension between tenor (autobiographical fact) and vehicle (myth) never relaxes for a moment. The poem is Romantic in essence, related directly to that genre of quest-romance so often described by Frye and Bloom—the journey toward home, the hero's necessary pilgrimage. *The Odyssey* remains the prototype of this genre, and one thing that never changes is the bereft condition of the traveler. He has lost an original state of bliss; like Dante's bewildered hero, the poet-pilgrim, he finds himself in a dark wood from which he must escape. In Blake's version of this basic myth, the contraries of existence constitute the dark wood that must be escaped. The modern hero has Milton's Satan for an ancestor, the Promethean figure who battles for his own redemption with little real hope for success. The High Romantics from Wordsworth through Yeats internalized this myth, which made the quest for self (and self-transcendence) the proper subject for poetry. The movement is from the discovery of the natural self to self-liberation through the redemptive powers of imagination, although, as Bloom says, "the imagination's freedom is frequently purgatorial, redemptive in direction but destructive of the social self."[19]

The "Lost Son" sequence is incomplete in that the quest never ends; the journey is regressive, and each step forward seems to precede two steps backward. The hero periodically lands on islands that promise to be home, but Circe and Calypso soon appear and he sees that Ithaca, self-realization, adulthood, and transcendental apocalypse are far away, an impossible shore. *The Far Field* represents the final stage in this mythic

journey. It is Roethke's *Paradiso*. But it has much more in common with
Emerson (and Whitman) than any European source. The title poem,
"The Far Field," is one further ring widening out from Emerson's central text, *Nature* (1836): "Crossing a bare common, in snow puddles, at
twilight, under a clouded sky, without having in my thoughts any oc-
currence of special good fortune, I have enjoyed a perfect exhilaration.
Almost I fear to think how glad I am. In the woods too, a man casts off
his years, as the snake his slough, and at what period soever of life, is
always a child. In the woods, is perpetual youth."[20] Roethke writes in this
vein: "For to come upon warblers in early May / Was to forget time and
death"—

> —Or to lie naked in sand,
> In the silted shallows of a slow river,
> Fingering a shell.
> Thinking:
> Once I was something like this, mindless,
> Or perhaps with another mind, less peculiar;
> Or to sink down to the hips in a mossy quagmire;
> Or, with skinny knees, to sit astride a wet log,
> Believing:
> I'll return again,
> As a snake or a raucous bird,
> Or, with luck, as a lion.
> (*CP*, pp. 199–200)

It was Matthew Arnold who called Emerson the friend and the aider of
anyone who would live in the spirit, and Roethke is the latest major
American poet to benefit from this help.

Emerson adapted from Coleridge the idea that the "ruin or the blank,
that we see when we look at nature, is in our own eye. The axis of vision
is not coincident with the axis of things, and so they appear not transparent but opaque."[21] Poetic vision, then, becomes the coincidental alignment of one's personal axis with that of nature's. It is seeing into the
heart of things. This liberates the poet from his dependence on culture,
for the source of real knowledge is within him already. In this ideal state
of transparency, the inner and outer realms come together. Everything
in nature remains itself, a separate thing, but a luminous symbol as well,
an analogue to the interior paradise. Roethke took over Emerson's so-
called doctrine of correspondences entirely, in one late poem announcing his experience of "A steady storm of correspondences!" (*CP*, p. 239).
According to this doctrine, every landscape becomes, in effect, a mor-
alized landscape. Because the ruin is in his own eye, the poet reads into

nature his spiritual condition, or better, he discovers the appropriate symbol in nature, whether it suggests joy or desolation.

Roethke liked to count himself "one of the happy poets" though his poems often move through purgatorial stages, sometimes willfully, as he acknowledges in "The Long Waters":

> And I acknowledge my foolishness with God,
> My desire for the peaks, the black ravines, the rolling mists
> Changing with every twist of wind,
> The unsinging fields where no lungs breathe,
> Where light is stone.
> I return where fire has been,
> To the charred edge of the sea
> Where the yellowish prongs of grass poke through the blackened ash,
> And the bunched logs peel in the afternoon sunlight. . . .
> (CP, p. 196)

This desire for the peaks and ravines is typically Romantic; as in Wordsworth, Roethke's periods of disintegration were a necessary part of the soul's progress from paradise lost to paradise restored. This involves a play of polarities such as one finds in Blake, Wordsworth, and Whitman, not a systematic dialectic of any kind, but as a critic has said of Wordsworth: "[one finds in him] a very strong habit of thinking in terms of paired opposites or contrarieties. Everywhere in nature, in individual man and in society, [he] saw a constant interplay of opposing forces."[22] It is the image of the journey that controls this dialectic of opposites in *The Prelude*, which Abrams calls "Wordsworth's account of unity achieved, lost and regained."[23] Like Dante's traveler who found himself lost, but to wonderful advantage in the end, Wordsworth undertook his fearful journey aided by the spirit of Coleridge, to whom the entire poem is addressed, and a number of guides who are analogous to Dante's Virgil or Beatrice:

> A Traveller I am,
> And all my Tale is of myself; even so,
> So be it, if the pure in heart delight
> To follow me; and Thou, O honor'd Friend!
> Who in my thoughts art ever at my side,
> Uphold as heretofore, my fainting steps.[24]

Roethke called on similar spiritual aid in "The Abyss":

> Be with me, Whitman, maker of catalogues:
> For the world invades me again,

And once more the tongues begin babbling.
And the terrible hunger for objects quails me:
The sill trembles.
(*CP*, p. 220)

In this moment of spiritual crisis, he demands a native guide, but one thoroughly apprised of the Romantic contrarieties: "I am not the poet of goodness only," said Whitman in *Song of Myself*, "I do not decline to be the poet of wickedness also."[25] "The Lost Son" poem itself describes the loss and partial restoration of unity, and the sequence of poems that follows traces the regressive journey of the poet-protagonist from adolescence back to the womb, into the perfect state of bliss that precedes the fall into creation. After *The Waking* (1953) Roethke begins "the long journey out of the self" (*CP*, p. 193) which takes him through the antithetical quest of his Yeatsean period into the Whitmanesque last poems of *The Far Field*. The details of this journey, archetypal in poetry, are the subject of this study.

In *Natural Supernaturalism* (a phrase adapted from Carlyle) Abrams reflects: "Life is the premise and paradigm for what is most innovative and distinctive in Romantic thinkers. Hence their vitalism: the celebration of that which lives, moves, and evolves by an internal energy, over whatever is lifeless, inert, and unchanging."[26] Roethke, like no other poet since Whitman, made the subject of his poetry the celebration of everything that moves with organic life, including the self in its dynamic interplay with the natural world. Nothing that lives can be less than amazing, as Whitman declared:

I believe a leaf of grass is no less than the journey-work of the stars,
And the pismire is equally perfect, and the egg of the wren,
And the tree-toad is a chef-d'oeuvre for the highest,
And the running blackberry would adorn the parlors of heaven,
And the narrowest hinge in my hand puts to scorn all machinery,
And the cow crunching with depress'd head surpasses any statue,
And a mouse is miracle enough to stagger sextillions of infidels.

Throughout *Song of Myself* the single leaf of grass is taken for the symbol of organic life, that which is most amazing in all creation: "A child said *What is the grass?* fetching it to me with full hands; / How could I answer the child? I do not know what it is any more than he."[27] He does not know exactly, but he thinks of it as the type of everything that flourishes and dies. This is the great Romantic metaphor and the source of that final optimism we attach to Blake, Wordsworth, Emerson, Whitman, and Roethke.

Whitman's acceptance of reality, his celebration of each separate fact, whether good or evil, coincides with his master's; Emerson wrote in his last chapter of *Nature*: "To the wise, therefore, a fact is true poetry, and the most beautiful of fables. These wonders are brought to our own door. You also are a man. Man and woman, and their social life, poverty, labor, sleep, fear, fortune, are known to you. Learn that none of these things is superficial, but that each phenomenon hath its roots in the faculties and affections of the mind."[28] Because the ruin or blank in nature is in our own eye, we must re-establish our line of vision, our axis of real sight, with the natural world. It is a question of aligning the essentially identical structures of subjective and objective realms (mind and nature). McIntosh points to a passage in Schelling behind this:

> So long as I am *identical* with nature, I understand my own life; I realize how this general life of nature reveals itself in the most various forms, in step-by-step developments, in gradual approaches to freedom. But as soon as I separate myself (and with me the whole ideal realm) from nature, nothing remains for me but a dead object and I cease to understand how a *life outside* me is possible.[29]

The fear behind this, of course, is the loss of contact with anything outside the individual mind, solipsistic withdrawal and detachment. So one must actively seek to contact nature; according to Emerson, to realize the correspondences; to make the natural world an extension of one's body; to connect the private self with the infinitely greater self which is transcendent.

This was Roethke's effort from his middle years to the end of his life:

> To have the whole air!—
> The light, the full sun
> Coming down on the flowerheads,
> The tendrils turning slowly,
> A slow snail-lifting, liquescent;
> To be by the rose
> Rising slowly out of its bed,
> Still as a child in its first loneliness;
> To see cyclamen veins become clearer in early sunlight,
> And mist lifting out of the brown cat-tails;
> To stare into the after-light, the glitter left on the lake's surface,
> When the sun has fallen behind a wooded island;
> To follow the drops sliding from a lifted oar,
> Held up, while the rower breathes, and the small boat drifts quietly
>   shoreward;

To know that light falls and fills, often without our knowing,
As an opaque vase fills to the brim from a quick pouring,
Fills and trembles at the edge yet does not flow over,
Still holding and feeding the stem of the contained flower.
(*CP*, p. 67)

This epiphany, summarized by the last two images—the rower in equipoise, gliding, and the transient flower in its vase, filled to brimming—is directly in the Emersonian line of vision. Contact with nature has been established, and the poet has found his identity *in relation to* nature, not outside of it.

Once the self gathers enough stability to engage nature in vital conflict, the transcendental journey out of the self begins. Roethke accomplished this selfhood in the *Praise to the End!* poems and the wonderful love elegies of his middle period ("Words for the Wind" and "Four for Sir John Davies" especially). His last volume comprises that "long journey out of the self," for in this book, *The Far Field*, Roethke's transcendental glimmerings find ultimate expression:

Near this rose, in this grove of sun-parched, wind-warped madronas,
Among the half-dead trees, I came upon the true ease of myself,
As if another man appeared out of the depths of my being,
And I stood outside myself,
Beyond becoming and perishing,
A something wholly other,
As if I swayed out on the wildest wave alive,
And yet was still.
(*CP*, p. 205)

Here he continues the Emersonian program taken up in various ways by poets like Jones Very, Emily Dickinson, Walt Whitman, Robert Frost, E. E. Cummings, and Hart Crane. (Even Stevens and Eliot were fevered with self-transcendence in their own, highly original ways.) Roethke, who was able to assimilate the most divergent influences, must finally be seen as the central American Romantic poet of the generation that includes Robert Lowell, John Berryman, Karl Shapiro, Richard Eberhart, and John Crowe Ransom. He is the celebrant of a uniquely American nature, a Romantic descended from Blake, Wordsworth, and Yeats, but one whose language is idiomatically American and whose meaning derives from the Emersonian tradition.

More so than many of his contemporaries, Roethke's poetry seems divided into periods marked by radical changes of style; but there are no real shifts of intention. Roethke's original symbol cluster remains the same. The few themes he took for his own at the beginning are never deserted, though they undergo constant revision or elaboration. The dream world Roethke imaged has a unity that reveals itself gradually as the work unfolds in time, centered on an autobiographical myth reflecting a deep Romantic bias. If we judge Roethke harshly, we must judge the tradition of Emersonian Romanticism in the same terms. Indeed, any argument for Roethke's greatness impels us to see him whole *and* in the context of this visionary line that, far from exhausting itself, continues as the lifeblood of contemporary poetry in America.

CHAPTER TWO

THE POET AS APPRENTICE

I am that final thing,
A man learning to sing.

Roethke, "The Dying Man"

In a late essay, Roethke referred to his own poetic apprenticeship:

> The poet's fidelity, as Stanley J. Kunitz has
> said, is to the poem. In my own case, many
> pieces are completed without asking for or
> accepting comment, but I have received valu-
> able criticism, from time to time, from peo-
> ple ranging from practicing poets and editors
> to semi-literates who profess to hate poetry.
> The writer who maintains that he works
> without regard for the opinion of others is
> either a jackass or a pathological liar. (*SP*, p.
> 35)

The fact is, few poets of Roethke's stature have
been so open-minded about criticism, so willing to play the role of apprentice, so indefatig-
able in the quest for mastery over the details of
their craft. To the end of his life he sought out
those whose advice might prove useful; this
was one aspect of his greatness. It is also true
that Roethke had a long way to go before he
could write as well as he ultimately did.

Roethke first began writing seriously as a
graduate student at Harvard in 1930, and from
the beginning his poems could be called autobiographical, although his treatment of this material was indirect, tentative, even self-deceived.
One extract from his earliest existing notebook
points to the problem:

He remembered his youth, his childhood. But most of all, he re-membered his childhood. Somehow this stood out more strongly than anything. There was something very fine in the suffering young boy. He had led a hideous life, but everything was natural there. His courage at the time was a fine, moral courage. Physically, he had been afraid of everything: of dogs, of thunder. Now he was afraid of the very idea of life. Sometimes he almost hated to be alive.[1]

Characteristically, he always speaks of himself in the third person when referring to something close to the bone, like his childhood. And the earliest poems cast nervous glances at the matters that really concerned him—the relations with his father, his struggle for ego—but there is no confrontation. It is one thing for a poet to recollect the past—this is easy; but the *re-creation* of the past which occurs in the mature poetry meant reliving the experience, and this could not have been easy.

Born in the heart of the Saginaw Valley in Michigan on 25 May 1908, Roethke witnessed the decline of American wilderness and the growth of a small but vigorous town. The lumber boom, which began in the 1840s, had lured immigrants to this remote area of the frontier from all over Europe. An immense flow of capital from the Eastern seaboard had brought Saginaw into prosperity; even as the forests dwindled, the busi-ness potential of the area attracted newcomers, such as the poet's grand-father, Wilhelm Roethke, who came to Michigan from East Prussia in 1872 with his three sons: Emil, Charles, and Otto. In the old country Wilhelm had been the chief forester on the estate of Bismark's sister, the Gräfin von Arnim. But in the new world, he would work for no one but himself and established the market garden which evolved into the green-house of his grandson's childhood. Otto Roethke eventually attained full control of the business, which he pursued with the same tenacity that his son lavished on *his* craft.

Inevitably, Roethke's intellectual and spiritual roots were deeply American. Recounting his interests and ambitions as an adolescent, he wrote:

I really wanted, at fifteen and sixteen, to write the "chiselled" prose as it was called in those days. There were books at home and I went to the local libraries (and very good ones they were for such a small town); read Stevenson, Pater, Newman, Tomlinson, and those maundering English charm boys known as familiar essayists. I bought my own editions of Emerson, Thoreau, and, as God's my witness, subscribed to the *Dial* when I was in the seventh grade. (*SP*, p. 16)

Apparently he was not encouraged by his father, who had no intellectual interests, but was by his mother, Helen Heubner Roethke: "[her] favorite reading was the Bible, Jane Austen, and Dostoyevsky" said her son (*SP*, p. 58). But Allan Seager warns that this later recollection of Mrs. Roethke may well have no factual basis.[2]

As I have said, Roethke looked to Emerson as his first master: his personal copy of *Nature*, dog-eared and heavily underscored, has a comment scribbled inside the title page which hails Emerson as one of "the great optimists" who revealed "the possibilities of the human spirit." It goes on: "One of the potencies of Emerson is that he appeals to your own initiative."[3] This was crucial to the young man interested in the possibilities of the spirit; he learned that he could discover *himself* in the woods, the self which contains everything necessary for the full life. Roethke wrote at the end of *Nature*: "After all, nature exists only for man, who is to be the master." Like Blake and the other Romantics, he affirms the belief that "without man, nature is barren." For him, nature becomes "a steady storm of correspondences" in which the world of the spirit unfolds, with "all shapes blazing unnatural light" (*CP*, p. 239).

A few years before his death, Roethke wrote to Ralph J. Mills, Jr., that "*early*, when it really matters, I read, and really read, Emerson (mostly prose), Thoreau, Whitman, Blake and Wordsworth."[4] From these poets the young student derived his notions of what poetry was all about; but he did very little writing of his own until he entered the University of Michigan in 1925, and then his work was mostly prose. The college essays that have survived from this period in his life show that he already had a sensible, modest approach to the craft: "I write only about people and things that I know thoroughly. Perhaps I have become a mere reporter, not a writer. Yet I feel that this is all my present abilities permit. I will open my eyes in my youth and store this raw, living material. Age may bring the fire that moulds experience into artistry." He tells of his feelings toward nature with a wonderful innocence, trying (unsuccessfully) to sound unaffected:

> I have a genuine love of nature. It is not the least bit affected, but an integral and powerful part of my life. I know that Cooper is a fraud—that he doesn't give a true sense of the sublimity of American scenery. I know that Muir and Thoreau and Burroughs speak the truth.
>
> I can sense the moods of nature almost instinctively. Ever since I could walk, I have spent as much time as I could in the open. A perception of nature—no matter how delicate, subtle, how evanescent,—remains with me forever. (*SP*, p. 4)

His prose style, reminiscent of Emerson, is remarkably clear and force-ful, and his predictions for himself stand up well under the harsh scru-tiny of hindsight.

The atmosphere in Ann Arbor in the mid-twenties was too pro-vincial for Roethke, who wanted to break into the larger world of letters. So, after an abortive semester at Michigan Law School, followed by a semester of graduate studies in the English department there, he left his native state for Harvard, ostensibly to study with the critic I. A. Rich-ards. He entered Harvard Graduate School in 1930 with hopes of gaining a Ph.D., but the depression squashed this plan and Roethke was forced to place himself in the precarious job market. He found a teaching po-sition at Lafayette College in Easton, Pennsylvania, and finally had the chance to get his poetic apprenticeship under way.

Rolfe Humphries (1894–1969), a poet and translator of Latin verse, lived not very far away in Belvidere, New Jersey. He was Roethke's senior by fourteen years and already a solid figure in the literary estab-lishment; more important, he was a craftsman of the first order (as his translations of Ovid, Lucretius, and Virgil demonstrate). Allan Seager writes: "Humphries was the first poet of ability with whom Ted could have a continuing association."[5] Roethke's own later testimony to his first mentor's helpfulness appears in his essay "Verse in Rehearsal," where he quotes from one of Humphries's letters offering detailed critical com-mentary on an early draft of the poem "Genesis," which eventually was published in *Open House*:

> This elemental force
> Was wrested from the sun;
> A river's leaping source
> Is locked in narrow bone.
>
> The love is lusty mirth
> That shakes eternal sky,
> The agony of birth.
> The fiercest will to die.
>
> The fever-heat of mind
> Within prehensile brute;
> A seed that swells the rind
> Of strange, impalpable fruit.
>
> This faith surviving shock,
> This smouldering desire,
> Will split its way through rock
> Like subterranean fire.

Humphries's comments are restrained yet exacting. He forces Roethke to weigh every word carefully and to control his tone and argument with precision:

> It is certainly in the historical and traditional manner but you can make more use of the manner, and exploit it to better advantage than you do here. If the editors have any intelligent reason for rejecting the poem, it may be that they are fighting shy of it on the ground of its conventional rhymes: desire-fire; shock-rock; mirth-birth; sky-die. It just misses breath-death, as it were, and is pretty trite. . . . And personally I am a little bothered by your monogamous adjective-noun combinations: six such combinations in the first eight lines, while each may be used advisedly, is a good deal to ask the reader to endure; or, if he can achieve such endurance, you condition him to a frame of mind which he has to throw off with a most violent wrench when he comes to "strange, impalpable fruit." (*SP*, p. 33)

The correspondence between Roethke and Humphries in the thirties is touching; Roethke was shy, unsure of his own talent, eager for approval and genuinely constructive advice; Humphries was fatherly, meticulous in his criticism, always encouraging. He became the first in a long line of surrogate fathers which would include Kenneth Burke and Robert Heilman, and one of the many whom the poet would call "Pa." One can see how Humphries candidly felt about his young friend in a 1935 letter to Ann Winslow, who was planning an anthology of younger poets and had questioned him about Roethke:

> As to Roethke in particular, I think what he writes is unusually sensitive, delicate, tentative, rather shy stuff. I could not, at this point, utter 300–500 profitable words about his writing unless I were to criticize his poems in the item rather than in the mass. . . . I should think it obvious that Roethke is nobody's damn fool; what is less obvious is his capacity for full-toned and robust expression. That metaphysical-personal-Elizabethan vein cannot yield ore inexhaustively. Techniquely, Roethke has a good deal to learn, and I suppose he knows it. If I am allowed to take down his pants in public, I might say, for one thing, that he should try to get along without adjectives for a while; for another—this seems to contradict the first—that it wouldn't hurt, for practice, to play up the sensuous at the expense of the intellectual, and to show more concern with sound and less with image. And there is a trick of sustaining the energy of a poem; he hasn't quite got this, always; sometimes condensation is needed, sometimes expansion.[6]

Looking back, we can see that Roethke learned several things from Humphries that would determine the later course of his work; if his first attempts at verse were overly intellectual, unmusical, and sluggish, his mature work shows none of these deficiencies. Indeed, as Blessing puts it: "In his great poems Roethke's 'meaning' . . . is always a celebration of the dance of being, the energy of life."[7]

Apart from friendship and sensible criticism, the best thing Humphries gave to Roethke was an introduction to Louise Bogan, whose poems the younger poet had loved for several years. She was to become his most personal counselor, extending her solicitude from his poems to his life in general. Much less formal than Humphries, her letters are variously scathing, witty, or affectionate, but always full of highly specific commentary on his work. One especially good letter of 1935 contains her critique of an early draft of "Open House," the title poem of his first book. Examining the final version of the poem, it is possible to see how Roethke utilized Bogan's advice to turn a hackneyed, dull poem into an nearly perfect lyric of its kind:

Now to tackle your last lines:

In language strict and pure
I stop the lying mouth

is perfect, really fine. But I don't like *lyric cry*: it's a cliche, as old Malcolm would say. And it seems to me what you need in the last line is a synonym for *open* or *apparent*, as opposed to the tongueless idea. A fine sounding word meaning *apparent* would, to my mind, bring the intensity of the last stanza to a practically unbearable point of crisis, and that, my dear, is as you know, the great triumph of the short lyric: that it can be brought up, at the end, into a sound that tears the heart in twain. Of course, you could have it, as you suggested: This is my (something) cry, and then, My rage, my agony. That is what you were working toward, I think. Or you could delete the colon after mouth, and say, I stop the lying mouth, *With* something or other. I like the colon after that swell line, however. I leave the job of writing the penultimate line to you—nice of me, isn't it—and I go back to a word meaning *apparent* that could be clapped in front of *agony*, to make the last line. And here are all the words the thesaurus gives: conspicuous, manifest, definite, explicit, apparent, notable, notorious, start-staring, literal, plain-spoken, producible, and above board. (I don't *really* think above board would do, but some of the others might!) Now go ahead, my dove. It's your poem, after all.[8]

Young poets rarely win such lavish attention from their elders, or such concrete advice. Suggestions of a more general nature occur in a subsequent, unpublished letter of 3 March 1936; as usual, Bogan is responding to a previous letter of Roethke's which contained new poems offered up for commentary: "I like your pieces, but I wish you had loosened up in them a little more: been more Theodore in them. Loosen them up, somewhat, if you haven't already sent them off. Forget the necessity of pure prose and let go."[9] If one recalls the rich expansiveness of Roethke's later poetry, which everywhere brims with "Theodore," it is clear that he was a most attentive student.

Louise Bogan also warned her apprentice against the enemy of all beginning poets: abstract diction. The following extract comes from a letter dated 14 December 1937: "The latest poem was what Edmund [Wilson] always calls 'very well written,' but it *was* too full of abstractions, and the form is too full of Yeats. And that long form, with short lines, needs some actual objects in it, to come off. You know how full of objects the poem about the man going up to cast flies in the stream, where the stones are dark under froth, is. That's what your poem needs. . . ."[10] *Actual objects*, of course, become the focus of Roethke's poetry in the forties, when the greenhouse world of childhood rushes into his consciousness with all "that anguish of concreteness." This redirection of vision toward the concrete *fact* is the beginning of Romantic poetics, for as Emerson said: "To the wise, therefore, a fact is true poetry." Abstract knowledge is equivalent to what Plato, in the *Republic*, calls the level of *dianoia* or knowledge *about* things; the poet achieves direct apprehension of the concrete fact, the level of *nous*, where subject–object separations disappear.

The young poet has to listen to advice, as I have been suggesting, but there is the obvious danger of mistaken advice; after a certain point, any poet finds himself on his own. In a letter of 3 August 1937, Bogan praises Roethke for eliminating some abstractions. In the unpublished extract from the letter which follows, Bogan also calls Roethke's attention to the matter of sound and silence in poetry:

> As for your poems, my pet: certainly the nonabstract words tightened and bettered the whole tone. I don't like *Wisdom of the Bold* for a title, however. And I wish you'd do some more realistic pieces, outside of your own gizzard—the automobile one was so good. *Against Disaster* I should shorten. If it were mine (and, of course, it isn't), I'd omit the last stanza and transpose the third and fourth, and leave it at that. In that way, there's room enough left for reverberation: the idea isn't beaten out flat, and you can hear it all better, in the silence made by the abrupt close.[11]

Roethke listened, and he learned how to manipulate the silent beats of a poem, something many lesser poets never think about. Roethke's best lyrics have a resonance *after* the close which reinforces the meaning of the final line or stanza, so that the reader, like the bemused passerby of Wordsworth's "Solitary Reaper," continues to hear the haunting music "long after it was heard no more."

The thirties was a decade when political activism was of principal concern to artists; writers like Auden, Spender, Orwell, Lorca, and Malraux had the center stage. So it was natural that Roethke should attempt a kind of *engagé* writing. But this was never his mode; he was, say his friends, comically uninformed on political matters, especially in the late thirties. He was only vaguely aware of the international catastrophe that had been gathering wind over Europe for a decade, though he made some attempts at political poetry. With great wisdom, Louise Bogan wrote on 28 June 1939 to warn him against writing poetry with any overt political interest. She makes overly generous remarks about his mediocre poem "Ballad of a Clairvoyant Widow," which appeared in *Open House*, then comes to her real point:

> The Clairvoyant Widow is good, too. One of the lenses of the telescope is on the Auden side, but not too much so. And I wish the Widow—who is a really evocative and strange conception—didn't go Simplified Left in the end. After two years of studying the proletariat at first hand, I should say that they don't resemble those New Masses pictures of Everyone Holding Chained Hands Up Toward the Heights, in the least. They are all different—like any class. Don't get too simplified. Life isn't like that. Don't let the Zeitgeist get you.[12]

Bogan liked to mother Roethke, and it seems clear enough from the younger poet's letters that he needed someone to do this. One moving example of his role playing is this little note of 25 May 1936:

> Dear Louise: It's three o'clock in the morning, and I've just finished reading, of all things, 'Time Out of Mind' by Rachel Field.
>
> Just twenty-eight years ago today little Theodore came into the world. Touching, isn't it? I've never thought much about the passage of time over my flesh, but this time it really gets me down. Twenty-eight years, and what have I done? No volume out and I can't seem to write anything. You can say what you want, but *place* does have a lot to do with productivity. Hell, I don't care what happens to me,—whether I go nuts or my entrails hang out; but I can't stand being so mindless and barren as I've been. . . . (*SL*, pp. 36–37)

He was asking to be knocked over the head, sympathetically; and Bogan liked doing this.

In the forties Roethke became such an accomplished craftsman that the advice Humphries and Bogan had been giving him was no longer so urgent. Still, the persona of moral counselor to Roethke appealed to Bogan, and Roethke didn't object, so the letters went on. Here is a brief sample from an undated letter of 1942 in which Bogan characteristically admonished Roethke for being adolescent:

> Auden respects and likes you thoroughly, I should say. He wrote that review, you must realize, against all his decisions not to review contemporaries. He thinks you are a good poet, a good teacher, and a fine person generally; but we agreed that you should *grow up*, and stop pretending that your childish side is melancholy, *which it isn't*. Now, worry over that one![13]

Roethke was thirty-four at this time and had been hospitalized for manic-depression, an illness that would plague him throughout his life. It seems that Louise Bogan either didn't understand Roethke's psychological problems or thought that by making light of them she could jolt him out of his melancholy states.

A third mentor of great importance to young Roethke was Stanley Kunitz. Kunitz was only three years his senior, but he had already established himself as a recognized poet; he had published one book, *Intellectual Things* (1930), a book Roethke had liked immensely even before he met its author. Typically, it was Roethke who actively sought out the person he thought could help him write better poems; the fact that Kunitz was so young did not seem to matter; the craft, as ever, came first. Kunitz later recollected their meeting:

> More than a third of a century has passed since he [Roethke] blew into my life like the "big wind" of one of his poems. I was living in the Delaware Valley then. He came, unannounced, downriver from Lafayette College, where he was instructor in English and— more satisfying to his pride—tennis coach. My recollection is of a traditionally battered jalopy from which a perfectly tremendous raccoon coat emerged, with my first book of poems tucked under its left paw. The introductory mumble that followed could be construed as a compliment. Then he stood, embarrassed and inarticulate, in my doorway, waiting to gauge the extent of my hospitality. The image that never left me was of a blond, smooth shambling giant, irrevocably Teutonic, with a cold pudding of a face, somehow contradicted by the sullen downturn of the mouth and the pale,

furious eyes: a countenance ready to be touched by time, waiting to be transfigured, with a few subtle lines, into a tragic mask. He had come to talk about poetry, and talk we did over a jug grandly and vehemently all through the night. There were occasions in the years that followed when I could swear that I hadn't been to bed since.[14]

Kunitz was delighted that a poet not much younger that he was (and one who had already published a number of poems in good magazines) sought out his criticism. The two got on very well, as their letters show, but during the thirties Kunitz retained the upper hand; the tone of his letters was affectionately stern, big-brotherly. The following letter of 31 January 1936 is among the best, a moving document; it was written shortly after one of Roethke's earliest breakdowns:

> I'm terribly sorry to learn of your illness. Being flat on one's back, I know, isn't a pleasant experience—how much longer will it be? —but it's a nice opportunity for meditation, dedication, and the gathering of peace to the heart. Your poem has more strength of spirit, more *will*, than anything of yours I've seen. That consciousness of your own value and direction is something to take with you out of the sickroom.
>
> I think you've let yourself be bothered too much by the venomous little pedants, sneerers, and fops that seem to crawl out of the floorboards and plumbing of the academies. They bite the creative because it is human. Save a drop of pity for them, but no more. The artist needs to respect life.
>
> Really, the world is not a hopeless place, despite all the crimes of power, stupidity, and avarice. The imagination of the race, however starved and terrorized, stubbornly continues to build its commonwealth, where a man can be decent, happy, and useful. That is why we—I mean the poets—are worthy: because we have preserved that possibility, defended the mind from our tongue and our strength, to help in the organization and inspiration of men of good will. That is why we must go beyond Eliotism and defeatism and the unplumbed, salt, estranging metaphysical sea, and identify ourselves with the movement of history, the mainstream of energy in our time. I see all kinds of exciting poems, speculations, and seeds ahead. Let me know how you think and feel. . . .[15]

This letter had straightforward designs on Roethke's flagging spirits, and he desperately needed this encouragement. Normally, the letters from Kunitz make few sweeping statements; they focus on specific problems in Roethke's newest poems with immense accuracy and sensitivity. Sometimes Roethke was very sensitive to this intense criticism, which often found echoes of other poets in his work. This letter of 30 October 1935 seems to have upset him:

> "My secrets cry aloud" ("Open House") is all of a piece, and a good piece, too. The change in the next-to-the-last line is for the better. I think, however, that in your second stanza you've caught an echo from one of the poems in my last poetry group. I don't mind in the least—but since you or some reviewer may—I'll take the chance now of offending you. Don't bother discussing this business, unless you feel I'm mistaken.[16]

There is no mistake on Kunitz's part, for "Open House" resembles his "The Guilty Man," in which he writes: "I stand within myself, myself my shield." Roethke followed with: "I'm naked to the bone, / With nakedness my shield." The theme of both is much the same: the need for openness, for relinquishing defense mechanisms that make it difficult to be true to oneself; but the linguistic parallels are more striking. Roethke always picked up rhythms, rhetorical gestures, and tropes from the poets he read and liked; for him, "writing poetry was like making love: it was an activity requiring a partner. All of his poems are literary love children, the issue of a union between Roethke's own vision and the work of other poets whom he admired."[17] This critic overstates the case, but not by much. Roethke, of course, would have denied all this vehemently. He wanted to be his own man, and he wrote to Kunitz full of regret that he had caught this echo from his friend. In a letter written in November 1935 Kunitz reassured him; here he is at his very best as mentor, full of benevolence and graceful wit:

> Don't be a damned fool. *The poem is your own.* Nobody else wrote it or could have written it. Furthermore, it's a good poem—the best one I've read in months, I think. I do want you to publish it and to forget about this nonsensical "fake business." Now I curse myself for having mentioned the matter at all. I did it, believe me, in no accusing spirit and wholly without malice, as one might dissect a moth to find, among its pulp and sap, the buried engine of its tropic life.
>
> As for the passage in question, I believe I got the idea and some of the phraseology from a paragraph in Thoreau. Rilke expressed the same sentiment, variously, at least a dozen times. I could not, therefore, lay claim to either the substance or the expression. All of us take what we can from the mother speech, who is a bitch.

> You persecute yourself too much. The poet's only fidelity is to
> the poem. One must know what one is doing, but one must not
> use that knowledge against oneself! That is the death of the will.[18]

Such a letter can only have bolstered the younger man's confidence; he
certainly kept the poem. But the problem of "influence" obsessed him
throughout his life, especially since critics liked to point out his affinity
with Yeats. Once in December 1937, he asked Kunitz to arbitrate on a
poem, possibly "The Summons," which seemed to fall under the Yeatsean shadow to an inordinate degree:

> Curse me if you will, Stanley, but here is one more poem. I won't
> send or show you another until I see you, I promise. I've been
> making a desperate effort to turn away from negation and "hatred"
> and this is the result. The shadow of Yeats is on the page, but is it
> too heavy? In other words, is it my poem or a series of echoes? I
> believe it mine for I had to fight through much to get even this on
> the page. God knows what I say isn't new, but is it worth saying in
> this way? I mean with this many abstractions?
>
> Oh hell, never mind *all* the questions. What's troubling me is the
> "influence" business. It's so easy to say: "Yeats: (1) three foot alter-
> nate rhymes (2) enumerations."
>
> Be patient with my frantic questioning. (*SL*, pp. 56–57)

With help from Kunitz, Roethke learned that at all costs the poet must
remain faithful to the poem, aware of himself as only an element, albeit
the crucial one, in the creative process; he realized that a poet must be
conscious of the tradition he writes from and appreciate the conventions
he shares with his fellow-speakers—what Kunitz calls "the mother
speech."

Although Roethke would turn increasingly to Kenneth Burke and
others for advice in the forties, Stanley Kunitz remained an irreplaceable
friend. Their relationship stands as one of the more fruitful "literary
friendships" in modern poetry. It is a testimonial to Kunitz, Humphries,
and Bogan that their common apprentice should have become the most
significant poet of his generation. Without them, he may never have
reached the level of technical accomplishment so evident in *Open House*.
He may never have felt so free to experiment with the breaking of
forms in *The Lost Son* and later volumes had he not first mastered them.
The example of Roethke as poet-apprentice should speak to a new generation of writers who wonder how a poet like Roethke accomplished,
even in free verse styles, the sense of *achieved* form. Each of his lines
opens out like a leaf, as if inheriting the one possible shape it could have.

We should thank his mentors for the counsel they made available when he was a talented beginner with much to learn before he could write anything like great poetry. Roethke went to these older poets as young Renaissance painters had gone to the studios of older masters; like them, he in time was able to fashion an unmistakable style of his own. In so doing, he went beyond anything Humphries, Bogan, or Kunitz might have guessed.

CHAPTER THREE

THE POETICS OF EXPRESSION

Why this endless self-exhortation, this savage introspection? Am I a Dostoevsky? Must I go through something terrible before I can become articulate?

Roethke, "Notebooks" (July 1933)

The beginning poet often has to accept the poetics of his master in order to gain his or her approval. From the letters quoted, it should be clear that Roethke needed approval rather desperately and went out of his way to get it. His early work fits neatly into the style of the period, the tightly rhymed and witty mode often called metaphysical. Roethke's best lyrics in this vein survive in *Open House*, which is the subject of chapter four. First, however, it is best to look at the poetics that Roethke adopted early in the thirties and never abandoned, a poetics of the kind M. H. Abrams in *The Mirror and the Lamp* calls "expressive," a Romantic poetics.[1] One doesn't normally think of Humphries, Bogan, and Kunitz as Romantic poets, of course, but as Eliot once said, in a Romantic age the best one can do is *tend toward* Classicism, which he did himself. By the time Roethke began writing poetry, the expressive poetics of Wordsworth and Coleridge had become almost a matter of course, the usual fate of once revolutionary ideas. Although the primary evidence of Roethke's Romantic poetics is in the poetry itself, the unpublished notebooks contain various ruminations about poetry which reinforce this evidence.

Roethke's poetics hark back to German Romantic theory and Coleridge, although his personal sources were Wordsworth and Emerson. Fundamental to this system is the concept of poet as prophet. The poet becomes a priest of the imagination, a secular clergyman. But the cost of this special role is alienation from the main- stream of society; the seer appears to outsiders as a madman, the *poète maudit* of nineteenth-century French letters. The example of Whitman shows how swiftly this Romantic idea took hold in America, for Whit- man was indeed at times a caricature of the prophetic bard. There is no doubt Roethke thought of himself as one of the "mad poets" and even embraced the idea. In the late poem "In a Dark Time" he rhetorically asks: "What's madness but nobility of soul / At odds with circum- stance?" (*CP*, p. 239). Frank Kermode sums up the conditions of this vatic role for the poet: "He must be lonely, haunted, victimized, devoted to suffering rather than action—or, to state this in a manner more ac- ceptable to the twentieth century, he is exempt from the normal human orientation towards action and so enabled to intuit those images which are truth, in defiance of the triumphant claims of merely intellectual disciplines."[2]

The true source of poetry for the Romantic poet is that divine energy celebrated by William Blake in *The Marriage of Heaven and Hell*: "Energy is the only life, and is from the Body; and Reason is the bound or out- ward circumference of Energy." As Socrates told Ion, poets "compose their beautiful poems not by art, but because they are inspired and pos- sessed." Shelley echoed this notion in the *Defense of Poetry* with his as- sertion that poetry comes not by labor but by the compelling afflatus of genius, that spirit of creation whose visitations are "elevating and de- lightful beyond all expression." Wordsworth did not go quite so far as either Plato or Shelley; still, he speaks of a strange, overwhelming joy at the source of the creative act in his famous Preface to *Lyrical Ballads* (1800). Not quite a seer, his ideal poet is nevertheless an exceptional man, "endowed with a more lively sensibility, more enthusiasm and tenderness . . . pleased with his own passions and volitions, and who rejoices more than other men in the spirit of life that is in him."

Roethke's ideas about the origins of his own poetry and about poetry in general unfold in the notebooks in an unsystematic way. The bulk of his published criticism is small and consists mostly of occasional pieces gathered together after his death by Ralph J. Mills, Jr. Nevertheless, both sources suggest that Roethke was interested in the details of poetics, that he was conscious of the tradition he wrote in, and that he was aware of certain contradictions between Romantic theory and the facts of literary composition.

In short, writing poetry was plain hard work for Roethke—as, in- deed, it had been for Shelley! A certain drudgery often attended his ef- fort to compose verse. He wrote these jottings in the summer of 1945:

"Am I saying anything new when I say that poetry is difficult: heart-breakingly so? . . . A bleakness about poetry-writing: like getting to the factory at seven in the morning."[3] Poets are unreliable sources for information about the way they write, but Roethke's daily journal entries appear more reliable than any of his public boastings. Long hours of meditation have always been a necessary prelude to the sudden clarity of vision which poets call "inspiration." Roethke describes the process: "after long meditation, the mind opens up with a sudden burst, and all things appear in a clear light."[4] The poet must give the impression of spontaneity, but he need not write spontaneously. It is clear from Roethke's rough drafts that he wrote quickly, especially in later years when he experimented with techniques of free association; nevertheless, his final version of each poem is hammered to perfection.

That Roethke was a conscious craftsman is obvious from the "Open Letter" he published in 1950. He writes that a poet,

> in order to be true to what is most universal in himself, should not rely on allusion; should not employ many judgment words; should not meditate (or maunder). He must scorn being "mysterious" or loosely oracular, but be willing to face up to genuine mystery. His language must be compelling and immediate: he must create an actuality. He must be able to telescope image and symbol, if necessary, without relying on the obvious connectives: to speak in a kind of psychic shorthand when his protagonist is under great stress. He must be able to shift his rhythms rapidly, the "tension." He works intuitively, and the final form of his poem must be imaginatively right. If intensity has compressed the language so it seems, on early reading, obscure, this obscurity should break open suddenly for the serious reader who can hear the language; the "meaning" itself should come as a drastic revelation, an excitement. The clues will be scattered richly—as life scatters them, the symbols will mean what they usually mean—and sometimes something more. (SP, p. 42)

This description of what a poet "must do" comes near to Wordsworth's formulation of emotion recollected in tranquility. Although Roethke could not in good conscience be called tranquil, the point remains: the poet must offer his meaning in the form of revelation. A poet's awareness of technique may very well contradict the notion of spontaneity (in Shelley's sense of the term). Nonetheless, a poet is no mere technician who gives his audience what often was thought but never so well expressed; he faces up to the mystery; he creates an actuality.

Romanticism has undergone endless permutations since its earliest manifestations in Germany and France, England and America, but certain characteristic ideas about poetry persist to the present. A few of them seem fundamental to a Romantic poetics and occur in Roethke. The dangers of such an exercise are obvious enough, but it is worthwhile to have a clear grasp of Roethke's usually implicit poetics before looking at the poems in any detail.

Romantic poetics are, first of all, expressive. Poetry, according to A. W. Schlegel, is not imitation but self-expression (from *ex-pressus* and *ex-primere*). It is by definition autobiographical; the poet writes from his own experience, expressing something from deep inside him, making the unconscious conscious. Thus we find Roethke quoting Yeats's friend, the poet A. E., in his notebook: "The supreme question about a work of art is out of how deep a life does it spring." We see him admonishing himself in another passage: "Make your poetry the reflection of your life." And in another jotting he says: "The poet writes the history of his own body." But his best formulation of this doctrine is: "Poetry is still the natural form of self-expression."[5] The notion of autobiographical necessity accounts for the predominance of the lyric mode in poetry since Romanticism took hold early in the last century; the lyric was for this same reason the main vehicle of expression for Roethke.

Another Romantic notion, parallel to the first, is that poetry represents a form of emotional, rather than intellectual, expression. Critics after Wordsworth commonly held this belief, and by the time John Keble occupied the Chair of Poetry at Oxford (1832), the belief was generally accepted. Keble writes: "Poetry is the indirect expression in words, most appropriately, in metrical words, of some overpowering emotion, or ruling taste, or feeling, the direct indulgence whereof is somehow repressed."[6] A twentieth-century version of this idea appears in the critical writings of I. A. Richards, who was Roethke's teacher at Harvard. Richards distinguishes between the "symbolic" or "scientific" use of words and the "emotive" use. The former is descriptive, mainly "for the support, the organization, and the communication of references." The latter is used "to express or excite feelings and attitudes," and this is where poetry enters, "the supreme form of emotive language."[7] A life-long admirer of Richards, Roethke wrote in his unpublished teaching notes the following proposition: "Poetry—the emotional equivalent of thought." He liked to think of himself as an intuitive, not an intellectual, poet, and while taking notes on Kierkegaard he made the following aside: "Why, damn it, do I insist on being a *thinker*? Why can't I just be a refiner of the medium, like Herrick, and let it go at that?" Another time he asked himself: "With good intuitive equipment, why think?" He believed that a poet should depend on the sureness of his emotions as the ultimate guide: "I like to think a thing part way through and feel the rest of the way." The distinction, raised by I. A. Richards, between emotive and scientific language, interested Roethke a great deal; he copied out this passage from an essay by Samuel Beckett in 1947:

> Poetry is essentially the antithesis of metaphysics: metaphysics purge the mind of the senses and cultivate the disembodiment of the spiritual; Poetry is all passion and feeling and animates the inanimate; Metaphysics are most perfect when most concerned with universals. Poets are the sense philosophers, the intelligence of humanity.[8]

One finds endless variations on this theme in Emerson, Whitman, Yeats, and other Romantic poets and critics, but the basic sentiment is Roethke's when he says: "Reason? That dreary shed, that hutch for grubby schoolboys!" (CP, p. 92). Or in the beautiful villanelle, "The Waking": "We think by feeling. What is there to know?" (CP, p. 108). For Roethke, poetry was the sensuous and concrete expression of emotion, a contrasting mode to the intellectual, abstract disciplines of science and philosophy. The difficult notion of "concreteness" plays a central role in Roethke's poetics. It recalls the immediate, hard reality sought after in his poems, a reality apprehended by the senses and transformed by the imagination. He says in his notebook: "It's the essence of poetic thought to be concrete."[9]

Another key premise for a Romantic poetics relates to diction. It was Hopkins who called poetry "the current language heightened," and in doing so, reformulated Wordsworth's argument in the Preface that ornamental figures of speech and inflated, "poetical" diction have no place in poetry. The poet need not deviate from normal speech patterns, for the poetry occurs in the choice of subject, not the level of diction. The subject itself naturally leads the poet "to passions the language of which, if selected truly and judiciously, must necessarily be dignified and variegated, and alive with metaphors and figures."[10] One finds the following remark in Roethke's teaching notes: "Plain words do the trick, yet there must be a sufficient heightening, an edge to the common speech, some stepping up of rhythm." And again: "Stick to observation: Look at things. Study what seems to be commonplace and it ceases to be commonplace."[11] As a meditative poet, Roethke's method was to focus his attention wholly on the subject, allowing the natural variety of simple diction and normal speech rhythms to suffice. The poet, says Emerson, is a *namer*: "the poet names the thing because he sees it, or comes one step nearer to it than any other."[12] So poetry becomes what D. H. Lawrence calls "an act of attention," a concentration of vision, not an inflated language. Romantic poetry, Kermode argues, is therefore dependent upon the image, "the Image as a radiant truth out of space and time." In keeping with the notion of poetry as emotive language, he emphasizes that image-making is not an intellectual act, except in so far as intellect is involved in that creative operation of the whole mind which is Imagination."[13] Roethke's poems demonstrate the importance of this idea for contemporary poetry. His best work is a naming, in ordinary speech sufficiently heightened, of the thing to which he stands nearest. And, as he said in his teaching notes, "the Romantic image often attempted to *approximate* or suggest the quality of the thing itself." He goes on to remark, à la Pound, that the image is not merely pictorial representation, rather it is "a unification of disparate ideas and emotions, a complex presented spatially in time."[14]

This leads us naturally to the mysterious Romantic concept of imagination, the faculty that resolves disparate ideas and emotions into the magical unity of an image. Because this unity depends on the concept of organic form, they will be discussed together. "The poet," said Coleridge in a famous passage from the *Biographia Literaria*, "described in *ideal* perfection, brings the whole soul of man into activity. He diffuses a tone and spirit of unity, that blends, and (as it were) *fuses*, each into each, by that synthetic and magical power, to which we have exclusively appropriated the name of imagination. This power . . . reveals itself in the balance or reconciliation of opposite or discordant qualities."[15] That art involves a "reconciliation of opposites" is central to Romantic theory; contrary elements must be passed through the crucible of imagination for the image to become a unifying agent. This image must not, however, be static. Emerson, who hymns the imagination in his essay "The Poet," elaborates: "But the quality of the imagination is to flow, and not to freeze. The poet did not stop at the color or the form, but read their meaning; neither may he rest in this meaning, but he makes the same objects exponents of his new thought." He explains that "all language is vehicular and transitive, and is good, as ferries and horses are, for conveyance, not as farms and houses are, for homestead."[16]

The great Romantic model for the creative process, which flows and does not freeze, is the botanical organism. It was the German Romantic J. G. Herder who drew attention to the metaphoric potential in the life cycle of the plant: "With what marvellous diligence a plant refines alien liquors into parts of its own finer self, grows, loves . . . then ages, gradually loses its capacity to respond to stimuli and to renew its power, dies. . . ."[17] The famous dialectical triad of Hegel is a version of this metaphor, the refinement of two contrarieties into a higher third. Blake's version of this idea was copied by Roethke several times into his notebooks: "Without contraries is no progression." Another time we find Roethke paraphrasing Blake: "A great deal of art arises out of opposition." And in Roethke's teaching notes: "Poetry [achieves] an integration of experience—what Richards called 'organization.' A fusion of all the forces of man." He defines poetry as "form that culminates in Unity of Being." And he describes the part played by the poet's eye in Emersonian terms: "The eye, of course, is not enough. But the outer eye serves the inner eye, that's the point." The "inner eye," which the imagination uses to see into the heart of things and to perceive the essential unity in disparate experience, must be kept open: "Every attempt to minimize or ridicule the free use of the imagination is a little murder of human life."[18]

So Roethke engaged in a life-long defense of the imagination. His struggle was against the chaos symbolized by the jungle aspects of his greenhouse Eden, the threat of "fifty summers in motion at once" (*CP*, p. 38). The poem is that momentary stay against confusion celebrated by Robert Frost; as the plant turns air, light, water, and mineral earth (the four primary elements) into a single, vital form, so the poet transforms the diverse materials of his life into a new whole. As T. S. Eliot says:

> When a poet's mind is perfectly equipped for its work, it is constantly amalgamating disparate experience; the ordinary man's experience is chaotic, irregular, fragmentary. The latter falls in love, or reads Spinoza, and these two experiences have nothing to do with each other, or with the noise of the typewriter or the smell of cooking; in the mind of the poet, these experiences are always forming new wholes.[19]

The Romantic imagination is linked by necessity to the concept of organic form.

Finally, the Romantics were evangelical visionaries, and this is an important part of their poetics. Wordsworth believed he was granted "an internal brightness" that was "shared by none." He took for his mission to speak "of what in man is human or divine." "I would impart it, I would spread it wide, / Immortal in the world which is to come."[20] Wordsworth took Milton for his bardic model, the poet whom the Romantics generally regarded as their father. American Romantics, like Roethke, more often look to Emerson or to the Whitman who called into the future:

> Poets to come! orators, singers, musicians to come!
> Not today is to justify me and answer what I am for,

But you, a new brood, native, athletic, continental, greater than
    before known,
Arouse! for you must justify me.[21]

The idea of salvation underlies this poetics, and Roethke writes directly
in this tradition; his poetry is secular religion or, in Carlyle's phrase,
natural supernaturalism. Art is what gives "shape to a random joy,"
Roethke writes, and "Being myself, I sing / The soul's immediate joy"
(*CP*, pp. 124, 126). Every Romantic poet has his particular revelation to
impart; nonetheless, "He is the poet," says Emerson, "who sees through
the flowing vest the firm nature, and can declare it."[22] Thus, in the poem
"Four for Sir John Davies" Roethke says to all poets: "Summon a vision
and declare it pure." In the magnificent last lines of his poem, he rejoices
in poetry's redemptive powers: "Who rise from flesh to spirit know the
fall: / The word outleaps the world, and light is all" (*CP*, p. 107).

CHAPTER FOUR

IN LANGUAGE STRICT AND PURE

I burned my life, that I might find
A passion wholly of the mind,
Thought divorced from mind and bone,
Ecstasy come to breath alone.
I broke my life, to seek relief
From the flawed light of love and grief.

                    Louise Bogan, *"The Alchemist"*

Roethke came to his expressive poetics rather indirectly. As has been suggested, one could hardly avoid Romantic ideas anyway; they were in the air. Yet the reaction to Romanticism had set in with T. E. Hulme, Pound, and Eliot. Auden appeared in 1930 with a new brand of anti-Romantic sentiment that deeply affected Americans like Bogan and Kunitz. The tightly structured, witty, "neo-Metaphysical" lyric came into fashion, and Roethke adopted this mode. Nevertheless, though less well realized, the themes of his early poems are much the same as those of his later work. The main themes—the need to establish a firm sense of self and the discovery of a correspondence between internal and external realities—dominate *Open House*. The book fails on many counts, and only a few of the lyrics suggest that Roethke was a potentially important poet. *Open House* would be of little interest today if Roethke had not later gone beyond the slick, cautious writing that characterizes this early work.

The book has all the usual faults of first efforts. It is self-consciously clever, derivative, and unevenly textured in spite of at least ten years of sustained attention that went into its making. Roethke had simply gone down the wrong path, relying too heavily on his masters and ignoring or repressing the genuine impulses of originality that would occasionally surface, especially in the poems of the late thirties. The first poem in *Open House* is the title poem, which has become a minor anthology piece. The tone of the first stanza is assertive, a bit strident, but it stays in the mind:

> My secrets cry aloud,
> I have no need for tongue.
> My heart keeps open house,
> My doors are widely swung.
> An epic of the eyes
> My love, with no disguise.
> (*CP*, p. 3)

The poet promises a great deal here, and the heavily end-stopped lines draw attention to the promissory element. Yet the next stanza goes even further as Roethke claims a greater capacity for honesty than can be taken seriously:

> My truths are all foreknown,
> This anguish self-revealed.
> I'm naked to the bone,
> With nakedness my shield.
> Myself is what I wear:
> I keep the spirit spare.

The final stanza grasps a theme Roethke would cultivate in later years, that of the relation between language and experience:

> The anger will endure,
> The deed will speak the truth
> In language strict and pure.
> I stop the lying mouth:
> Rage warps my clearest cry
> To witless agony.

Although the poem is technically accomplished, showing off Roethke's perfect musical sense and mastery of form, the speaker sounds like a poseur. Too many abstractions in the second and third stanzas wear away at the original effect of the conceit established in the first. Taken as the title poem, one might argue with Richard Blessing that "an open house suggests informality, a kind of unstructured, free-floating gathering in which guests come and go pretty much as they please."[1] If so, the title is misleading.

Karl Malkoff divines a remarkably complicated ground plan for *Open House*; he isolates the theme of selfhood and suggests that the five parts of the book explore the definition of self and view it from various angles.[2] But I must again agree with Blessing, who warns that this is overly complicated. Applying Occam's razor, let us assume that these were the best poems on hand when Roethke submitted the manuscript to Knopf. They group naturally into categories, but this matters very little. In *Open House* there is none of the overall singleness of voice and vision that pervades his later books. Still, Roethke looked back on his first volume with a certain affection: "It took me ten years to complete one little book, and now some of the things in it seem to creak. Still, I like about ten pieces in it" (*SL*, p.16).

Among the best of these lyrics is "Feud," which begins:

Corruption reaps the young; you dread
The menace of ancestral eyes;
Recoiling from the serpent head
Of fate, you blubber in surprise.

Exhausted fathers thinned the blood,
You curse the legacy of pain;
Darling of an infected brood,
You feel disaster climb the vein.

There's canker at the root, your seed
Denies the blessing of the sun,
The light essential to your need.
Your hopes are murdered and undone.
(*CP*, 4)

The poem opens a Freudian vein, and the method mimics the psychoanalytic. The subject is the separation of the self from ghosts of the family which persist in the unconscious long after they should have been subdued; Roethke argues, the "spirit starves / Until the dead have been subdued." If this were true, we would have none of Roethke's later poems. "Feud," with its wish to escape or suppress the past, points to Roethke's fundamental early mistake. Nobody can run away from home; the mature man makes his peace with old ghosts. The oblique nature of this poem, which remains impersonal on the surface because of its second person subject, is symptomatic. The poet controls his powerful emotions by driving a wedge between language and experience.

"Prognosis" continues the psychoanalytical theme, this time dealing with the image of Mother:

Though the devouring mother cry, " 'Escape me? Never—' "
And the honeymoon be spoiled by a father's ghost,
Chill depths of the spirit are flushed to a fever,
The nightmare silence is broken. We are not lost.
(*CP*, p. 5)

The confrontation with Mother, for Roethke, was less important than
that with Father, "Papa"; yet some of the finest passages in the *Praise to
the End!* sequence exploit the obvious Oedipal connections. Of the poems
in *Open House* dealing with family or childhood memories, "The Premonition" comes closest to Roethke's later, more direct poetry:

Walking this field I remember
Days of another summer.
Oh that was long ago! I kept
Close to the heels of my father,
Matching his stride with half-steps
Until we came to a river.
(*CP*, p. 6)

The poem begins with a memory, recalling a bright scene from childhood—an opening reminiscent of Wordsworth. The field, the boy with
his father, and the river would become dominant symbols in Roethke's
later work. The manner is straightforward, less clipped and strained than
other poems in *Open House*, again foreshadowing the later style. A luminous image ends the poem with a memory of how, as the father

. . . dipped his hand in the shallow:
Water ran over and under
Hair on a narrow wrist bone;
His image kept following after,—
Flashed with the sun in the ripple.
But when he stood up, that face
Was lost in a maze of water.

The image has become a symbol of mortality. One line alludes to
Donne's "Bracelet of bright haire about the bone" in "The Relique," a
technique of allusion that Roethke favored through his career.[3]
Most of the poems in Section I can be called competent lyrics in the
metaphysical style; they are full of conceits, compressed images, and
intellectual flexing. Irony and wit predominate, and the range of allusion
is considerable. La Belle tracks down references to Elinor Wylie, Bogan,
Hopkins, Donne, and Dickinson, among others. Nonetheless, the content has a strong Romantic bias. When Roethke, in "The Signals," claims

that "Sometimes the blood is privileged to guess / The things the eye or hand cannot possess," he expresses a basic Romantic idea, one popularized by D. H. Lawrence, whose work Roethke had been teaching throughout the thirties. And the strong influence of Emily Dickinson (which amounts to parody in Roethke's "No Bird") suggests that from the beginning he was writing in the mainstream of American Romanticism.

"The Adamant," which closes the first section of *Open House*, has many admirers, including Yvor Winters, who called this poem "one of the best things in the book and in recent poetry."[4] However, the rhythmical naiveté alone would be enough to condemn this poem; the intellectual naiveté apparent in the first stanza adds insult to injury:

> Thought does not crush to stone.
> The great sledge drops in vain.
> Truth never is undone;
> Its shafts remain.
> (*CP*, p. 9)

In this case, truth *is* undone. Objections notwithstanding, Roethke remained proud of this poem to the end.

In the second section, Roethke shifts the center of gravity from the inner world (a cloudy chamber indeed) to the outer, but the switch is deceptive. A close reading reveals the subtle dialectic established between the inner and outer worlds of self and nature. It is a Romantic dialectic, and Emersonian formulation. "The Light Comes Brighter" is the first poem in the section, set in early spring. As signs of green life begin to show through the frost covering, a direct link forms between inner and outer weather—a technique that Roethke will continue to use in later poems. The influence of Robert Frost is obvious in these poems, especially in "Slow Season" and "Mid-Country Blow," which are full of simple natural description:

> Now light is less; noon skies are wide and deep;
> The ravages of wind and rain are healed.
> The haze of harvest drifts along the field
> Until clear eyes put on the look of sleep.
> (*CP*, p. 12)

This scarcely goes beyond Georgian poetry, but the high level of technical sophistication should be noticed. "Slow Season" goes on to picture the deadening effect of late autumn on everything in nature, including the poet himself. Again, the Emersonian correspondence between internal and external spheres is drawn:

The shoots of spring have mellowed with the year.
Buds, long unsealed, obscure the narrow lane.
The blood slows trance-like in the altered vein;
Our vernal wisdom moves through ripe to sere.

Robert Lowell has separated American poetry into two categories: the raw and the cooked. "Slow Season," by this standard, is very well done. Roethke reworked these poems meticulously, usually improving them in the process. An early typescript of "Slow Season," for instance, ends with these three lines:

Buds, long unsealed, are litter in the lane.
The blood moves trancelike through the altered vein;
Our vernal wisdom has grown ripe and sere.[5]

The facile phrase "are litter in the lane" has been changed to the more suggestive "obscure the narrow lane." The dull verb "moves" in the next line has been replaced by the more accurate "slows." And the banal and nearly illogical line—"Our vernal wisdom has grown ripe and sere"—is transformed in the final draft to allow for a sense of process crucial to the poem's effect.

The influence of Imagist poetry was still strong in the thirties, and Roethke's nature poems abound in hard, clear images that would have pleased Pound and Amy Lowell. In this mode "The Heron" is a successful poem which follows a tedious descriptive poem called "The Coming of the Cold." It conjures the image of a heron standing on one leg in a pool of black water until

He jerks a frog across his bony lip,
Then points his heavy bill above the wood.
The wide wings flap but once to lift him up.
A single ripple starts from where he stood.
(CP, p. 15)

"The Bat" ends the section with an ominous note, forcing a connection between the bat and the human animal in the last, sharp couplet: "For something is amiss or out of place / When mice with wings can wear a human face" (CP, p. 16). This signals a change in mood, and one enters the third section with considerable disquiet.

The third section defines the self by the *via negativa*, the way of negation; but at this stage Roethke has yet to explore the harrowing negative way of his later, mystical poems of *The Far Field*. The specter of death haunts the poet in these poems, as in "No Bird":

Now here is peace for one who knew
The secret heart of sound.
The ear so delicate and true
Is pressed to noiseless ground.

Slow swings the breeze above her head,
The grasses whitely stir;
But in this forest of the dead
No bird awakens her.
(*CP*, p. 17)

Here Roethke evokes Emily Dickinson specifically, that death-haunted poet whose presence in *Open House* has been documented by La Belle.[6] The phrase "the forest of the dead" is lifted unabashedly from Dickinson's "Our journey has advanced" and shows Roethke's acceptance once more of Eliot's famous dictum: "Bad poets imitate; good poets steal."

Roethke never gives in to complete morbidness; rather, he celebrates the "narrow vegetable realm" that overwhelms mankind, as in the beautiful "Long Live the Weeds," which takes its title from Hopkins:

Long live the weeds that overwhelm
My narrow vegetable realm!
The bitter rock, the barren soil
That force the son of man to toil;
All things unholy, marred by curse,
The ugly of the universe.
(*CP*, p. 18)

One could be ungenerous and point out that Hopkins's line is by a long shot the best in the poem, but this would detract from the real energy of Roethke's vision, which meets the Hopkins image head-on and assimilates it. The poem ends by defining the self in terms of the following unattractive alternatives: "Hope, love, create, or drink and die: / These shape the creature that is I." The naiveté and abstractness of this conclusion, and the embarrassing contortion of normal syntax for the sake of a rhyme, are further evidence that Roethke matured slowly as an artist. He painfully acquired his skill.

"Epidermal Macabre" is more successful, examining the classic flesh-spirit dichotomy in a witty manner. Roethke begins with a proleptic assertion: "Indelicate is he who loathes / The aspect of his fleshy clothes"; yet this merely prepares the way for his later revelation:

I hate my epidermal dress,
The savage blood's obscenity,

The rags of my anatomy,
And willingly would I dispense
With false accouterments of sense,
To sleep immodestly, a most
Incarnadine and carnal ghost.
(*CP*, p. 19)

The oxymoronic last phrase, coupled with the word play on the root *carne*—the Latin word for flesh—demonstrates a growing sophistication on Roethke's part. Rosemary Sullivan notices that the poem imitates the form of Louise Bogan's "The Alchemist"—but there is nothing new about writing in regular tetrameter couplets. She concludes that "the younger poet's technique is not entirely adequate to the rigid structure."[7] But the brilliant last phrase—"carnal ghost"—allows the poet to have his cake and eat it too. As A. O. Lovejoy points out in his great study of Romantic epistemology, *The Reason, the Understanding, and Time*: "The reasoning characteristic of ordinary thought and natural science depends upon the setting up of sharp contrasts between things, upon propounding dilemmas and formulating irreconcilable oppositions. . . . Its entire thinking, in short, is based upon the logical principle of contradiction. But the higher insight of the Reason transcends these oppositions. It is all for embracing both sides of all questions."[8]

The last poem in this section strikes a more soundly autobiographical note than its predecessor. "On the Road to Woodlawn" refers to the graveyard in Saginaw where Otto was buried, the opening setting, in fact, for Roethke's major poem "The Lost Son." This brief lyric sketches a small town funeral, recalling the horse drawn procession of baroque hearses and the carriages smelling of perfume and varnish. Yet the poem lacks vitality; it has none of the terrible immediacy of Roethke's later poems about death, such as "Elegy for Jane," his most famous poem. The remoteness of "On the Road to Woodlawn" and of most of the poems in *Open House* can be attributed to Roethke's early inability to face those aspects of life most painful to him, the taproots of his later poetry. Even in his private journals, he cannot refer to himself directly and uses the third person, as in this entry from July 1934: "His life seemed always subject to a very few major influences. It was a small heaven—with very few stars: mother, and sister, and Stanley Kunitz, and drinking and Conrad Aiken and music. Sometimes mother vanished out of sight."[9]

Not until a decade later could he really confront his problems without evasions. In the forties, a sense of self-destructive guilt soaks through his most casual jottings as a few examples from the notebooks indicate:

I carry the guilt of too many lives.

The devil who has my heart
Will not let me be.

Afraid? Why hell, I've been afraid all my life—dogs, thunder, my cousin.

Anxiety—It is when we begin to hurt those that we love that the guilt with which we are born becomes intolerable . . . we hate ourselves in them.

My private conscience is terrible.

I'm in the pits still; in the mire, spiritually. I can't seem to throw off the sensuality that is a part of me. I don't want to throw it off. I'm not tempted, I'm a tempter. Maybe I'm even one of the party of the Devil. One of his seducing, fat charges.[10]

These are all confessions of a guilt that plagued Roethke from adolescence, but which he was late to acknowledge. The restricted forms of *Open House*, the limited scope of his diction—all based on the models he was imitating—provided no verbal outlet for his anxieties. He needed a more expansive form to deal with his needs, to feed his imagination to a white flame. When he found his *métier* in the "Lost Son" poems, the creative act became, for him, a kind of therapy, an incantation by which the poet sought to liberate himself from "the menace of ancestral eyes" (*CP*, p. 4).

The fourth and fifth sections of *Open House* reflect the immediate influence of W. H. Auden and are largely boring. Roethke would later become a tolerably good satirical poet, but the supposedly cutting poems here, like "My Dim-Wit Cousin," are a poor excuse for poetry. The poems of social protest in the last section, full of wearisome abstractions, posturing, and cliché ("Ballad of the Clairvoyant Widow" is the worst) remind us that Roethke never possessed Auden's capacity for manipulating ideas in poetry. And he knew this himself, as his notebooks show: "I like to think a thing part way through and feel the rest of the way. . . . Conceptual thinking is like believing in God—one wants to put it off as long as possible."[11] This Romantic prejudice against conceptual thought has been discussed already, but here we can find one of the problems with *Open House*. Roethke was an intuitive poet who had not yet learned to trust his intuitions. His gradual drift toward mysticism, which culminates in *The Far Field*, parallels his withdrawal from abstract modes of thought. He understood this by 1944, when he wrote in his notebooks: "Mysticism has the desirability of requiring no sustained thinking; instead, a constancy of belief and the capacity for intuitive leaps."[12]

But Roethke's enchantment with Auden continued throughout his life; he said in his notebooks in 1945: "Auden, for all his cleverness and posturing and thumb-turning episcopality, is one of the true sources of life."[13] Auden, who was best man at Roethke's wedding, was one of his closest readers and critics; Auden's insistence on sheer technical virtuosity, characteristic of his own work, had a lasting influence on Roethke. One can find many traces of Auden in Roethke: the idealized landscapes, the photographic aspect of his imagery, the colloquial phrasing assimilated into formal settings. But these were Auden's gift to all poets writing in the thirties and forties. When Roethke comes too close to Auden, as in "Lull (*November, 1939*)"—the result is more like parody than creative imitation:

> The winds of hatred blow
> Cold, cold across the flesh
> And chill the anxious heart;
> Intricate phobias grow
> From each malignant wish
> To spoil collective life.
> Now each man stands apart.
> (*CP*, p. 31)

Premonitions of war are followed by a final groping toward abstract summary:

> Reason embraces death,
> While out of frightened eyes
> Still stares the wish to love.

The poem reads like a very rough draft of Auden's famous "September 1, 1939."

One final poem of real interest in the book is the last, "Night Journey." Roethke used as tight a form as before, but the theme is so much his own that echoes of other poets disappear; the poem re-creates the experience of traveling by sleeper across America:

> Now as the train bears west,
> Its rhythm rocks the earth.
> And from my Pullman berth
> I stare into the night
> While others take their rest.
> (*CP*, p. 34)

The clickety-clack trimeter suggests the rhythmical sway of the train. The poet's eye catches "Bridges of iron lace, / A suddenness of trees, / A lap of mountain mist." Here, Roethke, following Whitman, again fulfills Emerson's prophesy that America would not wait long for a literature to celebrate its riches. Roethke ends his poem and book: "I stay up half the night / To see the land I love."

In a characteristically astute early review of *Open House*, Auden posed some crucial questions for Roethke:

> The only question which remains, and it concerns the poet rather than the reader, is: "Where is Mr. Roethke to go from here, having mastered with the help of Herrick, Marvell, and Blake, a certain style of expression? How is he to develop it, to escape being confined to short and usually iambic lyrics?
>
> It is possible, I think, that Mr. Roethke is trusting too much to diction, to the poetic instrument itself to create order out of chaos. For poetry is only an instrument. It can be sharpened, but it cannot, by itself, widen the area of experience with which it deals. Poe was quite right in saying that an instrument in poetry alone can only produce short lyrics, but wrong, I think, in concluding from this that only short lyrics are poetry. It is possible that Mr. Roethke has read quite enough English poetry for a while, and should now read, not only the poetry of other cultures, but books that are neither poetry nor about poetry, for every artist must be like one of his own characters who "Cried at enemies undone, / And longed to feel the impact of defeat." Otherwise, he may be in danger of certain experiences becoming compulsive, and either, like Emily Dickinson and A. E. Housman, playing more and more variations on an old theme, or like Rimbaud, of coming to the end of his experiences and ceasing to write.[14]

Fortunately, neither of these unhappy alternatives was realized. With ferocious energy, Roethke battled his way out of the corner where the aesthetics of *Open House* had left him, pushing his way at last into the open spaces of *The Lost Son*. Nobody, not even Roethke himself, could have guessed how good he would become, moving from style to style, dazzling his mentors. As he wrote in his notebooks: "The poem is a kind of death: it is finished, a complete, a comprehensive act. The better the poem, the more final the destruction."[15]

PART TWO

THE RADICAL VISION

CHAPTER FIVE

THE BROKEN MIRROR OF PERSEUS

The poem of the mind in the act of finding
What will suffice. It has not always had
To find: the scene was set; it repeated what
Was in the script.

Wallace Stevens, "Of Modern Poetry"

Roethke took the advice offered in Auden's review of *Open House*: he began to read widely
outside of the narrow discipline of poetry, ex-
ploring psychology (especially Freud and Jung),
anthropology and myth, Oriental religions and
mysticism, and such theologians as Paul Tillich
and Martin Buber. Leaving Penn State for Bennington College in 1943, he met the critic Kenneth Burke and found a new mentor. In *The
Philosophy of Literary Form* (1941) Burke remarks
that the myth of Perseus and the Gorgon Me-
dusa can by analogy teach us something about
the ways of poetry. He identifies the poet with
Perseus, the Greek hero "who could not face the
serpent-headed monster without being turned
to stone, but was immune to this danger if he
observed it by reflection in a mirror, enabling
him to confront the risk, but by the protection
of an indirect reflection."[1] Like Perseus, Roethke
had numerous personal serpents to slay. But the
art of *Open House* seems to have failed as a re-
flector; the classical notion of mimesis is less
therapeutic than the Romantic poetics of
expression. For the Romantic, poetry must not
mirror reality so much as *embody* it. Wallace
Stevens sheds some light on the process:

> There is always an analogy between nature
> and the imagination, and possibly poetry is

the strange rhetoric of that parallel: a rhetoric in which the feeling of one man is communicated to another in words of the exquisite appositeness that takes away all their verbality.[2]

In other words, poetry at its best dissolves the medium by embracing reality and the imagination directly, achieving that "exquisite appositeness" beyond "verbality" or language.

The modern Romantic poet is "the new Perseus" described by Geoffrey Hartman in *The Unmediated Vision*:

> It is said that Perseus, when he went to slay the Medusa, was given by Athene a resplendent mirror to escape the monster's direct glance, which would have turned him into stone. Perseus, accordingly, cut off the Gorgon's head, and from her blood there sprang the winged horse Pegasus which with one stamp of its foot produced Mount Helicon's sweet fountain, dear to the Muses. But the new Perseus is a different kind of hero. He disdains or has lost Athene's mirror, and goes against the monster with naked eye. Some say that, in consequence, he is petrified; others, that he succeeds but the fountain of Pegasus is a bittersweet brew.

Hartman argues that the modern poet seeks to gain "pure representation" of experience by means of a direct, sensuous intuition of reality. "The eye and the senses are made to supply not merely the ornaments but the very plot of truth. Consciousness becomes, in its contact with the physical world, the source and often the end of cognition." He suggests that not only the four poets examined in his study—Wordsworth, Hopkins, Rilke, and Valéry—but the majority of poets since the dawn of Romanticism have refused any but human and sensory intermediaries to knowledge. They seek what he calls "the Hellenic innocence of the senses," and rely on no arbitrary or traditional text: "Nature, the body, and human consciousness—that is the only text." This fact, the new priority of experience in the most personal sense, is another way of looking at the great Romantic effort to naturalize the supernatural. Yet a price must be paid for sacrificing the sacred texts. When the tension between sacred and profane reality is lost, the poet is driven back in upon himself, into a world where "symbols are only such by pretense, and the entirety of life is caught up in this pretense. Everything is *in potentia* equally sign and symbol."[3] The poet must discover his own meanings, risking unintelligibility "in the act of finding / What will suffice."[4]

The alternative to risking everything, as far as Roethke was concerned, was silence—Rimbaud's choice. But language was a form of consciousness Roethke could not repress; he wrote in his notebooks, quoting Hegel: "All consciousness is an appeal to more consciousness." Thus, he set himself the task of moving beyond the limited aesthetics of *Open House*; he decided to put down the mirror and become, in effect, the new Perseus, facing the Gorgon head of his past experience with a cold eye. The notebooks of this period (1943–1947) record the struggle for self-knowledge and a fresh language leading up to the publication of *The Lost Son*. The great personal myth of the greenhouse Eden evolved gradually as the poet looked into his past; his readings in psychology, guided by Kenneth Burke, presented him with a technique for tunneling into the unconscious. Roethke took experience for his text, experience filtered through the gauze of memory. He sought immediacy, "that anguish of concreteness," above all else, recognizing that a poet's task is not simply to record experience but to re-create it. Invoking Whitman, he wrote in his notebooks: "The poet writes the history of his body."[5] Taking "the body" in its widest possible meaning, Roethke began writing the history of his conscious life. This history unfolds in the three books to succeed *Open House*, and it is the subject of the next three chapters.

CHAPTER SIX

THE LESSON OF THE PLANTS

*Originally the ego includes everything; later it detaches from itself
the external world. The ego-feeling we are aware of now is thus
only a shrunken vestige of a far more extensive feeling—a feeling
which embraced the universe and expressed an inseparable connection of the ego with the external world.*

Freud, Civilization and Its Discontents

*A notion of centrality: there is a core to all things that even a child
knows, yet it is one of those ancient thoughts that can never become
a cliché.*

Roethke, "Notebooks" (July 1945)

As noted earlier, the life cycle of an organism—
birth, growth, maturity, decay, and death—offered the Romantics a paradigm for the human
life cycle, and the organic process was seen to
parallel the act of literary invention.[1] Kant, Herder, and Schelling stress the plant metaphor,
and Coleridge—adapting the concept of dynamic opposition between the subjective artist
and the object contemplated from Schelling's
System of Transcendental Idealism (1800)—explains creative genius in the same biological
terms. "The poet," says Coleridge, " . . . brings
the whole soul of man into activity, with the
subordination of its faculties to each other, according to their relative worth and dignity. He
diffuses a tone and spirit of unity that blends
and (as it were) fuses, each into each, by that
synthetic and magical power to which we have
appropriated the name of imagination." The
implicit biological metaphor in the word "synthetic" should be obvious. The poet, like the
plant, unites disparate elements: light, water,
minerals, and carbon dioxide. Images are taken

from the external world and transmogrified in the poet's mind, as Coleridge explains:

> images, however beautiful, though faithfully copied from nature, and as accurately represented in words, do not of themselves characterize the poet. They become proofs of original genius only as far as they are modified by a predominant passion; or by associated thoughts or images awakened by that passion; or when they have the effect of reducing multitude to unity, or succession to an instant; or lastly, when a human or intellectual life is transferred to them from the poet's own spirit. . . .[2]

Emerson, a devout student of Coleridge, reformulates the same theory in "The Poet," turning his master's idea inside out: "The Universe is the externization of the soul." He plays with the plant metaphor constantly, saying in one classic phrase that a poem is "a thought so passionate and alive that like the spirit of a plant . . . it has an architecture of its own, and adorns nature with a new thing."[3]

These ideas, central to all Romantic theory, will help us to understand the organization of Roethke's greenhouse poems—his greatest achievement. In short, Roethke abandoned the mechanical structures which mar even the best poems in *Open House*, structures imposed from without. He began to think in terms of the plant metaphor, the organic process, allowing each poem to develop from within, assuming a shape unique to itself, adorning nature with a new thing. The fourteen poems that make up the greenhouse sequence appear at the outset to be merely descriptive pieces, but far more is involved. Roethke's plants take on a strangely human aspect; they operate as symbols in a subtle way. As Coleridge demanded, the image of each flower is modified by the human life, the passion, transferred to it from the poet's own spirit. Many of the poems in this sequence approximate a particular psychological state. As the notebooks make clear, Roethke hunted the recesses of his mind for symbols adequate to his experience. He wrote in his notebooks, somewhat wearily, of "the long testing of the unconscious before one gets even a few symbols true to himself."[4] This long testing lasted from 1942 until 1948, when *The Lost Son* was published. But the earliest greenhouse poems started to appear in magazines in the early forties, revealing a new Roethke. By the process of regression and near withdrawal from the public eye, he managed to discover his source and develop a style completely his own. Exactly how Roethke did this remains to be considered.

The move from Penn State to Bennington was crucial. The new environment helped, but the presence of Kenneth Burke was the most important aspect of the change. By happy accident, Roethke moved into the same building with Burke, "Shingle Cottage." Burke was at Bennington three days a week: just often enough for Roethke to see him when he needed. Burke exercised a profound influence over his younger friend; the notebooks from these years are studded with ideas taken straight from Burke's major books up to 1941: *Counter-Statement* (1931), *Permanence and Change* (1935), *Attitudes Towards History* (1937) and *The Philosophy of Literary Form* (1941).[5] Also, the extant letters between Roethke and Burke give evidence of their intimacy during these years. Burke had early access to the manuscript of *The Lost Son* and acted as editor-mentor in much the same way as Humphries, Bogan, and Kunitz had done earlier. Burke's natural disposition was pedagogical, and the correspondence between them shows that he never restrained himself with Roethke, who always distrusted his own abilities and sought reinforcement.

In *The Philosophy of Literary Form* Burke asserts: "Critical and imaginative works are answers to questions posed by the situations in which they arose. They are not merely answers, they are strategic answers, stylized answers." He thinks of poetry as proverbial medicine; a proverb, he says, offers a means of sizing up a situation. Proverbs are ameliorative, and so are poems. He asks:

> Might we think of poetry as complex variants and recombinations of such materials as we find in proverbs? There are situations typical and recurrent enough for men to feel the need of having a name for them. In sophisticated work, this naming is done with great complexity. . . . And in all work, as in proverbs, the naming is done "strategically" or "stylistically," in modes that embody attitudes, of resignation, solace, vengeance, expectancy, etc.

Thus poetry becomes what Burke calls "symbolic action." He emphasizes the *physical* nature of speech, referring to Sir Richard Paget's mimetic theory of "language as gesture." He explains:

> According to Paget's theory, language arose in this wise: If a man is firmly gripping something, the muscles of his tongue and throat adopt a position in conformity with the muscles with which he performs the act of gripping. He does not merely grip with his hands; he "grips all over." Thus, in conformity with the act of gripping, he would simultaneously grip with his mouth, by closing his lips firmly. If now, he uttered a sound with his lips in this position, the only sound he could utter would be *m*. . . . Hence, *m* would be the proper tonality corresponding to the *m* as in contact words like "maul," "mix," and "slam."[6]

Burke's interest in the physical quality of words seems to have carried over into Roethke's new style; the language of the greenhouse poems, especially, is acutely physical, often mimetic. The style is entirely Roethke's own, though Hopkins—who had strong interests himself in the mimetic theory of language origins— comes to mind as a precursor. Roethke's notebooks from this period are full of Hopkins's poems copied out by hand, but this influence is indirect. Kenneth Burke was standing over Roethke in these years, literally and figuratively.

The idea that a poet should write about what concerned him most urgently, about his "burdens," related to Burke's notion of the poem as strategy. For him, a poem is cathartic; it resolves a problem or, at least, brings into balance contending forces. There is nothing original about Burke's idea, of course; one recalls the famous advice given by Malcolm to Macduff: "Give sorrow words," he urges, for "the grief that does not speak / Whispers the o'er fraught heart and bids it break." But the Romantic poets fixed on the cathartic function of poetry, as Abrams has shown, outlining the parallels between Romantic theories of poetry and Freud, reinforcing the earlier observation (taken from Norman O. Brown) that psychoanalysis, in effect, completes the Romantic revolution.[7] As we shall see, Roethke combines poetry and analysis in an original way, writing—as Burke urged him to do—about his burdens, giving expression to hitherto repressed emotions.

One other main tenet of Burke's poetics is the importance of synecdoche, which he calls the basic figure of speech. Art *is* artifice, of course, or illusion; Burke argues that there is nothing deceptive about this: "A tree, for instance, is an infinity of events—and among these our senses abstract certain recordings which 'represent' the tree. Nor is there any 'illusion' here. In so far as we see correctly, and do not mistake something else for a tree, our perceptions *do really* represent the tree."[8] Relating this to his poetics, Burke speaks of "associational clusters" or systems of symbols. The poet evokes reality by naming a few parts of reality, by relying upon a few key words as triggers. I think Roethke understood the synecdochic function intuitively, for he began to rely on "associational clusters" more heavily after 1942. He used a few key words over and over, expecting them to trigger something in the unconscious. Like Yeats or Stevens, Roethke developed a private range of associations for his special words. The color white, for instance, always connects with the realm of spirit in his later poems. As in Stevens, the color blue often represents the imagination; green connotes literal reality. As with most great poets, one poem informs another in Roethke's corpus, and you have to read all of him to understand the parts.

Burke's hermeneutics included a useful map of "levels of symbolic action." He discerns three levels: first, the bodily or biological level, which finds expression in kinesthetic imagery. Here the artist attempts to represent the rhythms of the organic life cycle, relying on sensory imagery to "symbolize" the pattern of "growth, decay, drought, fixity, ice, dessication, stability, etc."[9] *This* is the level upon which the greenhouse poems operate. Second, in Burke's system, comes the personal, intimate, or familiar level: the arena of human relations. Roethke moves up to this level in "The Lost Son" and later poems, confronting in turn his father, mother, sister, and lover. The third level is that of abstraction, of political or social discourse. As I have already said, Roethke rarely ventured into abstraction of this kind with success. He remained an introspective voyager, questing after personal salvation. In this sense, too, he is consummately Romantic.

Roethke took Burke's theories seriously; most important, he followed the advice to write about his personal history. In *Permanence and Change* we read: "Once a set of new meanings is permanently established, we can often note in art another kind of regression: the artist is suddenly prompted to review the memories of his youth because they combine at once the qualities of strangeness and intimacy."[10] The belief that childhood is the special province of the artist had common acceptance among Romantic writers. Indeed, Roethke quotes Thomas DeQuincey in his notebooks in 1943: "The infant is one with God and one with everything in our immense universe through the medium of love. . . . The adult mind must regain this vision, this secure unity."[11]

Freud refined this great Romantic belief in a primal state of unity with nature lost through maturation, and he invented psychoanalysis as a way to recover the past. In this sense Norman O. Brown is correct to suggest that psychoanalysis completes the Romantic revolution. He observes how the categories of primal unity, differentiation, and final harmony can be found in the Romantic poets. One recalls Wordsworth's classic summary of this view:

> There was a time when meadow, grove, and stream,
> The earth, and every common sight,
>   To me did seem
>   Apparelled in celestial light,
> The glory and the freshness of a dream.
> It is not now as it hath been of yore;—
>   Turn wheresoe'er I may,
>   By night or day,
> The things which I have seen I now can see no more.[12]

Nevertheless, says Brown, "these categories . . . remain in the Romantics arbitrary and mystical because they lack a foundation in psychology. The psychoanalytical theory of childhood completes the Romantic movement by filling this gap."[13]

One crucial aspect of Freud's theory, relevant to our understanding of Roethke's new poems, is the concept of regression. Freud develops this carefully in *The Interpretation of Dreams* (1900):

> What takes place in the hallucinatory dream we can describe in no other way than by saying that the excitation follows a retrogressive course. It communicates itself not to the motor end of the apparatus but to the sensory end, and finally reaches the system of perception. If we call the direction which the psychic process follows from the unconscious into the waking state *progressive*, we may then speak of the dream as having a *regressive* character.

Later in the same work Freud asserts: "In regression the structure of dream-thoughts breaks up into its raw materials." Thus, in dreams one goes back to original perceptions, recovering primary sensations of light, sound, and so on. This partly explains the strangely perceptual quality dreams often possess. For dream-thinking, Freud claims, exploits the deepest regions of memory; it reactivates the infantile mind and reinhabits the past. He concludes

> that dreaming is on the whole an act of regression to the earliest relationships of the dreamer, a resuscitation of his childhood, of the impulses which were then available. Behind the childhood of the individual we are then promised an insight into the phylogenetic childhood, into the evolution of the human race, of which the development of the individual is only an abridged repetition influenced by the fortuitous circumstances of life.[14]

Kenneth Burke saw the importance of Freud's theories for literary studies. In his essay "Freud—and the Analysis of Poetry," he begins with a confession: "The reading of Freud I find suggestive almost to the point of bewilderment." It would be foolish, Burke remarks, to equate psychology and literature, the Freudian perspective having been developed "primarily to chart a psychiatric field rather than an aesthetic one."[15] Yet the technique of art depends upon the workings of the unconscious, and the more a critic can learn about the psychology of literary invention, the better he will understand the literary product itself. As Lionel Trilling says in his essay on Freud in *The Liberal Imagination*: "Freud discovered in the very organization of the mind those mechanisms by which art makes its effects."[16] And Burke attempts to outline the specific mechanisms that obtain in poetic composition.

To begin, Burke turns to Freud's speculations on sexual puns and double-entendres, predicting that close analysis of poetic language will bear out many of Freud's ideas. Much of the ostensibly incomprehensible gibberish of Roethke's "Lost Son" sequence can be explained in terms of what Freud called "dream-language," a mode of expression which reaches into the unconscious and uses the inherent ambiguity of language to its fullest purpose. According to Freud—and Burke—art is a way of making the unconscious conscious. When hailed as "discoverer of the unconscious" late in life, Freud responded by saying that "the poets and philosophers before me discovered the unconscious; what I discovered was the scientific method whereby the unconscious can be studied."[17] Thus, Freud (and Freudian critics like Burke) established the close relation between art and the unconscious; this was attended by interest in wit, the element of play which bridges the gap between conscious and unconscious in language. Here, of course, the poet enters. He is first of all one who likes to "play with words," much as a child does. The great enemy of the unconscious, Freud said, is reason (the reality-principle) which restricts the free associational process so crucial to invention. Freud explains: "Wit carries out its purpose in advancing the thought by magnifying it and by guarding it against reason. Here again it reveals its original nature in that it sets itself up against an inhibiting and restrictive power, or against the critical judgement."[18] Seeing the importance of puns and double-entendres in poetry, Burke would often focus on patterns of word play in a text. And he succeeded in challenging his pupil, Roethke, who suddenly began to play with language in a daring way. The idea of a poem as the conscious reproduction of a dream state was new to Roethke, too, and it provides a key to some of the more difficult passages in *The Lost Son*. The difference between poetry and dreaming remains, of course, the element of conscious control. As Charles Lamb said long before Freudian criticism: "The poet dreams being awake. He is not possessed by his subject but has dominion over it."[19]

Burke also took up the concept of regression, noticing with typical brilliance that "regression . . . is a function of progression."[20] This recalls Roethke's notebook entry of January 1944: "I go back because I want to go forward." A year later Roethke quoted Kierkegaard in his notebooks: "Life can only be understood backwards; but it can only be lived forwards."[21] Through Burke, Roethke came to understand the mechanics of regression which chart the tortuous return of the poet-protagonist into the hinterlands of memory. *Praise to the End!* takes the poet back once again, even further, into the womb and beyond, pressing through into the eternity preceding existence, Blake's "Vale of Har." But the regressive journey harrows the traveler. For, according to Freud and Burke, birth is the first jolt to anyone. Burke laments the "change at birth when the foetus, heretofore enjoying a larval existence in the womb, being fed on manna from the placenta, so outgrows this circle of confinement, whereat it must burst forth into a different kind of world—a world of locomotion, aggression, competition, hunt." Burke continues: "In the private life of the individual there may be many subsequent jolts of a less purely biological nature, as with the death of some one person who had become pivotal to this individual's mental economy."[22] For Roethke, adolescence and the death of his father provided pivotal jolts from which he never fully recovered.

Regression, then, is the leitmotif of *The Lost Son*. The protagonist, seeking to restore unity, to be reborn, must dive into the past in order to cleanse himself and recover his identity. As Burke comments on this theme:

> In the literature of transitional eras, for instance, we find an especial profusion of rebirth rituals, where the poet is making the symbolic passes that will endow him with a new identity. Now, imagine him trying to do a very thorough job of this reidentification. To be completely reborn he would have to change his very lineage itself. He would have to revise not only his present but his past.

He stresses the role of psychoanalytical techniques in gaining access to this kind of literature: "In so far as art contains a surrealist ingredient (and all art contains some of this ingredient), psychoanalytic coordinates are required to explain the logic of its structure." Thus he demands the fullest biographical data that can be gathered about a writer, insisting that "we can eliminate biography as a relevant fact about poetic organization only if we consider the work of art as if it were written neither by people nor for people."[23]

The effect of Burke's general poetics on Roethke's notion of what a poem should do was profound. He abandoned the abstract, mechanical style of *Open House* and, in *The Lost Son*, began to chronicle a young man's regression into his own murky past, a mission of self-discovery. Burke's idea of a poem as "a symbolic proclaiming and formation of identity" describes the "Lost Son" poems accurately. And, wisely, Burke associates this kind of poem with Romanticism, adding that "the Romantic movement tended greatly to conceive of man's identity in nonsocial, purely naturalistic terms, specializing in such objective imagery as would most directly correspond in quality with subjective states."

The poem, he continues, enacts a symbolic "slaying of the old self" which is "complemented by the emergence of a new self."[24] The shape of this second book suggests that Roethke was an attentive student, and Burke certainly may be regarded as the spiritual father of *The Lost Son*. We can see why Roethke always called him "Pa."

Roethke's particular burden, the source of creative energy in *The Lost Son*, was his relationship with his father, Otto. He thought himself a failure in his father's eyes, long after his father had died. Otto wanted young Theodore to become a lawyer, and Roethke enrolled for one miserable term in the law school at the University of Michigan. He forsook law for poetry, and acquired an excess of guilt in the process. But this was only a small aspect of a larger guilt, one of mysterious origins, associated with his father's death. This guilt produced all manner of anxieties, including an obsession with death. It also was the source of Roethke's anxieties about God, who gradually replaces Otto in the poet's private pantheon. A highly selective anthology of entries taken from the poet's unpublished notebooks while he was working on the major part of *The Lost Son* opens a window into Roethke's mind:

1943

Our concern with death puts an edge upon life. It gives us dignity and purpose. It resolves us to condense more [into] our few hours.[25]

At 34, at last I find out what loneliness means.

Hunted the final night, dug in my own rich dark.

Innocence is the natural state from which man has separated to find corruption.[26]

I carry the curse of too many lives.

I have a great horror of thrusting myself on people or bothering them in any way.

Not all the dead are used: we must take what we can from them.

The devil who has my heart / Will not let me be.

Charlie and Otto Roethke
labored for sixty years
trying to make a greenhouse
that was truly theirs.[27]

1944

Thanatos: death defines love.

When a man comes to realize that something he has done is evil, then he has suffered a growth of the soul.

An almost insane terror of death.

The tough who crave but do not whimper for love.

Papa is holy.

What an irony that we love the concrete so much, yet this is the very thing that must pass away.[28]

The bones of my human guilt.

To write about one's past is not to escape but to understand the present.

"Without contraries is no progression" (Blake)

I go back because I want to go forward.[29]

What a miserable little talent I have! after all the ten years of effort.

Style is the ultimate morality of the mind.[30]

I learned the struggle in the stem.

Whose guilt I carry?

Make your poetry the reflection of your life.[31]

1945

Times when every simple act of life is a burden: times of NO THOUGHT.

"For it is the nature of man to deteriorate unless he recognizes the tendency and the source of his deterioration and expends actual effort to reduce them." (Yvor Winters)

Ah papa! It was seven long months before your guts leaked away.

Visit me: wrath and fury.
Blow out my veins.[32]

I don't believe there is a God, but to try to believe in one is one of the noblest human efforts.

Lawrence had the fierce sense of life—but notice this—a place became exhausted for him. He could not pull it out of himself.

I suppose it is a dangerous feeling of power you get from a successful duel with death. But God you have a pride in yourself when you *know* your fever has been 103.5–104 for five days and you can still bark orders and sit up and not lie down limp as a rag.

Afraid? why hell, I've been afraid all my life—dogs, thunder, my cousin.

Ah papa! He could snot his nose like an archbishop.

Something from this illness seems to have shaken loose powers; I am alive with ideas, some bad, no doubt, but there is more vehemence, more energy, more contempt, more love.

The will, that treacherous guide, often betrays our deepest self.[33]

I became to myself a barren land. (Psalms 19:12)

Lawrence . . . his particular psychological situation always linked to the life around him.

"One of the perils of the soul is the loss of the soul." (C. G. Jung)

The poem is a kind of death: it is finished, a complete, a comprehensive act. The better the poem, the more final the destruction.

Anxiety—It is only when we begin to hurt those that we love that the guilt with which we are born becomes intolerable . . . we hate ourselves in them.

A poem that is the shape of the psyche itself . . . in times of great stress, that's what I tried to write.[34]

Things, how they involve me!

The soul cannot be defiled.[35]

A constant attempt to see things in human form which are not human at all.

My private conscience is terrible.

An anguish of concreteness.

We must seek to go beyond the pleasure principle to come through to social and philosophical reality, yet preserving the freshness and naivete.

The dream has its own internal laws.[36]

Why am I afraid of death when so much of me is dead already?

The thought of oblivion reduces all happiness to ashes.[37]

Am I saying anything new when I say that poetry is difficult: heart-breakingly so?

A teacher: a wonderful capacity for being enthusiastic about the obvious.

A bleakness about poetry-writing: like getting to the factory at seven in the morning.

The poet: perceives the thing in physical terms.

All the present has fallen: I am only what I remember.[38]

"Actually, our human passions are always connected with antagonistic passions, our love with hate, and our pleasure with our pains. Between joy and the external cause there is invariably some gap and some obstruction—society, sin, virtue, the body, the separate self. Hence arises the ardor of passion. And hence it is that the ardor for complete union is indissolubly linked with a wish for death that brings release." [unidentified quotation]

We live by fictions and myths. They seem as necessary as food.

In many things I was the son of my father.

I feel beneath me the whole vast motion of the world.

To all men, at some times, comes the conviction that he is the center of the world.[39]

Happiness and gaiety are incidental, the inseparable counterparts of a capacity for grief and pity.[40]

. . . a haunting sense that I was an herbaceous plant, as large as a large tree, with a trunk of the same pith, and branched as large and shadowing. . . .

Poetry is still the natural form of self-expression.

For ten years I played the roaring boy when really I was the frightened boy.

A notion of centrality: there is a core to all things that even a child knows, yet it is one of those ancient thoughts that can never become a cliche.[41]

A man must resist some of the elements of his own age.

"Life can only be understood backwards; but it can only be lived forwards." (Kierkegaard)

The visible obscures delight.

I'm in the pits still; in the mires, spiritually. I can't seem to throw off the sensuality that is part of me. I don't want to throw it off. I'm not tempted: I'm a tempter. Maybe I'm even one of that party of the Devil. One of his seducing fat charges.[42]

Lost in a dismal place
I had suffered a soul's growth;
Shrunken, loose in my skin,
Out of myself I rose,
Hungry and haunted.

What was this greenhouse? It was a jungle, and it was paradise, it was order and disorder. Was it an escape? No, for it was a reality harder than the various suspensions of terror.

Snow: symbol of death, symbol of purity.

What is sown comes to life when it dies.

He'll come when. No, I know he won't come. He doesn't care about me anymore. No, I mean Him, the big He, that Great big three-cornered Papa.[43]

I became learned in the rhetoric of desperation.

Something within wants to get out.

When you're alone you either get something done or you fall apart.

The visible exhausts me. I am dissolved in shadow.
I felt myself falling into a dark swirl.[44]

How terrible the need for God.

A great deal of art arises out of opposition.[45]

Lawrence: analogies in the natural world.

I can no longer reject God because the metaphors are bad.[46]

Who killed Papa?

Conceptual thinking is like believing in God; one wants to put it off as long as possible.[47]

These excerpts are remarkable evidence of Roethke's passionate inner life. His obsessions, his burdens, stand out clearly: family guilt, death, the Romantic contrarieties, God, and poetry. Many of the passages have been quoted before, but looked at as a mosaic in this way, the poet's mind and sensibility emerge. The same energetic language that makes *The Lost Son* his greatest achievement can be found in the notebooks, which he quarried for poems. We learn a great deal about Roethke's reading, too, by his quotations; Blake, Lawrence, Jung, and the Bible exercise a special power over him. Roethke understood in his bones how thought and feeling must never be divorced, though—in true Romantic fashion—he enjoyed railing against "conceptual thinking" and reason. One central theme to emerge in these years was the importance of death for the living, how it "puts an edge to life." This key Romantic idea harks back to Keats especially, as in the "Ode to Melancholy" or to modern restatements of this theme, as in Stevens's "Sunday Morning," where he proclaims: "Death is the mother of beauty." The excerpts also show that Roethke did not want to leapfrog over the material world in favor of immutable spiritual realms. He preferred that "anguish of concreteness," crying out in a late poem: "Things, how they involve me!"

Having grown up around a greenhouse, Roethke was not isolated from the natural life cycle of plants. Now, approaching middle age, he sought to regain the insights of his childhood. He was coming to understand, perhaps remember, that "ripeness is all." Freud put this fundamental Romantic insight on a psychological basis, arguing in *Beyond the Pleasure Principle* that death is no accident, no external event; rather, "the goal of all life is death."[48] His suggestion that death-acceptance *implies* life-acceptance reflects the great psychologist's sane and detached way of looking at the world. Yet Roethke was not, and did not want to be, detached. The struggle of *The Lost Son* moves to reunion with the past, with the natural cycle. Roethke, in a sense, revises the myth of himself in these poems, becoming a modern version of Emerson's Orphic poet who says: "A man is a god in ruins. When men are innocent, life shall be longer, and shall pass into the immortal, as gently as we awake from dreams. Now, the world would be insane and rabid, if these disorganizations should last for hundreds of years. It is kept in check by death and infancy. Infancy is the perpetual Messiah, which comes into the arms of fallen men, and pleads with them to return to Paradise."[49] Hence, when Roethke says, in his notebooks, that he feels beneath him "the whole vast motion of the world," he shows an awareness of the powerful cycle of nature from which most men are detached. By analogy with the vegetal world, man comes to the belief that "what is sown comes to life when it dies." What Roethke learned as a child was the lesson of the plants, the cyclical movement wherein change is an illusion. Life itself continues, though it continually alters form. This is the "notion of centrality" Roethke mentions in his notebooks, the "core to all things that even a child knows."

In summary, the notebooks from these years reveal a man in the act of self-discovery; they report a strange voyage back to beginnings. Along the way, the poet-traveler meets various beasts he must slay, including his dead father and a number of old selves that refuse to sleep. He had one crucial lesson to learn: that life *includes* death and is magnified by it. Like Dante venturing into the underworld with Virgil as a guide, Roethke enters the unconscious with Burke leading him and with the spirits of Freud, Jung, and the Romantic poets in attendance. The goal of this quest finds perfect expression in the entry: "All the present has fallen: I am only what I remember." Here lies a reality beyond the mutable, what Roethke eventually called "the pure serene of memory in one man" (*CP*, p. 201).

CHAPTER SEVEN

THE GREENHOUSE POEMS

We are always demanding a framework, a metaphor, a legend.
    Roethke, *"Notebooks" (20 November 1943)*

In particular, what is a greenhouse?

                                                    Kenneth Burke

In a seminal essay, "The Vegetal Radicalism of
Theodore Roethke," Burke asks himself, "What
is a greenhouse?" and suggests the following
possibilities:

> It is not sheer nature, like a jungle; nor even
> regulated nature, like a formal garden. It is
> not the starkly unnatural, like a factory. Nor
> is it in those intermediate realms of institu-
> tional lore, systematic thanatopses, or con-
> venient views of death, we find among the
> reliques of a natural history museum. Nor
> would it be like a metropolitan art gallery. It
> is like all of these only in the sense that it is a
> museum experience, and so an aspect of our
> late civilization. But there is a peculiar bal-
> ance of the natural and unnatural in a green-
> house. All about one, the lovely, straining
> beings, visibly drawing sustenance from ul-
> timate, invisible powers—in a silent blare of
> vitality—yet as morbid as the caged animals
> of a zoo.[1]

In many ways the greenhouse is an ideal symbol, embracing the central paradox of art: that
art is not life, yet it must embody life. The
earthly paradise of an artist has to be ordered,
but it must somehow contain its opposite—
chaos—within itself. Tension—the vital element in all art—arises out of conflict, and in
Romantic theory the function of the imagina-

tion is to effect a proper balance or reconciliation of opposites. The greenhouse, literally, provides just the right contrarieties: light against darkness, order against chaos, life against death. Roethke was lucky to inherit this potent symbol from his Michigan childhood.

The first section of *The Lost Son* contains thirteen poems, plus the autobiographical vignette "Frau Bauman, Frau Schmidt, and Frau Schwartze" which was added to the greenhouse poems in later editions. This sequence, says Louis Martz, is "one of the permanent achievements of modern poetry."[2] These brief lyrics, all containing the image of a greenhouse at their centers, prepare the way for the longer, more difficult poems of the "Lost Son" sequence. *The Lost Son*, in contrast to *Open House*, is not just a collection of poems; it is a book and must be read whole, in sequence. It tells a story, the backward journey of the poet through memory toward self-realization. It is a version of what Bloom calls the interior quest-romance.

These poems represent a dramatic shift in style away from the formal lyrics of *Open House*. Roethke imposed no outward structure on them, allowing them to grow from within and seek their appropriate shapes. This is what "free verse" should mean: language exactly equivalent to reality, a skin pulled tautly over experience. It remains the easiest kind of poem to do badly and the most difficult to do well, because without formal restraints, the poet must have a perfect ear; he must *never* lose sight of his object for an instant. Roethke succeeds in this brilliantly. Each poem unfolds into what seems its one possible shape—like a plant, whose ultimate form is contained implicitly in the seed itself. Always the language of free verse has to be concrete. As Roethke observes: "The poet: perceives the thing in physical terms."[3] A mimetic theory of language underlies this notion; the objective of poetic diction in these terms is to reflect, imitate, the physical image. To achieve this effect, Roethke had to summon reserves of technical virtuosity learned in his apprentice years. The first fruits are the greenhouse poems, of which Burke has said: "No matter how brief the poems are, they progress from stage to stage. Reading them, you have strongly the sense of entering at one place, winding through a series of internal developments, and coming out somewhere else."[4]

The final thirteen (original) greenhouse poems in *The Lost Son* survived a winnowing process stretching from 1942 until their publication in 1948. Abandoned drafts of greenhouse-type poems scatter the notebooks from these years, and by browsing through them one learns about Roethke's huge effort to be concrete, to "perceive the thing in physical terms." Here is an early, uncollected poem called "Growth" (1943):

Around us abundant examples flourish
In the patience of sight, the response of seasons,
Swelling of seed, algae persisting in snow,
Soft snail-marrow jogging its acorn of shell;
For growth is a tadpole kicking, a wave-like
Weed-like motion of small beginning,
No dolphin-change or leaping.
Perhaps, further in time than solar calculation,
Some sport of the spirit, a psychic mutation,
Will unite pursuer with pursued, fish with otter,
And instinct enter the lost realm of understanding.[5]

Sloppy and unfocused, the poem dissolves into hopeless abstraction in the last four lines. Yet there is promise in the line "Soft snail-marrow jogging its acorn of shell," which combines concrete description with rhythms that suggest the primitive sense of unrestrainable life.

"The Snail" is an early unpublished version of a much later, considerably revised, poem called "A Light Breather" (1953). It was written, in the following draft, in 1944, anticipating in manner the greenhouse poems of *The Lost Son*. The poet avoids nearly all abstractions (the word "spirit" may be allowed for the conceit's sake) and generates a mimetic rhythm:

As a seed sings and beats like a fish
In soil moist and soft,
So moves the spirit
Still and inward,—
A snail:
Taking and embracing its surroundings,
Its house on its arched back,
Its horn touching a stone,—
A music in a hood,
A small thing,
Singing.[6]

Roethke had finally hit upon his own style; he had found a way of making his conceits physical and concrete. This poem was unsuitable, of course, for the greenhouse sequence, so Roethke tucked it away for later use. But he knew he had discovered a voice unlike anyone else's.

Roethke had learned how to whittle a poem to its bones. Here is a wordy early draft of a poem called "Propagation," which Roethke would divide into the first two lyrics of the greenhouse sequence, "Cuttings" and "Cuttings (*later*)":

Slivers of stem, minutely furred,
Tucked into sand still marked with thumb prints,
Cuttings of coleas, geranium, blood-red fuchsia,
Stand stiff in their beds.
Topsoil crusts over like bakery sugar.

But three inches beneath, in the damp sandy cradles,
Where the stem-end is cut diagonally like a string-bean,
The thin, flexible cells keep coaxing up water.
Even before fuzzy root-hairs reach for gritty sustenance,
One pale horn of growth, a nubly root-cap,
Nudges a sand-crumb loose,
Humps like a sprout,
Then stretches out straight.[7]

'Cuttings" is sleeker, more evocative:

Sticks-in-a-drowse droop over sugary loam,
Their intricate stem-fur dries;
But still the delicate slips keep coaxing up water;
The small cells bulge;

One nub of growth
Nudges a sand-crumb loose,
Pokes through a musty sheath
Its pale tendrilous horn.
(CP, p. 37)

The odd noun combination "sticks-in-a-drowse" reflects the continuing influence of Hopkins, as does the sensuous and concrete imagery. Monosyllables dominate the poem and internal alliteration forces the reader onward as the delicate shoot breaks upward through the topsoil. The poet himself stays out of the picture, but the poem imitates a psychic state; it can be read as a conceit with one half of the metaphor missing, the tenor presented without its vehicle (as in Blake's "Sick Rose"). The poem describes a state of consciousness which precedes the rational; it is a direct representation of the infantile nervous system, "polymorphously perverse" in Freud's sense of that provocative phrase. It is a poem about beginnings without fanfare, a poem of expectancy.

"Cuttings (later)" brings the poet-protagonist into focus. Roethke dramatizes the conflict of life against death in the plant world: "This urge, wrestle, resurrection of dry sticks, / Cut stems struggling to put down feet" (CP, p. 37). One critic calls attention to the "sliding of the metaphorical images by which the plants are rendered backward along the phylogenetic scale."[8] Indeed, the poem's metaphors descend the Great Chain of Being systematically: saint becomes suckling, and sobbing infant becomes fish. One senses at a very early stage in the sequence that the poet intends more than mere descriptions of a natural process. Blessing, somewhat vaguely, suggests that "the real *meaning* of these poems is the energy they convey."[9] Yet Blessing has singled out an important aspect of the greenhouse poems as a whole: they *move*. Whereas the lyrics of *Open House* can be thought of as photographs, the lyrics of *The Lost Son* are cinematic. Stanley Kunitz put it this way: "What absorbs his attention is not the intricate tracery of a leaf or the blazonry of the complete flower, but the stretching and reaching of a plant, its green force, its invincible Becoming."[10]

"Root Cellar" follows, taking us back further into the dank, steamy atmosphere of a greenhouse cellar, where the life force survives at the level of instinct:

> Nothing would sleep in the cellar, dank as a ditch,
> Bulbs broke out of boxes hunting for chinks in the dark,
> Shoots dangled and drooped,
> Lolling obscenely from mildewed crates,
> Hung down long yellow evil necks, like tropical snakes.
> (*CP*, p. 38)

The cellar, with its explicitly sexual imagery ("Shoots dangled and drooped, / Lolling obscenely"), may be read as a metaphorical equivalent of the unconscious mind. Here life persists at its most primitive level, gasping among roots and stems in a lively slime. "Nothing would give up life: / Even the dirt kept breathing a small breath." The life force thrives on opposition, importunately breathing. Sullivan points out the "terrifying and perverse" nature of Roethke's life impulse, calling the cellar "a chaos of aimless and bewildering multiplicity."[11] Yet there is something positive about the fact that "Nothing would give up life." It is strangely comforting to know that life *insists* on itself, albeit at this elemental level.

We come upon the actual greenhouse in "Forcing House," which describes the artificial environment working *against* the natural seasons of the planet. Here are "Fifty summers in motion at once, / As the live heat billows from the pipes and pots" (*CP*, p. 38). And in "Weed Puller," which follows, we are introduced to the protagonist, the "lost son," at his labors:

> Under the concrete benches,
> Hacking at black hairy roots,—

Those lewd monkey-tails hanging from drainholes,—
Digging into the soft rubble underneath. . . .
(CP, p. 39)

The boy ferrets among a variety of loathsome weeds, grubs, sticks, and fern-shapes, "Tugging all day at perverse' life." This labor resembles what Roethke called in the notebooks "The long testing of the unconscious before one gets even a few symbols true to himself."[12] In any case, the poem takes the form of descent into an underworld, whether or not we liken it to the unconscious; the last lines are explicit: "Me down in that fetor of weeds, / Crawling on all fours, / Alive, in a slippery grave."

The boy is not present in the next poem, "Orchids," one of the most accomplished in the sequence:

They lean over the path,
Adder-mouthed,
Swaying close to the face,
Coming out, soft and deceptive,
Limp and damp, delicate as a young bird's tongue;
Their fluttery fledgling lips
Move slowly,
Drawing in the warm air.

And at night,
The faint moon falling through whitewashed glass,
The heat going down
So their musky smell comes even stronger,
Drifting down from their mossy cradles:
So many devouring infants!
Soft luminescent fingers,
Lips neither dead nor alive,
Loose ghostly mouths
Breathing.
(CP, p. 39)

The conflict of opposites occurs more subtly here than before. Daylight governs the first stanza, while evening presides over the second. Similarly, the air is alternately warm and cold. The plants, like strange reptiles in a zoo, are awake, then asleep. The adder-mouthed creatures sway upward under the influence of sunlight, then recede to their mossy cradles when moonlight filters through the glassy roof. The gradual transformation of metaphor in the poem deserves attention; the snake imagery, signifying a very low point on the phylogenetic scale, gives way to bird imagery in the first stanza. By the second, the orchids have become "So many devouring infants!" The climbing is to a human level, albeit infancy. Yet a stronger transformation takes place in the last lines as the "Loose ghostly mouths" hover in suspended animation, "neither dead nor alive," waiting and breathing. The plants achieve a kind of spirituality, having become ghosts. (One recalls the Latin meaning of *spiritus*: breath.) By reversing direction along the scale of being, the poet sets "Orchids" in opposition to "Cuttings (*later*)," perhaps to suggest that a dialectical progression exists between the individual poems as a sequence. Malkoff, who reads the poems as a thinly veiled sexual autobiography, sees the dialectic of innocence and experience as a primary pattern in the sequence, and says of "Orchids" that "infancy here is not the age of innocence, but rather of demanding, grasping, undisciplined sexual urges."[13] While this is true, I think one loses the highly specific, concrete texture of this great lyric by treating its allegorical dimension as anything more than subliminal. It is first a poem about orchids.

"Moss–Gathering" brings the boy back to our attention. It narrates an experience familiar to Roethke as a child, that of going out into the countryside to gather patches of moss for lining cemetery baskets. The poem looks at the activity metaphorically. After cutting up squares from the earth's surface, the sensitive young man claims a certain feeling of remorse:

> As if I had broken the natural order of things in that swampland;
> Disturbed some rhythm, old and of vast importance,
> By pulling off flesh from the living planet;
> As if I had committed, against the whole scheme of life, a desecration.
> (*CP*, p. 40)

Only a poet plagued by guilt feelings could have reacted in this way to an apparently innocent task. Malkoff writes: "The 'gathering' itself takes place in a landscape with clearly sexual overtones; it is followed by a feeling of guilt at the onanistic action."[14] The phrase "pulling off flesh" certainly may have this level of association, yet the poem needs a wider reading. We meet the boy for the second time here, again in isolation, and again his response to the environment is individual. In both "Weed Puller" and "Moss–Gathering," nature is animate, threatening, ready to accuse or overwhelm the protagonist. Nature is never simply acted upon; it reacts, participating in the interplay of subject and object so crucial to Romantic poetry. La Belle points to Wordsworth's "Nutting," another Romantic poet's guilt-laden account of a childhood "desecration," as a precursor.[15] A passage toward the end of "Nutting" does parallel Roethke's last line:

Then up I rose
And dragged to earth both branch and bough, with crash
And merciless ravage: and the shady nook
Of hazels, and the green and mossy bower,
Deformed and sullied, patiently gave up
Their quiet being: and unless I now
Confound my present feelings with the past,
Ere from the mutilated bower I turned
Exulting, rich beyond the wealth of kings,
I felt a sense of pain when I beheld
The silent trees, and saw the intruding sky.[16]

Burke uses the next poem, "Big Wind," to illustrate his thesis that when reading the greenhouse poems "you have strongly the sense of entering at one place, winding through a series of internal developments, and coming out somewhere else." In this essentially narrative poem the poet begins by defining the situation with a rhetorical question:

Where were the greenhouses going,
Lunging into the lashing
Wind driving water
So far down the river
All the faucets stopped?—
(CP, p. 41)

There follows an account of efforts to keep the greenhouse together and functioning in the storm. The florists drain the manure machine and pump the stale mixture into rusty boilers, trying to keep the temperature high enough to save the plants. The greenhouse appears to be collapsing in high winds. The narrator explains:

Where the worst wind was,
Creaking the cypress window-frames,
Cracking so much thin glass
We stayed up all night,
Stuffing the holes with burlap.

This exact description of the physical work dominates the middle section of "Big Wind"; careful manipulation of line length and stresses pulls the reader forward through the poem like a piece of paper caught in a wind tunnel. The heavy use of present participles in a poem set in the past tense gives this memory poem its immediacy. And the poet ends with a vivid and perfect image-with-symbol: the greenhouse as a ship:

But she rode it out,
That old rose-house,
She hove into the teeth of it,
The core and pith of that ugly storm,
Ploughing with her stiff prow,
Bucking into the wind-waves
That broke over the whole of her,
Flailing her sides with spray,
Flinging long strings of wet across the roof-top,
Finally veering, wearing themselves out, merely
Whistling thinly under the wind-vents;
She sailed until the calm morning,
Carrying her full cargo of roses.

The poem moves, as a whole, from great instability to great stability, and the final image resolves the tensions generated earlier in the poem. This is, as Burke notes, perhaps the finest poem in the greenhouse sequence, yet it has had little sustained attention from critics. Malkoff tries to force the poem into a sexual interpretation and the result is ludicrous. He writes: "In 'Big Wind,' the protagonist confronts a more adult kind of sexuality. We have had hints of this before, particularly in the concluding lines of 'Cuttings (*later*),' but never was sexual intercourse itself so intimately related to the poem's central metaphor."[17] Nothing at all in "Big Wind" suggests sexual intercourse without stretching the imagination. Blessing is more sensible, seeing the poem as "a figure for the poet's life, that continuous activity of the mind pressing out to preserve itself from the violence of time and change," echoing, of course, a famous passage from Wallace Stevens's *Necessary Angel*.[18] For the subject of the poem is the problem of energy, creative energy. The poet, like the florist in "Big Wind," uses every possible source of imaginative energy to sustain his artificial world. But this is to exceed the literal boundaries of the poem. "Big Wind" enriches the context of the sequence as a whole; it thrusts the protagonist into a larger world, one where he is no longer on his own, where the excessive self-consciousness of "Weed Puller" and "Moss Gathering" will no longer suffice. While the poem has a completeness which makes it an ideal anthology piece on its own, within the context of *The Lost Son* it is functional. Father and son, working here in a desperate attempt to save their crop, are brought together in a touching way. It is the unity of their experience that matters to the poet recollecting the scene many years after his father's death. It is this harmony, broken by death, which the poet longs for during the rest of his life.

The last poems of the sequence widen the context of the protagonist still further. "Old Florist" draws a portrait of an elderly greenhouse attendant working at his job with loving patience, "That hump of a man bunching chrysanthemums / Or pinching-back asters, or planting azaleas, / Tamping and stamping dirt into pots" (*CP*, p. 42). The poem flashes a picture in ten lines made up of only one elaborate sentence. La Belle finds parallels here with Wordsworth's many solitaries, such as the Old Cumberland Beggar or the Old Leech-gatherer from "Resolution and Independence," men who "live near to nature and whose worthiness and wisdom are a result of active, direct association with nature."[19]

"Transplanting" describes a normal activity around the greenhouse and picks up an earlier theme: the struggle to be born. Aided by human skills, the plants appear under less pressure in this poem than in, say, "Cuttings." These plants, like children in the family atmosphere, are carefully attended; the controlled environment allows maturation to take place unhampered by the outside world. Of course, for the human organism, the shock of adolescence often comes from a first encounter with reality in an unadulterated form. Comparisons between the growth of the boy, the "lost son," and the plants seem inevitable, although the connection remains unspecific until the final poem, "Frau Bauman, Frau Schmidt, and Frau Schwartze." "Child on Top of the Greenhouse" occurs between "Transplanting" and "Flower Dump" as if to force the comparison by sheer association. In this brief lyric, composed entirely of participle phrases without main verbs, the reader enters the scene, as Blessing says, *in medias res*. The poem has one central image: the boy balancing dangerously on the slender beam that holds the glass roof together:

> The wind billowing out the seat of my britches,
> My feet crackling splinters of glass and dried putty,
> The half-grown chrysanthemums staring up like accusers,
> Up through the streaked glass, flashing with sunlight,
> A few white clouds all rushing eastward,
> A line of elms plunging and tossing like horses,
> And everyone, everyone pointing up and shouting!
> (*CP*, p. 43)

This portrait of the daredevil boy expands our knowledge of his character. It was very dangerous to climb on top of a greenhouse because the risk of plunging through the glass was great. The boy defies adult warnings, as well as accusations offered by the chrysanthemums, to become a hero. He needs the attention, and this ploy succeeds admirably in attracting that. Here is the artist-in-embryo, alienated from authority, from the natural world, exposing himself to destruction in the vain hope of glory. Roethke follows this poem, bathetically, with "Flower Dump," an emblem of decay. The pretentious exhibitionism of the child on the greenhouse roof contrasts with the compost heap, "Whole beds of bloom pitched on a pile" (*CP*, p. 43). This was the penultimate poem in the original sequence of 1948, followed by "Carnations," which makes an upswing from the fetid level of "Flower Dump." It tells of a "crisp hyacinthine coolness, / Like that clear autumnal weather of eternity, / The windless perpetual morning above a September cloud" (*CP*, p. 43). The sequence should have ended here, but later editions finish with "Frau Bauman, Frau Schmidt, and Frau Schwartze," an anecdotal poem written in a style out of keeping with the rest. The poem is more whimsical, less dense; the metaphor of the child-as-plant nurtured in the hothouse environment by florist-guardians is made too explicit. The poem is more allusive than anything going before it, referring to the three Fates (implicitly) and echoing Yeats's "The Magi" in a conscious manner. With this one reservation, the greenhouse poems are preferable to almost anything else in Roethke. He would write as well again, but never with more sheer verbal energy and concreteness.

A dozen short poems, grouped into two sections, follow the sequence of greenhouse poems. In style and method, they hark back to *Open House* and are therefore less interesting, but a few of them deserve attention. Especially important is "My Papa's Waltz," which leaves a strong impression of Otto Roethke that will carry over into the "Lost Son" poems. Otto appears as a huge, brutish man, full of whiskey and affection for his son, which he translates into an overly fierce playfulness. The boy's reaction is one of fear, although the poet's whimsical tone of recollection softens the response:

> The whiskey on your breath
> Could make a small boy dizzy;
> But I hung on like death:
> Such waltzing was not easy.
>
> We romped until the pans
> Slid from the kitchen shelf;
> My mother's countenance
> Could not unfrown itself.
>
> The hand that held my wrist
> Was battered on one knuckle;
> At every step you missed
> My right ear scraped a buckle.

You beat time on my head
With a palm caked hard by dirt,
Then waltzed me off to bed
Still clinging to your shirt.
(*CP*, p. 45)

In a brief space, the poet drops a large number of clues about his family and its tensions. The father is a man of high spirits, a drinker, a family man, a member of the working class, and someone feared by his son and wife. The wife stands to one side, disapproving but unable to stop the scene. The boy clings to his father for dear life, terrified by his physical power; though "Such waltzing was not easy" and his right ear scrapes a buckle at every missed step, he pretends that all is well. Why doesn't he cry or resist? What holds the mother back? Both recognize the deep love that underlies this outwardly rough behavior, the love that haunted Roethke throughout his life, forcing him to write "Who killed Papa?" in his notebooks almost twenty years after Otto's death. This tough Prussian father, with his simple and strong emotions, expected a great deal from young Roethke. And the sense of failure which dogged the poet till his death can be traced back to these unfulfilled expectations.

Two other poems of reminiscence help to deepen our image of the poet-protagonist: "Pickle Belt" and "Double Feature." Here we encounter the adolescent for the first time in specific terms. The former poem shows a young man at work in a pickle factory:

He, in his shrunken britches,
Eyes rimmed with pickle dust,
Prickling with all the itches
Of sixteen-year-old lust.
(*CP*, p. 46)

The latter recalls the familiar scene of a small movie theater where lovers fondle sweaty hands and sleep-heavy children lean against their mothers. The realistic details of this poem, and others like it in these sections, prepare the ground for surrealism in the "Lost Son" poems; without this gravity, the effect of weightlessness would be lost.

The last poem before "The Lost Son" is "The Waking," a title Roethke liked well enough to use again five years later. This bright lyric celebrates the sense of joy the poet feels while crossing an open field in midsummer. Again, it is a realistic, literal poem which prepares the way for the symbolism of the "Lost Son" poems and looks forward to *The Far Field*. Here is the child's view of nature:

This way! This way!
The wren's throat shimmered,
Either to other,
The blossoms sang.

The stones sang,
The little ones did,
And flowers jumped
Like small goats.

A ragged fringe
Of daisies waved;
I wasn't alone
In a grove of apples.
(*CP*, p. 51)

This sympathetic and responsive world surrounds and fills the poet. "And all the waters / Of all the streams / Sang in my veins / That summer day." Roethke, in effect, echoes Emerson's Orphic poet who maintains that "Nature is not fixed but fluid. Spirit alters, moulds, makes it. The immobility or bruteness of nature, is the absence of spirit; to pure spirit, it is fluid, it is volatile, it is obedient." In this ideal state, the poet knows himself to be the center of the world; the old subject–object dichotomy collapses. Again, quoting Emerson: "I become a transparent eyeball. I am nothing. I see all. The currents of the Universal Being circulate through me; I am part and parcel of God."[20]

Placed as it is before "The Lost Son," "The Waking" has strategic importance, invoking the ideal world that the poet-protagonist lost when his father died—when the descent into adolescence and adulthood began. The poem is a wish. It is a celebration of that primal innocence the poet seeks to recover from now on. The reader's emotions are lifted, temporarily, to make the effect of the fall in the next poem all the more vivid. One senses, like the reader in Book IV of *Paradise Lost*, that the "blissful bower" will soon be lost; "The Waking" gives way to a fitful, nightmare-ridden sleep.

CHAPTER EIGHT

THE LOST SON:

JOURNEY OF A HERO

All the present has fallen: I am only what I remember.
                    Roethke, *"Notebooks" (July 1945)*
For behold, the kingdom of God is within you.
                                    Luke 17:21

The "Lost Son" sequence includes the four long
poems that make up the fourth and last section
of *The Lost Son*, all of the poems from *Praise to
the End!* (1951), and the first poem of *The Waking* (1953). These poems, which are experimen-
tal in places to the point of unintelligibility,
have nonetheless acquired a permanent niche in
modern poetry. Roethke's method is that of free
association; he presses language into the service
of the unconscious to achieve the goal of all art:
the extension of consciousness. Thinking along
these lines, Roethke copied Hegel's famous dictum into his notebooks in 1947: "All consciousness is an appeal to more consciousness."[1]

In essence, this sequence describes the journey of the poet-protagonist into the hinterlands
of the unconscious mind, retracing steps that
have led him to the present; he has to recover
the past to "burn it up." The process was given
a scientific basis by Freud, who pioneered the
technique of *anamnesis* or filling in the memory
gaps by recollection. As Mircea Eliade explains
anamnesis: "The individual's return to the origin
is conceived as an opportunity for renewing
and regenerating the existence of him who un-
dertakes it."[2] It is clear that Roethke understood
this technique thoroughly; the "Lost Son"
poems are his attempt to incorporate psychoan-

alytic methods into his art. The danger here is of confusing life and art. Just as, for instance, the meditative religious poets of seventeenth-century England borrowed techniques of meditation from Ignatius, a psychoanalytic poet takes for his own certain Freudian techniques. Yet the meditative lyric *is not* meditation, nor is the psychoanalytic poem psychoanalysis. The "Lost Son" poems represent a version of the Freudian descent into the depths, a regression through time in search of what Freud called "primordial events," moments of personal trauma that occurred in the *illud tempus* of childhood and have been repressed. The process is curative in the same way that Romantic art is cathartic.

An explication of Roethke's difficult sequence requires two points of reference: the poet's subjective history, or the biographical elements in the poems, and the larger arena of shared experience represented by myth and archetype. The greatness of the sequence derives from the tension between these poles; it is a consummately autobiographical sequence, but it participates in the wider realm of archetypal journeys. C. G. Jung's distinction between the personal unconscious and the collective unconscious is useful here. Of the former, he says: "The materials contained in this layer are of a personal nature in so far as they have the character partly of acquisitions derived from the individual's life and partly of psychological factors which could just as well be conscious." These factors are, then, biographical or subjective. They employ a personal symbolism and may well be inaccessible to the outsider without some knowledge of the individual's family background and environment. Now, in addition to these personal elements of the unconscious there is the realm of collective unconscious: "These are the mythological associations—those motives and images which can spring anew in every age and clime without historical tradition or migration." This is the world of dreams. It includes the deepest layers of the human mind and provides a common point of reference for all people in all times. Jung explains this concept further in *Archetypes of the Unconscious*: "I have chosen the term 'collective' because this part of the unconscious is not individual but universal; in contrast to the personal psyche, it has contents and modes of behavior that are more or less the same everywhere in all individuals. It is, in other words, identical in all men and thus constitutes a common psychic substrate of a suprapersonal nature which is present in every one of us."[3]

The Lost Son illustrates the uses of mythology for modern man whose old myths have been rendered obsolete by science and by the general disintegration of culture. Writers think of this century as a time when "You cannot say, or guess, for you know only / A heap of broken images."[4] The modern artist can no longer enjoy the supporting myths that past epochs offered their creative people. Instead, myths have to be fashioned from the materials at hand, some of which are necessarily subjective. Roethke's main source of material was his own life, and he wrote about his life-crises in a fresh way. His images of the greenhouse, the father-florist, and the open field come directly from his personal experience. Yet these personal images take on greater meaning when framed by a mythic pattern. It is as if the poet placed a sheet of rice paper over the archetypal pattern of a face, but drew his own features into the portrait. As Thomas Mann said: "Myth is the foundation of life, the timeless *schema*, the pious formula into which life flows when it reproduces its traits out of the unconscious."[5]

All of the "Lost Son" poems participate in a central myth in some way, what Joseph Campbell has called a "monomyth":

> The mythological hero, setting forth from his commonday hut or castle, is lured, carried away, or else voluntarily proceeds, to the threshold of adventure. There he encounters a shadow presence that guards the passage. The hero may defeat or conciliate this power and go alive into the kingdom of the dark (brother-battle, dragon-battle; offering, charm), or be slain by the opponent and descend in death (dismemberment, crucifixion). Beyond the threshold, then, the hero journeys through a world of unfamiliar yet strangely intimate forces, some of which severely threaten him (tests), some of which give magical aid (helpers). When he arrives at the nadir of the mythological round, he undergoes a supreme ordeal and gains his reward. The triumph may be represented as the hero's sexual union with the goddess mother of the world (sacred marriage), his recognition by the father-creator (father-atonement), his own divinization (apotheosis), or again—if the powers have remained unfriendly to him—his theft of the boon he came to gain (bride-theft, fire-theft); intrinsically it is an expansion of consciousness and therewith of being (illumination, transfiguration, freedom). The final work is that of the return. If the powers have blessed the hero, he now sets forth under their protection (emissary); if not, he flees and is pursued (transformation flight, obstacle flight). At the return threshold the transcendental powers must remain behind; the hero re-emerges from the kingdom of dread (return, resurrection). The boon that he brings restores the world (elixir).[6]

This sounds rather specific as a general myth, but as Campbell emphasizes, the changes rung on this simple scale defy description. Any given tale may isolate one aspect of the cycle, such as the flight motif or the atonement with the father, or a number of independent cycles may be strung together (as in the *Odyssey*). Characters or separate episodes may be fused. But the basic monomyth remains in the background, offering a framework, a principle of organization.

The most commonplace version of the monomyth is the initiatory journey, a rite of passage. This latter term refers to any ceremony of birth, puberty, marriage, or burial which arises in one form or another in all societies, past and present. They are designed to assist the individual at a liminal stage, a transitional phase of his life. Anthropologists have concentrated on the rites of primitive societies, wherein survival itself is often in question; in this situation, rites and ceremonies contribute to social cohesion, translating the personal life-crisis into public, more general concern. Also, these rites reveal to each member of a given society his or her role as warrior, bride, priest, or chieftain. As Campbell explains: "The whole society becomes visible to itself as an imperishable living unit. Generations and individuals pass, like anonymous cells from a living body; but the sustaining, timeless form remains."[7]

In *Rites and Symbols of Initiation* Eliade discusses the most fundamental initiatory rite of passage: the puberty rite practiced by primitive or archaic societies, which "represents above all the revelation of the sacred— and, for the primitive world, the sacred means not only everything that we now understand by religion, but also the whole body of the tribe's mythological and cultural traditions." We have lost much of the ceremony, making this passage all the more difficult, but the crisis remains. "The Lost Son" itself re-creates the puberty rite in modern terms. The boy is separated from his father (by the father's death, although this is concealed) and from the greenhouse ambience (home, womb). He descends into the dream world of the unconscious, represented on a literal level as an escape into the surrounding swamplands. Here the adolescent hero faces a series of obstacles (tests) which he must overcome; he reaches the nadir of his journey, represented by a pit. In this dark, mythical zone he becomes aware of the vital forces within him (sexuality, manhood) and returns to reconcile himself with Otto (atonement). But things can never be the same for him now. Eliade's comments on the meaning of archaic puberty rites are relevant here to what Roethke has attempted in the poem: "In a great many cases puberty rites, in one way or another, imply the revelation of sexuality—but for the entire premodern world, sexuality too participates in the sacred. In short, through initiation, the candidate passes beyond the natural mode—the mode of the child—and gains access to the cultural mode; that is, he is introduced to spiritual values."[8] Through initiation, then, the boy becomes a man; he gains full access to the pleasures and responsibilities of adulthood. The ritual is instructive and symbolic, admitting the individual to a new role in his society. It is a slaying of the child in the initiate, a severance from the parents, an assertion of manhood. This is painful, and "The Lost Son" registers this pain. The hero returns, but the success of this journey, though real, is scarcely obvious until one has reconsidered the entire "Lost Son" sequence.

Eliade finds three distinct phases in the puberty rite, all of which are found in Roethke's poems: (1) separation from the family; (2) ordeals which may involve symbolic death; (3) resurrection of the initiate and return to the tribe. This is the exact sequence of events in "The Lost Son." Separation, ordeals, symbolic death, and return follow in imitation of this mythic pattern. And one finds an especially primitive element in the imagery. Eliade's account of an Australian puberty rite has striking parallels in Roethke. In this rite, the adolescents are captured by their elders, often masked so as not to be recognized, and taken into the wilderness. There they are buried beneath branches in the dark and told that they are about to die, that they will be killed by a divine being. "The very act of separation from their mother," says Eliade, "fills them with forebodings of death." The terrifying darkness is unrelieved by stars, moonlight, or fire. Then comes the hideous whirring sound of the bull-roarers, blown by the elders, in the distance, symbolizing the approaching divinity who will murder the boys. "This experience of darkness, of death, and of the nearness of Divine Beings," he explains, "will be continually repeated and deepened throughout the initiation." The novices die to childhood. And when they are uncovered, they believe themselves to be "new men." They are told the legends of the tribe, the secrets of sex, and other sacred mysteries, then allowed to return to the village. "When the lads finally come back to the camp, the mothers touch them to be sure they are really their sons. Among some Australian tribes mothers mourn over the initiands as the dead are mourned."[9]

"The Lost Son" itself, the central poem in the series of poems which imitate the regressive pattern, opens with a section entitled "The Flight." This alerts the reader to the escape motif that dominates the first part of this poem. It begins quickly, *in medias res*, and in the first person; the adolescent here has been *lured* by the otherworldly cries of the dead:

> At Woodlawn I heard the dead cry:
> I was lulled by the slamming of iron,
> A slow drip over stones,
> Toads brooding wells.
> All the leaves stuck out their tongues;
> I shook the softening chalk of my bones,
> Saying,

Snail, snail, glister me forward,
Bird, soft-sigh me home,
Worm, be with me.
This is my hard time.
(*CP*, p. 53)

Roethke wrote in his notebooks in 1944, not long before beginning this poem: "The motion of a poem: it must get underway quickly."[10] He does this well here, at the same time establishing the associational, dreamlike quality of the style. Without any biographical glosses, one still catches the anxiety of the protagonist who has heard voices from the dead, for whom leaves come to life, who asks the snail, the bird, and the worm to be his guides through this "hard time" that he anticipates. "The softening chalk of my bones" suggests mortality—the fear of death associated with initiatory journeys. The imagery throughout is hallucinatory, nightmarish. A further dimension comes into play if one knows that Woodlawn is the graveyard where Otto Roethke was buried, having died at a crucial period in his son's life. The sequence as a whole has its origins in the effect of Otto's death on Roethke at this painful juncture. Like most epic heroes setting out, the poet-protagonist calls for divine help on the journey: "Snail, snail, glister me forward." The poet explained his own intentions in a later essay: "Everything that lives is holy: I call upon these holy forms of life. One could even put this theologically: St. Thomas says, 'God is above all things as causing the being of all things.' Therefore, in calling upon the snail, I am calling, in a sense, upon God" (*SP*, pp. 24–25).

The poem continues with the hero waiting for what Campbell names "the call to adventure." There is a moment of hesitation before entering the dark wood:

Fished in an old wound,
The soft pond of repose;
Nothing nibbled my line,
Not even the minnows came.

Sat in an empty house
Watching shadows crawl,
Scratching.
There was one fly.

The hero fishes for a direction. He dips into the pond (perhaps a symbol for memory) and broods over an "old wound." Because the father has died, the house is empty. Like Dante before him, the pilgrim needs a

Virgil to show him the way into the abyss and out again. He becomes frantic for supernatural aid of some kind:

> Voice, come out of the silence.
> Say something.
> Appear in the form of a spider
> Or a moth beating the curtain.
>
> Tell me:
> Which is the way I take;
> Out of what door do I go,
> Where and to whom?

The answers he receives, as if given by an oracle, are cryptic:

> Dark hollows said, lee to the wind,
> The moon said, back of an eel,
> The salt said, look by the sea,
> Your tears are not enough praise,
> You will find no comfort here,
> In the kingdom of bang and blab.

One can only guess at the meaning of these lines. Perhaps "lee to the wind" means "shelter from the strongest currents; protect youself." Roethke commonly associates the wind with spirit (*spiritus*), but this advice is unspecific. Likewise, the moon's response cannot be pinned down with any ease. Traditionally, the moon is a feminine principle, whereas the eel is likely to be male. It makes sense that one should recommend the other. The salt, as one might expect, offers the sea as a possible direction to move in. One associates the sea with prelapsarian consciousness, that timeless state that precedes birth and follows death. The sea also is a womb, the source of all being, and perhaps, the void. Its polysemous nature as a symbol detracts from the salt's advice to "look by the sea." In any case, these cryptic suggestions are of little use to the hero; the "kingdom of bang and blab" is the waking world, where hints are necessarily oblique, where the true logos cannot be heard or recognized for all the noise.

The poem picks up in rhythm as the regressive journey gets underway, as the hunt begins:

> Running lightly over spongy ground,
> Past the pasture of flat stones,
> The three elms,

The sheep strewn on a field,
Over a rickety bridge
Toward the quick-water, wrinkling and rippling.

Hunting along the river,
Down among the rubbish, the bug-riddled foliage,
By the muddy pond-edge, by the bog-holes,
By the shrunken lake, hunting, in the heat of summer.

The imagery recalls the wilderness of Eliade's description. The hero must cross a bridge—another commonplace symbol in regressive journeys. Eliade writes: "The symbolism of the funerary bridge is universally disseminated and extends far beyond the bounds of shamanic ideology and mythology. This symbolism is linked, on the one hand, with the myth of a bridge (or tree, vine, etc.) that once connected earth and heaven and by means of which human beings effortlessly communicated with the gods; on the other hand, it is related to the initiatory symbolism of the 'strait gate' or of a 'paradoxical passage.'" [11] Clearly, the latter instance applies here.

Suddenly Roethke intrudes a twisted nursery rhyme, one of his own invention modeled after Mother Goose. The jingle depicts a gnomic figure that is bigger than a rat, "less than a leg," and feels like an eel in catskin rolled in grease:

It's sleek as an otter
With wide webby toes
Just under the water
It usually goes.

The hero seems to be moving backward, into the arena of childhood, where such fantasies are common; he has also entered the realm of dream, where monsters are not infrequent. The regressive journey is well under way. This is the stage of Campbell's monomyth where "unfamiliar yet strangely intimate forces" exist ambiguously as threats (tests) or magical aids (helpers).

The second section of "The Lost Son" is called "The Pit," corresponding to what Campbell marks off as "the nadir of the mythological round." Again, the title of the section gives a sign. The nursery is left behind, and the language shifts to a more appropriate rhythm as the hero dips into the nether regions of the unconscious. One thinks of the Australian initiands, covered with branches, calling out for help. Roethke employs a question-answer dialectic, but again, the answers are Delphic riddles:

Where do the roots go?
  Look down under the leaves.
Who put the moss there?
  These stones have been here too long.
Who stunned the dirt into noise?
  Ask the mole, he knows.
I feel the slime of a wet nest.
  Beware Mother Mildew.
Nibble again, fish nerves.

The three questions all relate to the identity of the hero. Where are his roots? Who put flesh on his bones? Who made the inanimate clay (dirt) animate? The answers are never direct, but always suggestive. La Belle singles out Blake's *Book of Thel* as a source, for Thel's motto begins: "Does the Eagle know what is in the pit? / Or wilt thou go ask the Mole?"[12] In other words, if you want to find out about the unconscious, the realm of instincts, ask somebody who lives there. The "slime of a wet nest" is threatening, an image at once suggesting birth and decay, as does Mother Mildew. And with this word of caution, the hero moves on: "Nibble again, fish nerves." He has slid back on the scale of creation to a point where, more like a protozoan than a human, he inhabits a world of pure instinct.

The trials which attend the hero on his descent follow in the next section, "The Gibber." The title points to chaos, "Gibberish." But a gibber, in working-class slang, is also a key. As in traditional initiation ceremonies, the goal of these trials is the dissolution of the old identity, the fracturing of ties with father and mother. One primary way of breaking down the old identity and starting over is the symbolic regression to the womb, a version of the backward journey examined by Eliade in *Myth and Reality*: "The *regressus ad uterum* is accomplished in order that the beneficiary shall be born into a new mode of being or be regenerated. From the structuralist point of view, the return to the womb corresponds to the reversion of the Universe to the 'chaotic' or embryonic state. The prenatal darkness corresponds to the Night before Creation and to the darkness of the initiation hut." So regression involves a disintegration of the established order (and identity) in an attempt to regain the limbo of the womb, the chaos that precedes creation. Relating this to myth, Eliade says the regression usually features "a hero being swallowed by a sea monster and emerging victorious after breaking through the monster's belly, or initiatory passage through *vagina dentata*, or the dangerous descent into a cave or crevice assimilated to the mouth or the uterus of Mother Earth."[13] Roethke uses the latter at the outset of "The Gibber" where the hero overlooks the *vagina dentata* (toothed gate):

> At the wood's mouth,
> By the cave's door,
> I listened to something
> I had heard before.
>
> Dogs of the groin
> Barked and howled,
> The sun was against me,
> The moon would not have me.
>
> The weeds whined,
> The snakes cried,
> The cows and briars
> Said to me: Die.

These stanzas point to the hero's anxiety, which is partly sexual ("Dogs of the groin") and partly filial (sun as father, moon as mother). Roethke's sense of guilt dominates the passage. An unsympathetic nature (represented by weeds, snakes, briars) calls out to the hero: Die.

So the regression gets fully underway:

> What a small song. What slow clouds. What dark water.
> Hath the rain a father? All the caves are ice. Only the snow's here.
> I'm cold. I'm cold all over. Rub me in father and mother.
> Fear was my father, Father Fear.
> His look drained the stones.

The change in line length alters the pace of the poem, and in a radical way Roethke takes up the dream language which characterizes the later poems in the "Lost Son" sequence. The hero presses down into the semicoherent limbo which is like an uneasy calm before a storm. It is a premonition stage. The central reference here is from Job, the only direct quotation in the poem. Job's intensely searching question reveals his isolation from God: "Hath the rain a father?" (Job 38:28); it has the same effect of Christ's mournful "God, my God, hast thou forsaken me?" The answer, for Roethke, is "yes." The father cannot be denied, just as the lost son cannot deny Otto, who gave him life and who controls its atmosphere as he controls the greenhouse temperature. Roethke's Father here, both Otto and God, is *Yahweh*, not the softer and ethereal *Elohim*. This Father has to be placated, assuaged. He demands sacrifice and obedience. And one look from his powerful figure is enough to drain all natural (sexual) impulses: "His look drained the stones." The regression to the womb remains more a wish than a realization: "Rub me in father and mother." Yet the return is underway, for the language becomes less rational as the hero drops further backward into his past.

The final goal of regression, Eliade concludes, is "to cure oneself of time."[14] By slipping back far enough, one arrives eventually at the point where time began. By retracing steps, the source of creation is encountered. The hero of Roethke's poem aspires to this condition in the next segment of "The Gibber":

> What gliding shape
> Beckoning through halls,
> Stood poised on the stair,
> Fell dreamily down?
>
> From the mouths of jugs
> Perched on many shelves,
> I saw substance flowing
> That cold morning.
>
> Like a slither of eels
> That watery cheek
> As my own tongue kissed
> My lips awake.

Again, the poet avoids making much literal sense. Words like "gliding," "beckoning," "poised," and "dreamily" suggest a feminine principle in contrast to Father Fear in the preceding segment. Like all women figures in Roethke, this one is vague; she may be mother or lover, perhaps both. She may well represent the desire of the quester, in Campbell's terms, for union—or reunion—with the goddess-mother of the world. In any case, the experience, conjured in dream imagery, leads to a release of energy, both psychic and verbal. The poet's own tongue kisses his lips awake.

The next stanzas, which bring "The Gibber" to an end, signal the break-up of the old self; the method recalls the Elizabethan rant (as Roethke himself pointed out in his "Open Letter"):

> Is this the storm's heart? The ground is unstilling itself.
> My veins are running nowhere. Do the bones cast out their fire?
> Is the seed leaving the old bed? These buds are live as birds.
> Where, where are the tears of the world?
> Let the kisses resound, flat like a butcher's palm;
> Let the gestures freeze; our doom is already decided.
> All the windows are burning! What's left of my life?

The poem continues in this vein, wherein the hero declares that his old self is in tatters. The leitmotif is destruction; the ground "unstills" itself under the hero's feet; his body is consumed in flames: "All the windows are burning!" But, in the midst of this crumbling of the old order ("Goodbye, goodbye, old stones, the time-order is going"), a glimpse of the new one can be discerned. The hero asks, "Do the bones cast out their fire?" and "Is the seed leaving the old bed?" The sexual imagery recalls the initiatory rite of passage described by Eliade, where the initiand learns about sex for the first time. But Roethke's hero rebels, momentarily, and cries: "I want the old rage, the lash of primordial milk!" He wants to regress still further before going forward. The conflict present in the hero's unconscious finds curious expression in the lines:

Money   money   money
Water   water   water

The two words are, perhaps, in opposition, *money* being an artificial and negative term and *water* representing life and renewal. On the other hand, Roethke might have agreed with Wallace Stevens, who said that "poetry is a kind of money." In any case, the line, "I run, I run to the whistle of money," which precedes the couplet, sets up a negative context for the word *money*, helping us to delimit the possible range of meaning.

This section as a whole ends with a partial annihilation of the old self, and Roethke once again uses the question-answer dialectic that often reappears at crucial moments in the "Lost Son" sequence. The hero's undoing seems complete in the last stanza:

These sweeps of light undo me.
Look, look, the ditch is running white!
I've more veins than a tree!
Kiss me, ashes, I'm falling through a dark swirl.

The color white nearly always anticipates a redemption scene in Roethke. White is also associated with regeneration, the realm of Blake's Generation, where sexual reproduction guarantees a kind of eternity—but hardly a redemption. The "dark swirl" of the hero may be the abyss of timelessness. Having descended the memory scale and re-encountered many primal images, the hero has burnt up some of his past, the unwanted self, the memories that persist and inhibit free access to the present. The ashes point to the burning up of the old self. Now the hero must bring a new self before the Father for reconciliation—atonement.

On the barest literal level, the boy has simply run away into a wild landscape, had some nightmarish hallucinations, and probably masturbated. In the next section, "The Return," the literal aspect of the poem reasserts itself. We come out of the shadowy regions of the unconscious, although the mythic pattern remains consistent. The stage in the mono-myth where the hero reunites with the father-creator fits "The Return." The boy straggles back from his adventures in the dark wood and re-turns to the greenhouse womb:

> The way to the boiler was dark,
> Dark all the way,
> Over slippery cinders
> Through the long greenhouse.

First he encounters the roses, personified, "breathing in the dark." The boiler fireman works by a single light. The weeds sleep undisturbed. Then suddenly he remembers an earlier encounter with his father. Past and present converge in a flashback:

> Once I stayed all night.
> The light in the morning came slowly over the white
> Snow.
> There were many kinds of cool
> Air.
> Then came steam.
>
> Pipe-knock.

Roethke described this section as "a return to a memory of childhood that comes back almost as in a dream, after the agitation and exhaustion of the earlier actions" (SP, p. 38). The "pipe-knock" refers to the violent knocking of the pipes which accompanied the infusion of steam. It also calls up an image of the pipe-smoking Otto, banging his pipe against a bench. The exact meaning is unimportant here; it signals the approach of Papa:

> Scurry of warm over small plants.
> Ordnung! ordnung!
> Papa is coming!

Indeed, Papa embodies the many aspects of the German word: *ordnung*, meaning order, power, and control. This point in "The Lost Son" inev-itably recalls Eliot's *Waste Land*, which ends with the episode from the Upanishads where Thunder gives the command of "Datta, dayadhvam, damyata" or "give, sympathize, control": all forms of giving.[15]

The section finishes with the night dissolving, the flowers and weeds coming back to life—the conscious world—after a deep sleep; the morning light returns and purifies the natural world:

A fine haze moved off the leaves;
Frost melted on far panes;
The rose, the chrysanthemum turned toward the light.
Even the hushed forms, the bent yellowy weeds
Moved in a slow up-sway.

The sensitivity to natural cycles that Roethke associates with his hero is deeply Romantic, of course. As Emerson said: "The greatest delight which the fields and woods minister, is the suggestion of an occult relation between man and the vegetable. I am not alone and unacknowledged."[16]

The final section of the poem opens with a recollection, and it is untitled:

It was beginning winter,
An in-between time,
The landscape still partly brown:
The bones of weeds kept swinging in the wind
Above the blue snow.

This is the stage of the hero's "illumination." The landscape widens for the first time, and daylight has arrived—not a full light but a strangely muted glow representing frozen possibilities. The season is winter, traditionally the season of death and tragedy. The hero meditates, remembering a place where "The light moved slowly over the frozen field." Toward the end of the poem the meditation turns Eliotic in the most open way, recalling "Ash Wednesday," a poem about intense spiritual anxiety:

Was it light?
Was it light within?
Was it light within light?
Stillness becoming alive,
Yet still?

The answer will not be forthcoming at this point. One has to read the complete sequence to understand the movement backward and forward which ultimately leads to a firm sense of progress and the establishment of a new self. Roethke explained this process himself:

I believe that to go forward as a spiritual man it is necessary first to go back. Any history of the psyche (allegorical journey) is bound to be a succession of experiences, similar yet dissimilar. There is a perpetual slipping-back, then a going-forward; but there is *some* "progress." Are not some experiences so powerful and so profound . . . that they repeat themselves, thrust themselves upon us, again and again, with variation and change, each time bringing us close to our own most particular (and thus most universal) reality? (*SP*, p. 39)

Still, "The Lost Son" is self-contained. It fulfills the mythological round, though the hero's final resolution here remains temporary:

A lively understandable spirit
Once entertained you.
It will come again.
Be still.
Wait.

The other poems in the sequence repeat, less grandly, the same heroic journey or dwell on some particular phase of it. But "The Lost Son" remains the central poem in Roethke's canon. All his other poems must be interpreted in its light, with attention to the key symbols as they appear in this poem. The figure of Papa as father-God, the greenhouse itself, the open field, the mother-lover, and the light and wind symbols are present and active in "The Lost Son." The later work will unfold from this poem, isolating certain points of the monomyth, widening the context and import of the individual symbols. In short, this poem is a watershed, akin to *The Waste Land* in Eliot's corpus. Shaping his version of the heroic journey, Roethke has rescued for himself one of the great myth cycles; and by linking this cycle with an initiatory rite of passage, he enables himself to write, as Kenneth Burke suggested he do, about his burdens. The autobiographical aspect lends the poem a particularity which might have gone unrealized within such a grand mythic structure; indeed, the real tension in the work is drawn between the concrete autobiographical specifics and the larger mythic frame. Overall, "The Lost Son," together with the greenhouse poems, stands as Roethke's major contribution to modern poetry and the center of his own work.

One should recall that Kenneth Burke was all this time acting as Roethke's mentor, especially during the composition of "The Lost Son." The poem would have been less successful without Burke's intervention, for Roethke simply did not know enough about psychology or myth at this point to use them as deftly as he did. Burke's advice was constantly sought by the poet, and a few letters survive to reveal something of the nature of this important friendship. One letter from Burke just after he read the first draft of "The Lost Son" is especially revealing:

> I agree with you that your poem is something to be emphatic about. Surely it is your farthest step in the direction of the eschatological. It gives well indeed the sense of turmoils and trammels, and vaguely balked expectation. And there are many lines that open up possibilities as one reads.
>
> I hope that you won't mind my hanging on to this copy, for a while at least. I think I can use it in the stuff I still want to write on the search for essence. (In the next Kenyon, I think, will appear some observations from the Grammar I did of this nature on Peer Gynt and Proust; but in the Symbolic I'd like to go into the matter further and your present poem seems to me one hundred per cent the exemplar of one of the ways.)
>
> It is interesting that you selected Eliot in particular to be furious about, in your letter. And I think the choice is quite significant. For do you not see that, for all the vast differences, you end on the vigil, the watching and waiting in silence? Eliot gives this much the traditional Christian interpretation. He could rub himself in father and mother by adding the intellectual matrix of the Church. This call beyond imagery to reason you are feeling, yet embattled to resist. You would glumly resist incorporation in some cause or movement or institution as the new parent. Hence your search for essential motives drives you back into the quandaries of adolescence (the age par excellence of waiting). The battle is a fundamental one; which is probably why one gets the feeling that this poem marks the end of one phase and the beginning of another, being thus a kind of "last poem" (hence my feeling that I can use it when on the Symbolism of the ultimate, the essential—which for reasons I explain in the Kenyon excerpt, leads to imagery of *temporal* return).
>
> You are confronting the need of a new dimension. You fear the loss of your identity whenever you attempt to incorporate it. You particularly resist Eliot because he did incorporate it (though unquestionably at great cost, as judged by the criteria of the aesthetic prevailing prior to this incorporation). So you sullenly arrest yourself, and hold yourself to the continued contemplation of that one station. Knowing the dangers of an ideational framework, you would maintain a kind of Chronic Throw-back—which, however

uncomfortable it may be for you, is of great interest to me in my search for the documents, since it does serve to make your poem so intensely and thoroughly an example of its kind.

I think your way of replacing Charlie was a great improvement. The only line I disliked in the poem was, "In the kingdom of bang and blab," though I can't explain just what bothers me about it. I guess it's because it suggests to me Stuart Chase's terms for de-bunking whatever expressions he considers meaningless. In the bot-tom stanza of page 2, the beginning and ending on "hunting" seems too symmetrical to me. For my slightly lop-sided taste, it would seem better if "hunting" were brought up into the line above, thus: "By the shrunken lake hunting, in the heat of summer." But though I agree that "hunting" should be repeated in that stanza, I can't see that a thing is gained by the repetition of "resound" in the line you inserted on page 5. The only other thing that bothered me was a question (not very strong) whether the quasi-Gothic jin-gles on the crawling things were wholly effective. (I mean such as the "serpents and hogs" lines on p. 4; though I see, looking again, that "crawling things" doesn't quite accurately classify the lot.)[17]

Typically, Roethke accepted most of the changes recommended by Burke—although he wisely kept the suggestive phrase "In the kingdom of bang and blab." Earlier letters show that Burke had full access to Roethke's rough drafts of *The Lost Son*—and we can only rejoice in this accidental crossing of two lively minds, one creative and the other crit-ical. It is also fortunate that Roethke, who was searching for a new men-tor, happened upon a man of Burke's sophistication.

The "Lost Son" sequence up to 1948 includes three moderately long poems which continue the cyclical movement established in the central poem itself: regression alternating with progression. "The Long Alley" is a tortuous poem, but an important one in the sequence. It takes up where the vigil left us with the illumination only partial. The light of summer had yet to occur. "The Long Alley" opens with images of a river, perhaps the same river where the fishing took place in "The Lost Son"; in any case, the progress of the hero seems, temporarily, more like regress:

A river glides out of the grass. A river or a serpent.
A fish floats belly upward,
Sliding through the white current,
Slowly turning,
Slowly.

The dark flows on itself. A dead mouth sings under an old tree.
The ear hears only in low places.
Remember an old sound.
Remember
Water.
(*CP*, p. 59)

The associations of father with guilt and death surface yet again. The
fish is dead (father symbol), and the "dead mouth" is probably the de-
ceased Otto buried under a tree, unwilling to let go of his son, even
from the grave. Sexual guilt again accompanies the ghost of Father Fear:

This slag runs slow. What bleeds when metal breaks?
Flesh, you offend this metal. How long need the bones mourn?
Are those horns on top of the hill? Yesterday has a long look.

Cinder, slag, metal, sulphurous water, and other remnants of factory
production permeate the first section of "The Long Alley." Roethke
links industrialism in its most sordid aspects to repressed or wasted sexuality, as in the third section of "The Lost Son" ("I have married my
hands to perpetual agitation / I run, I run to the whistle of money"). The
question, "Are those horns on top of the hill?" is sufficiently ambiguous
to combine both elements of the analogy.

The hero repeats the leading question at the outset of the next section:
"Lord, what do you require?" With no response forthcoming, he appeals to the goddess-mother, the feminine principle:

Come to me, milk-nose. I need a loan of the quick.
    There's no joy in soft bones.
For whom were you made, sweetness I cannot touch?
    Look what the larks do.
Luminous one, shall we meet on the bosom of God?
    Return the gaze of a pond.

The interior dialectic reappears, as before, when the hero is balked. The
questions are the same in essence: how can the hero find gratification for
his desires? The responses are maddening: "Look what the larks do" is
unequivocal. They sing. "Return the gaze of the pond" proposes narcis-
sism. This advice causes isolation and despair. "When the appeal fails,"
says Rosemary Sullivan, "the poet is thrown back to the lonely solipsism
of sexual hunger."[18] The resulting frenzy finds expression, as it did in
"The Lost Son," in nursery rhymes and riddles.

The note of despair carries over into the third section. The boy-hero asks, "Can feathers eat me?" and reveals a terror of the natural world. He admits that he has exhausted the rich depths of memory for a time: "There's no clue in the silt." So he enters the game of social interaction. The central stanzas of this section play on the rhythms and rhymes of childhood:

> A waiting ghost warms up the dead
> Until they creak their knees:
> So up and away and what do we do
> But barley-break and squeeze.

The children's game of barley-break continues in this fashion. In brief, it requires three couples, who pair off into three separate but contiguous squares. The couple in the middle has to catch the end couples as they attempt to cross the dangerous central zone untouched. Significantly, the middle plot is referred to as hell. Roethke played the game as a boy, but now it may well represent the frantic catch-as-catch-can adult world of sexual encounters. And the poem itself is an entry into the brutal adolescent world of partially satisfied sexual longings. "The Long Alley" focuses on that part of the mythic round concerned with winning a bride, though the myth recedes to a mere tracery behind the concrete imagery of the poet's youth.

The fourth section describes a certain relief from sexual and spiritual anxiety. It recounts what seems to be a kind of rebirth, the goal of all puberty rites. And it parallels that section of "The Lost Son" entitled "The Return." Here one finds "The long alleys of strings and stem" which give the poem its title. The boy experiences a lyric moment, another partial illumination or epiphany:

> Light airs! Light airs! A pierce of angels!
> The leaves, the leaves become me!
> The tendrils have me!

The reunion with the physical universe, with nature, has the traditional Romantic effect of amelioration. The frenzy of sexual and spiritual alienation seen earlier in the poem is relieved by contact with the material world.

And, in the fifth and final section, the poem's antagonisms are nearly resolved:

> Bricks flake before my face. Master of water, that's trees away.
> Reach me a peach, fondling, the hills are there.
> Nuts are money: wherefore and what else?

Send down a rush of air, O torrential,
Make the sea flash in the dust.

Call off the dogs, my paws are gone.
This wind brings many fish;
The lakes will be happy:
Give me my hands:
I'll take the fire.

Read outside of the context of Roethke's developing symbolism, this "conclusion" would seem incoherent. But for the hero of *The Lost Son*, this is a crucial moment of self-awareness. The importunate ghost of Father Fear remains "trees away." And the adolescent has accepted his sexuality as a natural part of life ("Reach me a peach, fondling . . ."). The false equation of sexuality with materialism is replaced with a fresh valuation of sex: "Nuts are money." The protagonist asks for wind and rain, although his urges are still self-directed and autoerotic at the end: "I'll take the fire." The resolution, again, is partial, but progress has been made. The hero is not running away from his desires, which is a start in the right direction.

Again, Kenneth Burke's private comments to Roethke in a letter of 12 August 1946 are worth noting:

> Delighted to hear from you. And many thanks indeed for the poem ("The Long Alley"), which I have copied for my subsequent ponderings.
>
> It is very lovely. Or rather, becomes so, up out of the convincingly and newly expressed depression. The great girlies-posies-fishlets amalgam in part 4 goes over very well.
>
> But it does take many readings, before things begin to emerge as satisfactorily as one cries for. (The general tenor, I think, is clear enough at first—and perhaps that is enough for meeting the minimum requirements of communication.) I wish I had a chance to ask you about details. (Incidentally, some comments you made, in an earlier letter, about a progression in one of your hothouse poems, suggested a lot to me. So don't hesitate to say something about the *ars poetica* whenever it occurs to you. After all, you are more up on your ways than anyone else can be—and one can easily miss, or fail to evaluate properly, something that seems obvious to you.)
>
> Above all, I'd like to ask you something about the structure. At first, noting that it was a five-stanza poem, I began trying to build it about part 3 as fulcrum (looking for the same kind of form I

thought I saw in the Keats Ode). But later, I decided rather that One and Three are in order, and Two and Four in another order. I.e., I would consider Two as antiphonal to One, Four as antiphonal to Three, and Three developing the motive of Two. Whereupon, Five would be the resolution of the two orders (a kind of "irresolute resolution"?).

I call Five an "irresolute resolution" because, although things seem to be clearing up, with the poet getting ready for the next time, the new fire must be taken in the *hands*, it thus being a not wholly communicative fire, but somewhat self-involved still. Would you agree? To review the whole series of summarizing lines, however, is to see that such a quality must be retained even at the last, if only for purposes of consistency. (By the summarizing lines, I mean: "My gates are all caves . . . Return the gaze of the pond . . . I'm happy with my paws . . . The tendrils have me . . . I'll take the fire." Indeed I wonder whether it might not be a good idea, for editorial purposes, and for pointing a direction in a way not alien to the quality of the poem itself, if you used these lines as titles for the five stanzas, instead of merely using numbers.)

My only complaints are:

"Slowly turning, / Slowly" seems spoiled by the second "slowly."

Similarly, I begrudge the repetition of "remember" in the next stanza.

Where you establish a tonality so thoroughly as you do, such purely mechanical repetitions seem bothersome to me. In another kind of poetry, where they were more necessary, I don't think I'd object to them.

I'd be happier (slightly) if "Can you name it? I can't name it" had just the second half.

As the author of a book on the grammar of who, what, when, where, how, I object to your one moment of weakness where you fall into my territory, in the line, "Wherefore and what else." I can't see that it conveys anything at all. And suspect that you put it there simply because you wanted to use up some time, so that the line would be the same length as its compatriots.

As for the beginning of that same line, "Nuts are money," it suggests wayward notions to me, alien to the quality of your poem. I once knew a guy who said the same thing, but he meant it in a Petronius sort of way.

Incidentally, as regards the ultimate equational recipe in your work, the "nuts are money" formula (taken seriously, not in the above suggested burlesque) has started me on a line of speculations I am still vague about. In your Phase One, you had money and water in antithetical relation (or, at least, so I tentatively thought). But in this last stanza of Phase Two, where fires would be asked to burn under water, the aqueous tree-harvest becomes equated with mazuma. You got me to thinking about starting some new book-keeping at that point. Any advice, that can assist me in my system of psychic accountancy, would be appreciated.

However, in sum total, let me once again congratulate you on the poem as a whole. It sounds very appealing indeed. And you are certainly working out an interesting language, which I do want to try to learn well enough to be able to find my way about town.[19]

Burke is as perceptive and sympathetic as ever. His technical comments testify to his acute understanding of the poetic process, of poetic structure. His hearty endorsement of Roethke's first radical experiment with the language itself could only have been reassuring, for Roethke has pressed language to the boundaries here, as he continues to do in the rest of the sequence. "The Long Alley" demands a close attention to the mythic structure and a willing suspension of linear logic. The poet has invented—as did Joyce before him in *Finnegans Wake*—a language of his own and a private symbology which is internally consistent, yet unintelligible out of the context of Roethke's mythos. As W. K. Wimsatt said: "Poetic structure is always a fusion of ideas with material, a statement in which the solidity of symbol and the sensory verbal qualities are somehow not washed out by the abstraction."[20]

"A Field of Light" follows directly upon "The Long Alley" and perpetuates the stage of illumination represented by "I'll take the fire." There is a brief, initial regressive note, however. The poem opens with the hero's coming to a stagnant lake where moss and leaves float on the surface of the water, where strange eyes peer upwards from the bottom. This is the third poem in a series to begin with a phase of indecision and brooding near water. In this odd state of mind, the poet "Reached for a grape / And the leaves changed; / A stone's shape / Became a clam" (*CP*, p. 62). The hero proceeds to the usual question-answer phase, recalling the Job story again: "Angel within me, I asked, / Did I every curse the sun? / Speak and abide." The answer, as ever, lies in an embracing of the physical world: "Alone, I kissed the skin of a stone; / Marrow-soft, danced in the sand." As Emerson says: "In the presence of nature, a wild delight runs through the man, in spite of real sorrows. Nature says,—he is my creature, and maugre all his impertinent griefs, he shall be glad with me."[21] This leads to what Emerson called "exhilaration," the transcendental oneness with the natural world—correspondence—a condition of sympathetic intercourse between a man and his environment. This condition of ecstatic vision finds wonderful expression in the last lines of Roethke's poem:

> My heart lifted up with the great grasses;
> The weeds believed me, and the nesting birds.
> There were clouds making a rout of shapes crossing a windbreak
>   of cedars,
> And a bee shaking drops from a rain-soaked honeysuckle.
> The worms were delighted as wrens.
> And I walked, I walked through the light air;
> I moved with the morning.

The moment of illumination comes, notably, in the field of light. The image goes well beyond the fifth section of "The Lost Son," that "in-between time" when the sun travels near the sky's rim. The frozen field has been transformed into a landscape buzzing with life: weeds, nesting birds, bees, flowers, worms, and wrens populate the scene. The paradisiacal state of childhood, as seen in the earlier poem "The Waking," is reinhabited. The union of the hero with his surroundings recalls the prelapsarian condition of the child, who has not yet grown *out of* harmony. A child is still close enough to his point of entry into the material world (birth) to apprehend the eternal in the temporal. But the adult has to fight to regain this apprehension. Significantly, Roethke copied De Quincey's famous statement into his notebooks not long before he wrote the "Lost Son" poems: "The infant is one with God and one with everything in our universe through the medium of love. . . . The adult mind must regain this vision, this secure unity."[22] This recapturing of a lost condition was called "radical innocence" by Yeats. Or, as Emerson put the same idea, "Infancy is the perpetual Messiah, which comes into the arms of fallen men, and pleads with them to return to paradise."[23]

"The Shape of the Fire" completes the sequence up to 1948. Making a sharp turn away from the illumination of "A Field of Light," the hero tunnels inward, attempts one further regression. This five-part poem repeats what is by now a familiar pattern: dark places into light, chaos into order, regression to progression. The first two sections are full of infantile images. The hero is wrapped in the watery drowse of a womb, but this womb is no place of rest; from the moment of conception, not just birth, life is a struggle with desires which must be either satisfied or repressed. The most basic urge, hunger, preoccupies the speaker, who asks:

What's this? A dish for fat lips.
Who says? A nameless stranger.
Is he a bird or a tree? Not everyone can tell.
(CP, p. 64)

Already, the interior dialectic of question and answer begins. The voice in the above passage cannot distinguish between food and mother. Sullivan, who reads the whole poem as "an attempt to convey the crisis of mental breakdown," argues that the first line above and a later one, "My meat eats me," refer to "the self-cannibalism of psychic distress in which the interior self feels consumed and suffocated by the alien body."[24] Perhaps; but more important, the poem re-enacts a kind of birth. Here is the prenatal state described in symbolist terms:

Water recedes to the crying of spiders.
An old scow bumps over black rocks.
A cracked pod calls.

In "The Vegetal Radicalism," Burke reports a student of Roethke's noting that the line "An old scow bumps over black rocks" echoed the heartbeat of the mother "as the foetus might hear it dully, while asleep in the amniotic fluids."[25] Since Burke's essay was published well within Roethke's lifetime, and the poet never had anything but praise for the article, there is no reason to doubt this interpretation. And certainly the next stanza is the voice of a prenatal child: "Mother me out of here." Then "Shale loosens" and the birth takes place. Finally, "A low mouth laps water" and "The arbor is cooler." The infant bids farewell to the womb state, and "The warm comes without sound."

In the second section Roethke uses the nursery rhyme once more to suggest a particular stage of development. The imagery of the cradle prevails, and the doctor (or father) comes to poke the child, who observes, in the haze of inchoate consciousness:

Time for the flat-headed man. I recognize that listener,
Him with the platitudes and rubber doughnuts,
Melting at the knees, a varicose horror.

But the child remains little more than a beast who

Must pull off clothes
To jerk like a frog
On belly and nose
From the sucking bog.

The amphibious associations of "frog" and "bog" point to a very low stage of phylogenetic development. One could believe that the hero has again regressed, entered the womb where, during the gestation period of the foetus, ontogony recapitulates phylogeny. Yet the third section of the poem is the fulcrum on which the whole poem turns:

> The wasp waits.
>> The edge cannot eat the center.
> The grape glistens.
>> The path tells little to the serpent.
> An eye comes out of the wave.
>> The journey from flesh is longest.
> A rose sways least.
>> The redeemer comes a dark way.

Here we see the influence of Burke again, who thought of proverbs and aphorisms as the core of all poetry. There are no literal connectives between the proverbs in the stanza above, so we are left to our own resources. The wasp, representing alien aspects of the natural world, is in temporary abeyance. But the edge cannot eat the center, which seems a good thing. This cryptic line may well refer to the mother who cannot destroy what is inside of her, or it may mean that the body cannot destroy the heart. Certainly the glistening grape is a symbol of ripeness, of the attractive side of the physical and sensual world. The path, similar to the Way of Truth in Taoism or Christ's "I am the way, the truth and the life," does not control the serpent. One recalls the Satan of *Paradise Lost*, whose protean shape permitted him to enter Eden in various guises. The journey from flesh to spirit is clearly a long and harrowing one, and redemption, seen in the rose image and in the redeemer who comes a dark and mysterious way, seems far away. The eye in the wave, perhaps, is the artist's vision of order in the midst of chaos, the still point of the turning world, a type of the rose which sways least of all. The dark way, the return to the womb, offers a glimpse of the eternal. Far from being merely a tangle of contradictory phrases, Roethke's litany of aphorisms moves *from* fear *to* the possibility of redemption, not in a linear way, but in the associational dream logic that we gradually learn to follow as the "Lost Son" poems unfold.

The last two sections of "The Shape of the Fire" celebrate the momentary recovery of the past, that prenatal paradise where

> Death was not. I lived in a simple drowse:
> Hands and hair moved through a dream of wakening blossoms.
> Rain sweetened the cave and the dove still called;
> The flowers leaned on themselves, the flowers in hollows;
> And love, love sang toward.

Not surprisingly, the poem (and *The Lost Son*) ends inside a greenhouse. The flowerheads are illuminated with the sunlight; the rose awakens, rising from its bed "Still as a child in its first loneliness." And the hero rejoices in the knowledge that he has gained by the underworld descent. Light, as ever, is the symbol of grace abounding. The hero has accomplished his journey. Having sustained the ordeals of his rite of passage, he is reborn, spiritually, coming to know

> . . . that light falls and fills, often without our knowing,
> As an opaque vase fills to the brim from a quick pouring,
> Fills and trembles at the edge yet does not flow over,
> Still holding and feeding the stem of the contained flower.

This paradisiacal image appropriately completes *The Lost Son*, which is his most essential writing, the center of his work, and the book that informs the poetry which follows in the next fifteen years. As Louis Martz puts it, "Roethke never surpassed the achievement of *The Lost Son*, though many of his later poems are filled to the same brim. In these green images Roethke reached the center of his memory and found his wholly individual idiom."[26]

CHAPTER NINE

FROM THE KINGDOM OF

BANG AND BLAB

*Thus, what we need is an irrational language with a new vocabu-
lary, something like what modern art is trying to find for an expression of the subconscious.*
                    Otto Rank, Beyond Psychology;
                    copied by Roethke into his notebooks.
What a whelm of proverbs, Mr. Pinch!
                    Roethke, "Praise to the End!"

With the publication of *The Lost Son*, Roethke
emerged from relative obscurity, attracting
public attention on both sides of the Atlantic.
Critics praised his adventurous new methods,
so he was encouraged to press on with the "Lost
Son" sequence, evolving what Rank called an
"irrational language." The next two books followed quickly, *Praise to the End!* coming in 1951
and *The Waking* in 1953. The same techniques
of associational logic and infantile language
witnessed in *The Lost Son* are now given full
play; indeed, Roethke takes his poetry to the
very edge of intelligibility, using the same general mythos of the regressive journey as an organizing principle. The continuing sequence
occupies the whole of *Praise to the End!* and finishes with "O, Thou Opening, O" in *The Waking*. Together with the greenhouse poems, the
"Lost Son" sequence represents the emotional
center of his work.

Finishing his job at Bennington in 1948,
Roethke went back to Penn State for a final
term, then moved to the University of Washington in Seattle, where he stayed until his
death in 1963. Hè lost the company of Ken-

neth Burke but now gained the emotional support of his new department chairman, Robert Heilman. The critical brilliance of Arnold Stein
also was at hand. In short, he felt ready to begin again the regressive
journey. The first poems he wrote in Washington recapitulate the primal
experiences already encountered by the lost son. But the regions of the
poet's mind which they explore are a labyrinth into which the reader
must venture, unlike Theseus, without a thread to unravel.

"Where Knock Is Open Wide" resumes the "Lost Son" sequence in
Praise to the End!, taking its title from Christopher Smart's *Song to David*
(Part 77). The poet takes the infantile language utilized in earlier poems
a step further. Father, mother, pets, and the usual nursery rhymes are
here:

> Once upon a tree
> I came across a time,
> It wasn't even as
> A ghoulie in a dream.
>
> There was a mooly man
> Who had a rubber hat
> The funnier than that,—
> He kept it in a can.
> (*CP*, p.71)

The echo of Joyce's *Portrait of the Artist* is deliberate; that novel begins:
"Once upon a time and a very good time it was there was a moocow
coming down along the road and this moocow that was coming down
the road met a nicens little boy named baby tuckoo. . . . "[1] The technique
is identical. Both writers understand the potential for nuance and ambiguity inherent in so-called baby-talk. But whereas baby-talk in *A Portrait of the Artist* leads rapidly forward into maturity, Roethke's language
presses backward.

The title is suggestive. As Ralph J. Mills, Jr., has noticed, "Roethke's
piece, which presents the sensations and thoughts of earliest childhood,
seems to use the line from Smart to imply birth and entry into the
world."[2] Indeed, the hero has regressed back into the womb, and his
rebirth into a strange and woeful world is the subject of this poem. The
first section ends with this inquiry:

> What's the time, papa-seed?
> Everything has been twice.
> My father is a fish.

The association of father and fish (sperm) has become familiar by now; the lost son's psychic fishing has turned up another recollection of Otto. The hint of reincarnation of the father *in* the son may help to explain "Everything has been twice," as well as the connection with "papaseed."

Like Smart, Roethke darts from reference to reference, constantly altering rhythms to suggest the infant's short span of attention. The poet thwarts any attempt at linear coherence, imitating a child's way of thinking. The second section becomes directly autobiographical when Uncle Charlie, whom Roethke disliked, enters the drama. Until he killed himself, Charlie had shared ownership of the greenhouse in Saginaw with Otto. This suicide fascinated Roethke at odd moments throughout his life, and perhaps it underlies these stanzas:

> I sing a small sing,
> My uncle's away,
> He's gone for always,
> I don't care either.
>
> I know who's got him,
> They'll jump on his belly,
> He won't be an angel,
> I don't care either.

"They'll jump on his belly" is a child's version of hell, unlike the tortures reserved for suicides in Canto 13 of Dante's *Inferno*.

The wildly exaggerated fears of childhood absorb the hero in the third section of the poem; he cries out to God (father) for assistance in a language full of obscure puns and private imagery:

> God, give me a near. I hear flowers.
> A ghost can't whistle.
> I know! I know!
> Hello happy hands.

This may be the child's prayer for birth, for the synethesia of "I hear flowers" suggests a very early stage of development where sight and hearing have yet to be distinguished; indeed, "A ghost can't whistle" is almost a plea for incarnation. "Hello happy hands" points out the guiltless masturbatory joys of an infant's world, where desire and gratification follow as the night the day.

Section Four recalls the stage of return and reunion with Papa in "The Lost Son." As before, it follows a "chaos-passage" and some kind of partial illumination. The pattern is all too familiar now. But the unexpected occurs as the boy remembers a fishing trip with his father that ended in humiliation:

> We went by the river.
> Water birds went ching. Went ching.
> Stepped in wet. Over stones.
> One, his nose had a frog,
> But he slipped out.
>
> I was sad for a fish.
> Don't hit him on the boat, I said.
> Look at him puff. He's trying to talk.
> Papa threw him back.
>
> Bullheads have whiskers.
> And they bite.

No single experience is more classic in American boyhood than the fishing trip with one's father. And few themes dominate the literature of American Romanticism more than that of man—or boy—against nature. One could follow the theme in its various manifestations from James Fenimore Cooper, Mark Twain, and Thoreau through Hemingway's "Nick Adams" stories and James Dickey's *Deliverance*. In Roethke's vignette, the reality of experience shatters the idealized myth. The poet's technique, as we have seen, is mimetic; the first stanza approximates the fitful nature of memory. The lines jerk along, omitting the usual connectives which render speech intelligible. In the second stanza the sensitive child confronts the father, who discourages any manner of sympathy with the creature. But the child reads things differently. He sees the father as asserting his authority and feels afraid, quashed. The father, in this scene, lacks understanding; for him, a fact is a fact: "Bullheads have whiskers. / And they bite." Yet the child is offended. No reconciliation can follow immediately from this harsh recollection. Instead, the hero conjures images of the father-florist's death, mingling affection, wonder, and grief. He feels separation and isolation, not atonement:

> He watered the roses.
> His thumb had a rainbow.
> The stems said, Thank you.
> Dark came early.

This is one of the few poems in the "Lost Son" sequence in which regression does not lead to some form of progression, to some insight or illumination. After a frightening portrait of the dead father in the fifth section of "Where Knock is Open Wide"—"He was all whitey bones / And skin like paper"—the child concludes, grimly:

> One father is enough.
>
> Maybe God has a house.
> But not here.

From this unfruitful meditation on the father, Roethke proceeds to a four-part poem on the mother. "I Need, I Need" opens with a re-creation of the infantile mentality seen in the oral stage:

> A deep dish. Lumps in it.
> I can't taste my mother.
> Hoo. I know the spoon.
> Sit in my mouth.
> (*CP*, p. 74)

The title bears close resemblance to Blake's inscription "I Want! I Want!" for the ninth design in his series *For Children: The Gates of Paradise* (1793), which traces a man's progress from infancy to adulthood.[3] "I Need, I Need" goes a step further than the prenatal imagery of the first section of "Where Knock Is Open Wide." Now, the child is certainly born; all desires will not be gratified instantly; hence, need arises. The womb world of continuous nutrition is removed: "I can't taste my mother." From this point onward, some needs will be met and some will not: "The Trouble is with No and Yes / As you can see I guess I guess." And so, desire becomes wish in the childlike rhyming of the second section:

> I wish I was a pifflebob
> I wish I was a funny
> I wish I had ten thousand hats,
> And made a lot of money.

The brief third section reveals the deep craving for Papa which a mother's love cannot satisfy:

> Stop the larks. Can I have my heart back?
> Today I saw a beard in a cloud.
> The ground cried my name:
> Good-bye for being wrong.
> Love helps the sun.
> But not enough.

The son ("sun") needs more. While the father, like God, remains "in a cloud," the son is separated from him. So he turns to the earth for help:

> When you plant, spit in the pot.
> A pick likes to hit ice.
> Hooray for me and the mice!—
> The oats are all right.

The child-hero returns to the natural world, where the elements, fire and ice, respond: "It's a dear life I can touch." The poem ends with the lines: "I know another fire. / Has roots." The fire in the root is sexual desire, the need suggested by the title.

"Bring the Day!" follows, adapting the faintly perceived insights of the two previous poems. The nursery jingles that open the poem set the celebratory tone:

> Bees and lilies there were,
> Bees and lilies there were,
> Either to other,—
> Which would you rather?
> Bees and lilies there were.
>
> The green grasses,—would they?
> The green grasses?—
> She asked her skin
> To let me in:
> The far leaves were for it.

In this magical world the herrings sing to each other, whispers become kisses, and the grasses and wind offer sympathetic advice. The hero feels assimilated into the natural process ("When I stand, I'm almost a tree"). The poem ends on a note of joyous expectation:

> The spiders sail into summer.
> It's time to begin!
> To begin!

The image of the self-as-tree is central to the poem that follows, "Give Way, Ye Gates." Malkoff associates this phase of the child's development with Freud's anal-aggressive category: "the struggle toward individuality is taken up more aggressively; the child is now less dependent upon others than before, and he is that much less threatened by separation from them. . . ."[4] Now the slightly older hero tries to put down roots; he revives the oedipal dream and courts his mother, hoping to supplant the dead father. The mother is also a religious symbol (blue being the Virgin's color): "Mother of blue and the many changes of hay." The son informs her: "We're king and queen of the right ground. / I'll risk the winter for you." Further on, he makes the lover's proposal of union: "We'll swinge the instant!" The peculiar word "swinge" combines "swing" and "singe" in a vivid way, creating a nexus of erotic possibilities. Later still, he is explicit:

> In the high-noon of thighs,
> In the springtime of stones,
> We'll stretch with the great stems.
> We'll be at the business of what might be
> Looking toward what we are.

In the brief third section the tone and pace shift as the hero addresses himself:

> You child with a beast's heart,
> Make me a bird or a bear!
> I've played with the fishes
> Among the unwrinkling ferns
> In the wake of a ship of wind;
> But now the instant ages,
> And my thought hunts another body.
> I'm sad with the little owls.

Childhood as an idyll recedes. The wish to become a bird or a bear cannot be fulfilled. The body of his mother must be given up as the boy matures. Melancholy overwhelms him. But the fourth, last section affirms that this delving into the past has not been without benefit:

> The deep stream remembers:
> Once I was a pond.
> What slides away
> Provides.

In "Sensibility! O La!" the adolescent hero of *The Lost Son* returns, hence the language and imagery grow more coherent. The jerky rhythms and associational logic remain, but the literal sense of the poem again moves within our grasp. Now the hero confronts his own sexuality head-on. He prepares to *make use* of his new found powers. The first section pictures an adolescent fantasy of Venus (representing ideal woman) riding in on the waves, couched in a bizarre, pseudoarchaic language, perhaps to suggest the mock-heroic quality of the fantasy: "In the fair night of some dim brain, / Thou wert marmorean-born" (*CP*, p. 81).

The reality of physical lovemaking seems far away. But the next section forces reality back into the poem:

A shape comes to stay:
The long flesh.
I know the way out of a laugh;
I'm a twig to touch,
Pleased as a knife.

In effect, the hero revels in his great new phallic dimension. He is a knight now, brandishing a mighty sword.

Unfortunately, the ghost of Papa (guilt) breaks in to thwart these moments of glory in the third section: "There's a ghost loose in the long grass!" Even Mama will not let the son be; the son shouts back at her, "Mama! Put on your dark hood; / It's a long way to somewhere else." At last, the hero refuses to succumb to these importunate ghosts and protests: "I'm somewhere else,— / I insist! / I am." This is a rare moment of ontological assertion for the hero, an important barrier for him to have crossed.

The first half of *Praise to the End!* concludes with "O Lull Me, Lull Me" which affirms the new sense of identity discovered at the end of the previous poem. The sexual imagery is subdued now; the hero once again asks for advice: "Tell me, great lords of sting, / Is it time to think?" (*CP*, p. 83). But the question, like so many of the hero's queries, is proleptic. He answers himself with new confidence: "I know my bones." And the poem moves on, through its second half, in celebration of the self-discovery. Nature suddenly appears sympathetic as the hero sings, "The air, the air provides. / Light fattens the rock." This childlike belief in the responsiveness of nature harks back to many other ecstatic passages in earlier poems, demonstrating a fundamental insight gained by the lost son in his regression, which is that the capacity for joy must not be relinquished in favor of adult sobriety. Roethke reasserts this great Romantic theme. He comes down, as did Blake, Wordsworth, and Emerson, on the side of radical innocence *earned* through experience. The ground thus far lost in the sequence has been regained, and the last stanza of the poem brings the hero to another "irresolute resolution" (in Burke's phrase). After making a final appeal to Mother Earth ("Soothe me, great groans of underneath"), the adolescent hero declares:

I'm all ready to whistle;
I'm more than when I was born;
I could say hello to things;
I could talk to a snail;

I see what sings!
What sings!

"The effect," says Roy Harvey Pearce of this stanza, "is of a man finding and piecing together his knowledge of himself, which is a product of his knowledge of the natural order."[5]

When Roethke published *Praise to the End!* he included the earlier poems from the sequence published in *The Lost Son*, that is, "The Lost Son," "The Long Alley," "A Field of Light," and "The Shape of the Fire," most of which concern the hero in adolescence. They are therefore placed chronologically in *Praise to the End!* at the beginning of Part Two, following the infancy poems of Part One. Three new poems of adolescence complete the sequence up to 1951.

The title poem—"Praise to the End!"—alludes to Wordsworth's poetic autobiography, *The Prelude*, making Roethke's sympathies with the Romantic view of nature and childhood explicit. Both poets trace the spiritual path of the sensitive artist from childhood to maturity. In the relevant passage, Wordsworth exclaims:

> Ah me, that all
> The terrors, pains, and early miseries,
> Regrets, vexations, lassitudes interfused
> Within my mind, should e'er have borne a part,
> And that a needful part, in making up
> The calm existence that is mine when I
> Am worthy of myself! Praise to the end![6]

Like Wordsworth, Roethke believes that early miseries are necessary in the process that leads to a mature self. La Belle has observed how "both poets repeatedly liken the structure of their poems to a difficult journey."[7] Both journeys, of course, remind us of Dante's famous pilgrim for whom "la diritta via era smarrita." In *The Prelude* and the "Lost Son" sequence the journeys are literal and symbolic. As W. K. Wimsatt has said, it is in the nature of Romantic poetry for the metaphoric level to be concealed or embedded within the literal image or experience.[8]

"Praise to the End!" itself has a central place in Roethke's sequence, for in it the hero rehearses the difficult primal scenes once more in summary fashion. The first section re-examines the sexual guilt felt by the adolescent hero, who finds himself, like Dante's pilgrim, in another dark wood:

> It's dark in this wood, soft mocker.
> For whom have I swelled like a seed?

What a bone-ache I have.
Father of tensions, I'm down to my skin at last.
(CP, p. 85)

Literally, the boy is "down to his skin" and full of sexual tensions for
which masturbation seems the only release. So he cries out, "Father,
forgive my hands." On another level, onanism represents the despair of
solipsistic withdrawal from genuine eros, which by definition involves
another person.

The second section presents a nostalgic view of childhood and the
child's guiltless sexuality:

Once I fished from the banks, leaf-light and happy:
On the rocks south of quiet, in the close regions of kissing,
I romped, lithe as a child, down the summery streets of my veins,
Strict as a seed, nippy and twiggy.

The regressive descent continues, signaled by a return to nursery rhymes
and infantile images of father and mother. Then the hero complains, "An
exact fall of waters has rendered me impotent." He has been "asleep in
a bower of dead skin." So, in the following section, he returns to the
primal fishing scene already mentioned.

The boy is now thirteen, walking in the "goldy grass." He revisits the
scene of the fishing trip, dreaming that this time he *is* the suffering fish
and that Jesus tosses him back into the water to save his life: a daring
transposition of the original scene from "Where Knock Is Open Wide."
This leads to renewed confidence for the boy-hero, who declares: "I feel
more than a fish. / Ghost, come closer." The lost son has now come
closer to terms with the dead father than ever before.

The final section of "Praise to the End!" suggests a relinquishing of
selfhood:

Wherefore, O birds and small fish, surround me.
Lave me, ultimate waters.
The dark showed me a face.
My ghosts are all gay.
The light becomes me.

Malkoff says, "the final section . . . ends with emphasis on regression
rather than progression."[9] The hero again slides back along the scale of
creation, merging with the animal and fish worlds, then the sea (the
unconscious) itself, and finally, light. This kind of regressive journey
prefigures a later line, "The journey from self is longest." This last sec-

tion is, literally, ecstatic (from Greek, *ek-stasis*); the hero stands beside himself.

The last regressive movements occur in "Unfold! Unfold!" which takes its title from Henry Vaughan, the meditative poet whose mysticism and attraction to childhood qualify him as a Romantic precursor. In this poem, Roethke "unfolds" his backward vision and summarizes his method: "By snails, by leaps of frog, I came here, spirit" (*CP*, p. 89). The reader feels that illumination is impending, at first; then the hero dips into the unconscious once again. The hero hides and refuses to move into the open field, where rapture and illumination usually occur; the slime is comforting, protective. Also, the hero fears the loss of identity which accompanies mystical experience, the absorption of self (which he has struggled to attain) into the body of nature. Like Lear, the speaker stands on a windy cliff crying:

> Eternity howls in the last crags,
> The field is no longer simple:
> It's a soul's crossing time.
> The dead speak noise.

The simple crossings of barley-break are gone; the sense of play has disappeared. And the hero is stumped.

As usual, advice comes out of nowhere, perhaps from the unconscious. The alternatives are put before him bluntly: "It's time you stood up and asked / —Or sat down and did." Perhaps the ghost of Papa is talking, for the hero's response, in the third section, seems ungenerous: "What a whelm of proverbs, Mr. Pinch!" He realizes, with amazement, the extent of his regression:

> I was far back, farther than anybody else.
> On the jackpine plains I hunted the bird nobody knows;
> Fishing, I caught myself behind the ears.
> Alone, in a sleep-daze, I stared at billboards.

It has become far too easy to depend on the past: "Easy the life of the mouth." So he asks himself pointedly: "What else has the vine loosened?" In other words, what has come of all this probing?

The revelations of the fifth section bring no surprises. The hero exults:

> Sing, sing, you symbols! All simple creatures,
> All small shapes, willow-shy,
> In the obscure haze, sing!

Roethke's stanza is quintessential Emerson; the hero discovers that all of nature is emblematic, that every object in creation has a corresponding spiritual fact, that nature is itself a mirror in which the poet reads himself. Wordsworth came to much the same conclusion in *The Prelude*; while crossing the Alps as a young man, he suddenly understood that:

> The unfetter'd clouds, and region of the Heavens,
> Tumult and peace, the darkness and the light
> Were all like workings of one mind, the features
> Of the same face, blossoms upon one tree,
> Characters of the great Apocalypse,
> The types and symbols of Eternity,
> Of first and last, and midst, and without end.[10]

Reconciliation with Papa also occurs in this last section of "Unfold! Unfold!" The leaves begin to shake in the wind, "A slow sigh says yes." The father (Papa-Otto-God) acknowledges the son and approves of him, although the son scarcely believes his ears and inquires: "Is it you, cold father? Father/For whom the minnows sang?" Papa answers proverbially:

> A house for wisdom; a field for revelation.
> Speak to the stones, and the stars answer.
> At first the visible obscures:
> Go where light is.

This advice points to the mystic way of redemption, embracing a view of the universe that, as Sullivan writes, "is less a philosophical conception than an animistic belief in a single creative propulsive energy, the soul of things, animating all living matter, including the human and subhuman in its embrace."[11] The visible world, at first, obscures; but meditation reveals the spiritual fact behind the object—an idea extended by Roethke in his last book, *The Far Field*.

The hero can now accept himself, the discovered self. And, in the last stanzas, he rehearses the lesson of the plants as if to be certain of his knowledge:

> What grace I have is enough.
> The lost have their own pace.
> The stalks ask something else.
> What the grave says,
> The nest denies.

This primitive belief in the power of nature to renew itself in a cyclical way has, paradoxically, issued from the hero's confrontation—and acceptance—of his father's death. Again, to refer back to Freud and Norman O. Brown, death-acceptance implies life-acceptance. The hero has been freed—at least in this fiction—from his obsession, cured of the past. The last three lines embody this insight: "In their harsh thickets / The dead thrash. / They help."

"I Cry, Love! Love!" brings the sequence, in *Praise to the End!*, to a close. It contains the hero's final effort to summon the love that binds, which makes us whole. The beginning mingles childhood recollections of uncertainty with joy: "I hear a most lovely huzza: / I'm king of the boops!" (*CP*, p. 92). This near-nonsense language gives way rapidly to more rational (mature) contemplation in the second section. The traditional Romantic bias toward intuition over intellection livens the opening rant:

> Reason? That dreary shed, that hutch for grubby schoolboys!
> The hedgewren's song says something else.
> I care for a cat's cry and the hugs, live as water.
> I've traced these words in sand with a vestigial tail;
> Now the gills are beginning to cry.

The poet describes and criticizes the regressive method itself in the last two lines quoted above; he has relied upon instinct alone, successfully, but the gills are "beginning to cry." The poetics of descent contains within it the need for reversal.

The speaker-hero then loses himself in a world of things that cries out for sensory recognition, unleashing "That anguish of concreteness!"— one of Roethke's most evocative phrases. This anguish accompanies a deep joy, as the hero says: "I proclaim once more a condition of joy." But one interesting aspect of this nearly mystical rapture is Roethke's firm grip on the material world; he never gives himself quite over to transcendental reality, though he sways in that direction at many points. *Love*, however, remains the subject of the poet's declamation in this poem, and—in Augustine's great phrase—love calls us to the things of this world. Says Roethke's hero in amazement: "Behold, in the lout's eye, / Love."

The concluding section takes us to a lakeside, the familiar pond of memory. Above it, bats weave among willows, veering out over the still water. A fish leaps and disturbs the moonlit image on the water's skin:

> The shine on the face of the lake
> Tilts, backward and forward.
> The water recedes slowly,
> Gently rocking.

And the hero queries: "Who untied the tree?" It was someone he met before he lived, no doubt the Father himself, who let loose the son (symbolized by the tree) into creation, his fallen state. The language of this section is, like the title itself (which comes from Oothoon's lament in *Visions of the Daughters of Albion*), Blakean throughout. This poem foreshadows the magnificent love poems of Roethke's last two major books, *Words for the Wind* and *The Far Field*. For the step beyond self-love (where Onan reigns unchallenged) and true love, which reaches out to the Other, is the subject of Blake's *Visions*, just as the hero of Roethke's poem finally understands, "We never enter / Alone."

Although "I Cry, Love! Love!" points toward a resolution of the hero's dilemma, which began with the father's death and prompted his descent into the unconscious, this poem did not provide a strong ending to the sequence. Roethke therefore added a further poem in his next book, *The Waking*. "O, Thou Opening, O" offers a summary of all previous illuminations, all of which take the form of aphorisms or proverbs (after Burke's advice). Even the poet seems dazzled by the process:

Dazzle me, dizzy aphorist.
Fling me a precept.
I'm a draft sleeping by a stick;
I'm lost in what I have.
(*CP*, p. 97)

We should recall that the "Lost Son" sequence, like Wordsworth's *Prelude*, recounts the "growth of a poet's mind." As such, the language of the sequence takes on new interest, for the poems represent not only a psychic but a philological delving as well. As Emerson writes in "The Poet," "the poet is the Namer or Language-maker, naming things sometimes after their appearance, sometimes after their essence. . . . The poets made all the words, and therefore language is the archives of history."[12] Every word was once a brilliant picture, Emerson goes on to say, with emphasis on the primacy of imagery. What Roethke has been doing in these poems can be seen as "naming" in Emerson's sense; the hero attempts to recover the past in his language, in his imagery. He names the original pictures; he reaches back into origins of language in primitive rhymes and nonsense syllables. And the hero–poet's growth is reflected in the growing sophistication of diction and verbal agility, culminating in "Dazzle me, dizzy aphorist." For, as Norman O. Brown has said, "Aphorism is the form of eternity."

We see the poet as dizzy aphorist again in the second section of "O, Thou Opening, O"—which is a curious thing indeed. It is prose, of a very unique kind:

And now are we to have that pelludious Jesus-shimmer over all things, the animal's candid gaze, a shade less than feathers, light's broken speech revived, a ghostly going of tame bears, a bright moon on gleaming skin, a thing you cannot say to whisper and equal a Wound?

This "pelludious Jesus-shimmer over all things" is the result of the poet's "naming," his repossession of the original picture-language, the "light's broken speech revived." Roethke's method parallels that of Joyce in *Finnegans Wake*, of which Harry Levin has written: "We used to lament that words were such a shadowy approximation of objective reality. We have learned to look upon them as objects of immediate apprehension, more real in themselves than their penumbras of meaning."[13] Joyce, by conceding the priority of the word to its object, refreshes our sense of language as an artistic medium. And so does Roethke.

The prose section continues, multiplying the religious associations with phrases such as, "I'm tired of all that, Bag-Foot. I can hear small angels anytime." Like Blake, Roethke prefers to make his own myths rather than be enslaved by another man's. Religions in their institutional forms never interested Roethke, who was nonetheless a deeply religious man. The hero of Roethke's poem rejects the worn-out dogmas of old Bag-Foot (another father figure). He rages against all authority derived from power (Bag-Foot is Big-Foot or God). "Who ever said God sang in your fat shape?" he questions, and we are aware of Otto's presence behind the mask of God. This is the stage of separation; the hero finally understands: "A son has many fathers."

The final section testifies to the wisdom accumulated throughout the long sequence. The hero apprehends fresh possibilities, saying:

> You mean?—
> I can leap, true to the field,
> In the lily's sovereign right?
> Be a body lighted with love,
> Sad, in a singing-time?
> Or happy, correct as a hat?

All of these will be part of the life to come: ecstatic identification with nature, physical love, and the joy of song. These intimations of future happiness bring on a profound release:

> I'm twinkling like a twig!
> The lark's my heart!
> I'm wild with news!
> My fancy's white!
> I am my faces,
> Love.

Self-discovery has led to self-acceptance: "I am my faces." One of the last lines in the poem is the aphorism, "Going is knowing," which looks forward to the beautiful villanelle, "The Waking," from which the book's title is drawn. "I learn by going where I have to go" is the refrain of that poem—a summarizing proverb which directs the hero out of the dark wood toward the field of light. The heroic journey is a long and arduous one, but it *must* be undertaken. One learns by going. There is no other way.

Looking back at the sequence as a whole, one marvels at Roethke's achievement. "The Lost Son" itself remains the center of the whirlpool, catching all manner of flotsam and jetsam in its spiral. The other poems emanate from this focus, where nearly all of Roethke's major symbols are present and active. Although obscurity often frustrates the reader (and *Finnegans Wake* again comes to mind), the rewards of persistence are considerable. After several readings, the sequence becomes more intelligible; the symbols begin to inform each other, and the strange dream imagery coheres. If one keeps the basic myth of the hero's initiatory journey in mind, the more opaque passages will not obstruct one's progress. For this sequence is Roethke's contribution to Romantic quest literature; the quest is interiorized, turning the hero's motion inward, allowing Roethke full possession of Freudian and Jungian insights.

The poems dealing with infancy and childhood tend to be the most difficult, employing the ancient technique of regression. The poems of adolescence often imitate patterns associated with rites of passage, provoking a great deal of tension as the hero crosses various thresholds. The sequence, taken as a whole, is Roethke's most original achievement, if not *quite* his best (priority still belongs to the greenhouse poems). Yet one must not overlook the therapeutic effect of these poems on the developing artist; they became, in effect, a psychic autobiography in which the poet recovered, in a Freudian sense, his own lost past. To go forward, the poet had first to go backward. He had to confront reality without an intervening mirror, taking experience for his own text, transforming himself into the New Perseus described by Geoffrey Hartman. After writing the "Lost Son" poems, Roethke felt much freer from the bondage of his past and, especially, of his guilt over the death of Otto Roethke. These poems, stretching from *The Lost Son* to *The Waking*, demonstrate once more that an important common ground exists between poetry and psychoanalysis.

PART THREE
THE LONG JOURNEY
OUT OF THE SELF

CHAPTER TEN

THE LESSON OF THE MASK

"Put off that mask of burning gold
With emerald eyes."
"O no, my dear, you make so bold
To find if hearts be wild and wise,
And yet not cold."

"I would but find what's there to find,
Love or deceit."
"It was the mask engaged your mind,
And after set your heart to beat,
Not what's behind."

"But lest you are my enemy,
I must enquire."
"O no, my dear, let all that be;
What matter, so there is but fire
In you, in me?"

Yeats, *"The Mask"*

The main subject of Romantic poetry has continued to be the growth of the poet's mind.
Wordsworth, while preaching against the self-
absorption of the Solitary in *The Excursion*, remains at the source of this modern tradition,
and the hero of his *Prelude* stands as a prototype
for the Romantic poet: a man alone with himself, on the skirts of society, deeply aware of the
gulf between self and nature, and dedicated to
the redeeming powers of the imagination. The
Romantic poet, like the Archangel Michael in
Book 12 of *Paradise Lost*, offers us "a paradise
within," an inner Eden wherein seer and seen
are one. The saving movement is first inward
toward self-discovery, then outward, beyond
the individual mind. This progress depends
upon Blake's dialectic of contraries, what Harold Bloom calls the "antithetical quest," and
what Roethke began in *The Waking* and contin-

ued until his death. One version of this quest arises in Yeats's doctrine of the masks, an ancient idea given new expression, which Roethke adopted in what I call his middle period.

Blake, too, realized the pitfalls of self-absorption, that most dangerous side effect of self-discovery. He named this side effect the Spectre of Urthona—embodied in the last of his epics, *Jerusalem*—and went so far as to claim that if man would build the earthly, paradisiacal city of Golgonooza, he must relinquish selfhood altogether. He prays:

> O Saviour, pour upon me thy spirit of meekness & love:
> Annihilate the Selfhood in me, be thou all my life!
> Guide thou my hand which trembles exceedingly upon the rock of
>   ages,
> While I write of the building of Golgonooza. . . . [1]

The imagination can win autonomy only by extinguishing the self, Blake argues. The poet must escape from the prison of self-consciousness if he will be saved.

Yeats, who writes in the same tradition as Blake and, in fact, was one of his first editors, thought the doctrine of the mask could be of use in liberating the imagination from the strictures of selfhood. As Richard Ellmann has said, "The doctrine of the mask is so complex and so central in Yeats that we can hardly attend to it too closely."[2] He goes on:

> Browning had spoken of "two soul-sides, one to face the world with," and one to show the beloved. But Yeats's doctrine assumes that we face with a mask both the world and the beloved. A closely related meaning is that the mask includes all the differences between one's own and other people's conception of one's personality. To be conscious of the discrepancy which makes a mask of this sort is to look at oneself as if one were somebody else. In addition, the mask is defense armor: we wear it, like the light lover, to keep from being hurt. So protected, we are only slightly involved no matter what happens. This theory seems to assume that we can be detached from experience like actors from a play. Finally, the mask is a weapon of attack; we put it on to keep us a noble conception of ourselves; it is a heroic ideal which we try to live up to.

One finds a wide-ranging variety of masks in Yeats's verse, from the wandering Oisin of his "Celtic Twilight" phase to the revolutionary nationalist Owen Aherne and his contrary, the mystical philosopher Michael Robartes. Often his masks are versions of the self, the embittered lover of "No Second Troy" or the "smiling public man" of "Among School Children." A poet *always* has a persona, but the more conscious he is of this fact, Yeats thought, the better. For literature participates in that realm of play where the conditional "as if" holds first place.

For an artist, especially the poet, the mask demands that willing suspension of disbelief not demanded of, say, a priest at the communion table. It demands the possibility that one can move outside of the narrow self-consciousness that Blake decried. It may require self-annihilation. But the artist, like the religious convert, understands that one must first be lost in order to be found; one has to make Roethke's "long journey out of the self." As Campbell says,

> we are to enter the play sphere of the festival, acquiescing in a game of belief, where fun, joy, and rapture rule in ascending series. The laws of life in time and space—economics, politics, and even morality—will thereupon dissolve. Whereafter, recreated by that return to paradise before the Fall, before the knowledge of good and evil, right and wrong, true and false, belief and disbelief, we are to carry the point of view and spirit of man the player (homo ludens) back into life. . . . [3]

If one recalls the struggle of the lost son to come to some sense of self, it is doubly impressive that Roethke should have learned the lesson of the mask and sought a way *out* of this self. However, the "Lost Son" period (1943–1953) seems to have worn Roethke down; having probed his past life so deeply, further work in this direction seemed unlikely to yield much more. Perhaps the near unintelligibility of parts of *Praise to the End!* worried him; he wanted to be read and understood. For whatever reason, Roethke changed his course again. He began an arduous process of self-transcendence, first by reaching out to someone with love, then by meditation and mysticism.

In another way, these new directions are a logical extension of his autobiographical mythos. Roethke merely extends the self discovered in *The Lost Son* and *Praise to the End!* to include adult patterns of behavior. He brings the hero into the present. The adolescent hero becomes the adult lover, the professor, the poet, and the mystic of later phases. The greenhouse image recurs, and Otto Roethke reappears. The poet's growing awareness of God seems an extension of affection and fear from the poet's biological father to God, who is Father in the abstract. The open field as a symbol displaces the greenhouse, just as the poet moves outside the prison (greenhouse) of his self-consciousness into the clear light of nature (open field).

A crucial aspect of the mask in Roethke's sense of that term involves his relation with his precursors, which is highly complex. Whereas he was merely *imitating* his precursors in *Open House*, in his later volumes he wears them like masks; he *becomes* each precursor, merging his own self so completely with another's that an amalgam voice is born. In a poem like "Four for Sir John Davies," for instance, Roethke flaunts the mask with great daring:

> I take this cadence from a man named Yeats;
> I take it, and I give it back again:
> For other tunes and other wanton beats
> Have tossed my heart and fiddled through my brain.
> Yes, I was dancing-mad, and how
> That came to be the bears and Yeats would know.
> (*CP*, p. 105)

One good way to escape the self is to become another. Here, Roethke gets into Yeats's skin, plays at being Yeats, just as Yeats played at being Oisin or Michael Robartes.

In his last book, *The Far Field*, the mask of Whitman takes precedence, although Yeats and Blake are not abandoned. The last book completes the myth of the lost son, reviving the metaphor of the journey in a fresh context. The journey, again, is regressive, but the illuminations now become the emotional center of these poems, just as the descent theme preoccupied the poet at an earlier stage. Roethke's belief in nature as a symbol of the spirit pervades these expansive final poems, most of which celebrate American landscapes in a way reminiscent of Emerson, who said: "O Poet . . . Thou shalt have the whole land for thy park and manor, the sea for thy bath and navigation, without tax and without envy; the woods and the rivers thou shalt own, and thou shalt possess that wherein others are only tenants and boarders."[4] Roethke's last meditations fulfill the Emersonian prophecy, constituting an imaginative repossession of the natural world which, in turn, allows a repossession of the spirit. *The Far Field* contains some of Roethke's very best writing, especially in "North American Sequence" and "Sequence, Sometimes Metaphysical," which display "not only some of his finest work," according to Ralph J. Mills, Jr., "but a number of the most astonishing mystical poems in the language."[5] "Once More, the Round," the ecstatic epilogue to Roethke's posthumous volume, completes Roethke's long journey out of the self with the cosmic dance wherein all conflicts find resolution:

> What's greater, Pebble or Pond?
> What can be known? The Unknown.
> My true self runs toward a Hill
> More! O More! visible.

Now I adore my life
With the Bird, the abiding Leaf,
With the Fish, the questing Snail,
And the Eye altering all;
And I dance with William Blake
For love, for Love's sake;

And everything comes to One,
As we dance on, dance on, dance on.
(*CP*, p. 251)

CHAPTER ELEVEN

LOVE'S PROPER EXERCISE

Dauncing (bright Lady) then began to be,
When first the seedes whereof the world did spring,
The Fire, Ayre, Earth, and Water did agree,
By Loves persuasion, Natures mighty King,
To leave their first disordered combating;
And in a daunce such measure to observe,
As all the world their motion should preserve.

Since when they still are carried in a round,
And changing come one in another's place,
Yet do they neyther mingle nor confound,
But everyone doth keepe the bounded space
Wherein the Daunce doth bid it turne or trace;
This wondrous myracle did Love devise,
For Dauncing is Love's proper exercise.

Sir John Davies, Orchestra (1956)

Nineteen fifty-three marks another turning point in Roethke's career. *The Waking: Poems 1932–1953* was published, completing the "Lost Son" sequence with its first poem, "O, Thou Opening, O" and announcing a new, highly formal style which derives from Yeats and the Elizabethan, Sir John Davies. Also, on 3 January 1953 Roethke married Beatrice Heath O'Connell, surprising his family and friends, who had come to think of him as a confirmed bachelor. His own attitude toward his marriage was one of unabashed delight. He wrote to an old friend, the Canadian poet A. J. M. Smith:

> I got married—don't faint—on January 3 to Beatrice O'Connell of Winchester, Va., and N.Y.C. Auden was best man & Bogan the matron of honor (the only attendants except for her ma & pa & brother). She's v.

pretty (26); Irish & German & no fool. You'll both like her, I know.
I've known her for nearly ten years. (*SL*, p. 183)

True, he had known Beatrice for nearly ten years, but only slightly.
She had been his student at Bennington in the mid-forties and had
admired him from a distance. Their acquaintance had lapsed until a
chance meeting in December 1952. They met this time in New York,
where Roethke was appearing at the Poetry Center, and the courtship
lasted a matter of weeks. Auden, who was best man, offered the new-
lyweds his villa on Ischia for a honeymoon, and they accepted, sailing to
Naples in March. They stayed until the end of May, in relative seclu-
sion; during this period Roethke wrote his finest love poem, "Words for
the Wind," and began the long journey out of the self. The "Lost Son"
period was certainly over. The hero had won the bride, and he was
ready to experiment with various masks; he was ready to extend himself to another.

After Italy, the Roethkes traveled by way of Geneva and Paris to England, where Roethke befriended Dylan Thomas and did a broadcast
for the B.B.C., called *An American Poet Introduces Himself and His Work*
(30 July 1953). The talk was well received, and Roethke was gaining in
confidence every day. He returned to America buoyed up by his accom-
plishments, the warm reception he had received in England, and the love
of Beatrice.

But the mental illness which had plagued him in earlier years would
not let him be. He was overtaken by one of his "manic phases" in late
autumn and was forced to spend two weeks in the Columbus Hospital.
He recovered quickly this time, but it was obvious now that no measure
of worldly success would protect him against these bouts of extreme
anxiety; in fact, his anxiety tended to increase with public acclaim. Yet
it was typical of Roethke to turn failures to his advantage as a poet. He
liked to identify with other "mad" poets of the past: Christopher Smart,
Blake, and John Clare especially. He took on the persona of a visionary,
taking pride in his madness, using his altered mental states to probe the
boundaries of sanity.

It was also during this period, the mid-fifties, that Roethke came into
his own as a teacher. Whereas the notebooks of the "Lost Son" period
are an indispensable guide to the poet's thinking at the first turning point
of his career, his teaching notes from the University of Washington provide essential clues to the thought underlying the later poetry. We learn
what books he was reading, what he was telling his students, and how
his own work was planned. We continue to see his obsession with technique, his concern for tradition, and his effort to learn about fields out-

side of literature. Burke had introduced him to psychology; now he began reading widely in philosophy, religion, and mysticism. Ideas come into his poetry again, though often without much success.

In a memoir written shortly after the poet's death, Robert Heilman recalls the poet as a teacher-colleague:

> As a colleague he was a man of great conscience. He was not useful in ordinary ways in the department of the university; he was not a committee man. But he was not aloof, indifferent, a great man who could not be bothered. He was profoundly concerned about the department, more so, perhaps, than some people who took their own good citizenship for granted. . . . He could sound ferocious about those who seemed untalented or lacking in some way or who seemed to be pursuing only private ends, and yet have a very kindly feeling for someone in whom he sensed warmth and the right devotion.[1]

Similar reports of Roethke's integrity as a teacher have come down from his students, many of whom have become well-known poets in their own right, especially Richard Hugo, David Wagoner, James Wright, and Carolyn Kizer. In his brief and brilliant essay, "The Teaching Poet," the professorial mask turns suddenly transparent:

> Let's say no one would claim to make poets. But a good deal can be taught about the craft of verse. A few people come together, establish an intellectual and emotional climate wherein creation is possible. They teach each other—that ideal condition of what once was called "progressive education." They learn by doing. Something of the creative lost in childhood is recovered. The student (and the teacher) learn a considerable something about themselves and the language. The making of verse remains a human activity. (SP, p. 45)

Looking over the teaching notes of his last decade, one discovers the intimate relationship that existed between his roles of poet and teacher. Rather than conflicting, as one might expect, they serve each other in the best possible way. Roethke needed the live audience before him to bring out his best, to get him going every day, to keep him alert and reading widely. He seems to have taken as much in inspiration from his students as he gave out. Also, being a teacher forced him to redefine his terms constantly, the terms of his art and of his self. A good teacher, like a good poet, has to invent his own language and be perpetually reborn to himself with every class.

Certainly Roethke won the devotion of his students. He urged them to *feel* things as passionately as they could. An excerpt from his teaching notes gives some hint of what his classes were like:

> You will notice that we don't begin with a great many rules and precepts: but we do begin! Another way to look at it: as a teacher I'm like a little kid who has done something bad. I don't tell about it all at once: it has to break out gradually.
>
> This course is based on the assumption that these particular old forms have served many minds nobly. They may be able to catch *some* of the things you have to say. At any rate, they will give you practice. We begin, to continue the child analogy, with small things. Now along with this I want you to follow your own impulses about the shapes of poems. Put down ideas in your notebooks. Expand them into poems. Always try to get a rhythm, a shape that seems to fit the material.[2]

Here is a teacher who can do what he professes; these notes tell us a great deal about Roethke's working methods, as teacher *and* poet. And his method, as poet, bears a striking resemblance to that of Yeats. The poet begins with an idea (gained through experience or reading); he puts it into abstract prose and later expands it into poetry, always seeking "a rhythm, a shape that seems to fit the material." The notion of fitting the shape to the idea comes out of the Romantic metaphor of the plant.

Roethke's teaching notes and his poetic notebooks, from *The Waking* onward, reveal a growing interest in mysticism. Even in the early forties, the poet dabbled in Oriental literature. Perhaps his interest in Yeats was responsible for his branching out. In any case, Roethke never fell head over heels for any sect, as did Yeats, but he believed himself a true mystic. And his conception of the universe takes on a Neo-Platonic hue in later years—another Yeatsian inheritance.

The notebooks of the forties contain many references to such contemporary scholars of mysticism as E. Allison Peers and Evelyn Underhill (a disciple of the Baron Friedrich von Hügel, an important influence on Yeats). The following notes on the mystical expansion or progress of consciousness, taken directly from Underhill, appear in Roethke's notebooks in 1946:

1. Awakening—to a sense of reality.
2. Purgation of the self, when it realizes its own (unprojecting) divine.
3. An enhanced return to the sense of the divine order, after the Self has achieved detachment from the world.

4. Dark Night of the Soul.
Sacramental perception.

Singleness: Discovery of singleness of self is the same as discovery of God in oneself.[3]

These are the kinds of "ideas" out of which Roethke fashioned his poems.

It will be useful to review the stages of mystic consciousness before turning to Roethke's middle and later poems. Underhill divines five progressive stages on the "scale of awareness." (1) Awakening of the self to consciousness of the Absolute, marked by feelings of intense joy, exhilaration; (2) Awareness of the gulf between the self and the Absolute, which leads to purgation or the attempt to eliminate extraneous factors that stand between the self and God; (3) Illumination: the contemplative state par excellence, characterized by a clear vision of Absolute Reality, a sense of the Divine Presence in creation; (4) Dark Night of the Soul: extreme awareness of the Divine Absence. This resembles the second stage but is a higher exponent of it. The feelings of personal satisfaction which accompany the third stage must be lost before the final stage can be prepared for; (5) Union: the goal of all mystic quests. This stage follows the surrender of selfhood in the fourth stage. It demands more than mere perception of the Absolute; it requires mergence. Self-consciousness gives way to complete consciousness. Serenity predominates, but not necessarily ecstasy.[4]

As Underhill observes, the poet rarely goes beyond the stage of Illumination. Roethke probably never went further, though he may have thought he did. It would be easy to mistake certain phases of the manic-depressive syndrome for mystical apprehension of the Absolute or, surely, the Dark Night of the Soul. The dynamics of mysticism imply a Platonic universe, also a fundamental presupposition of Romanticism.[5] The mystic posits a spiritual world running parallel to or contained within the material world; the mystical moment is that cutting across or rending of the veil, that "intersection of the timeless in time."

Using the language of Emerson, Roethke interpreted the world of nature as "a steady storm of correspondences" (*CP*, p. 239). And in his earliest notebooks one finds an appreciation of Plato's (and Emerson's) metaphysics: "Plato: the true order of going . . . is to use the beauties of earth as steps along which he mounts upwards for the sake of that other Beauty."[6] This basic mystical premise underlies much of his later verse, for in the poems after 1953 there is always the sense that one is being shown the particulars of reality only to suggest a higher reality. Roethke's metaphysics reflect the influence, too, of Blake's mentor, Jacob Boehme, the German mystic, who wrote in his *Confessions*: "Dost thou think my writing is too earthly? If thou wert to come to this window of mine thou wouldst not then say that it is earthly. Though I must indeed use the earthly tongue, yet there is a true heavenly understanding couched under it, which in my outermost moving I am not able to express."[7] Malkoff finds numerous points of affinity between Roethke and Boehme, including the doctrine of correspondences, the image of the self as a tree, and the symbolic field of light.[8] Indeed, in "The Pure Fury" the poet says, "Great Boehme rooted all in Yes and No; / At times my darling squeaks in pure Plato" (*CP*, p. 133). If good for nothing else, these lines point to Roethke's interest in Boehme and his great original, Plato.

In *The Waking*, there is one important addition to Roethke's symbol cluster: the image of Woman as lover. In Roethke's love poetry he almost never has a specific woman in mind, though presumably Beatrice was his later inspiration. He appeals, instead, to the archetype, what Jung called the "primordial image." Significantly, Roethke transcribed huge passages from Jung into his teaching notes. One key passage relating to the "primordial image" follows:

> The primordial image or archetype is a figure, whether it be dae-mon, man, or process, that repeats itself in the course of history wherever fantasy is fully manifested. Essentially, therefore, it is a mythical figure. If we subject these images to a close investigation, we discover them to be the formulated resultants of countless typi-cal experiences of our ancestors. They are, as it were, the psychic residua of numberless experiences of the same type.[9]

The primordial image of Woman first appears as the mother of the "Lost Son" poems. In *The Waking* she becomes the lover. In her new guise, in "The Visitant," we cannot even be sure if the transformation has been completed. The visitant is female, but she remains insubstantial, wraithlike:

> Slow, slow as a fish she came,
> Slow as a fish coming forward,
> Swaying in a long wave;
> Her skirts not touching a leaf,
> Her white arms reaching towards me.
> (*CP*, p. 100)

Not until the beautiful "Elegy for Jane" does Roethke's Woman receive an earthly habitation and a name. In this elegy the girl's death, in a riding accident, is no more the subject of the poem than Edward King's is the subject of Milton's *Lycidas*. The girl's death is rather the occasion for a poem calling up a certain emotional state; the poet's feelings of grief and pity transcend the occasion. Roethke compiled the elegy from fragments scattered over many years through the notebooks; it begins, in the manner of meditative poetry, with a memory evoked in concrete terms:

> I remember the neckcurls, limp and damp as tendrils;
> And her quick look, a sidelong pickerel smile;
> And how, once startled into talk, the light syllables leaped for her,
> And she balanced in the delight of her thought,
> A wren, happy, tail into the wind,
> Her song trembling the twigs and small branches.
> (*CP*, p. 102)

The phrase "a sidelong pickerel smile" first appears in the notebooks of 3 March 1945. Roethke, like many writers before him, used his notebooks as a phrase bank, saving up good images or expressions to be rescued at a later date. In this elegy, Roethke associates the girl with elemental aspects of nature: the plant tendrils, the pickerel, the wren; this has the salutary effect of defusing the pathos of her death. The Romantic views death as merely a stage; the lesson of the plants points to some kind of rebirth. Hence, the subject of the poem becomes, in effect, the poet's *response* to the girl's death and his ambivalent emotions at her graveside. Roethke pushes the technique of association to the extreme here, taking his imagery further down the scale of being, ending up with the mold itself:

> The shade sang with her;
> The leaves, their whispers turned to kissing;
> And the mold sang in the bleached valleys under the rose.

The technique is traditional, going back all the way to Bion's *Lament for Adonis* and Moschus's *Lament for Bion*, Hellenic poems of the second century B.C. in which the vegetation god, Adonis, plays a central metaphoric role. Roethke, perhaps not consciously (though he surely knew Shelley's *Adonais*, modeled on Bion's elegy), turns his Jane into a vegetation goddess. Her death occasions this poet's strongest lamentations:

> If only I could nudge you from this sleep,
> My maimed darling, my skittery pigeon.
> Over this damp grave I speak the words of my love:
> I, with no rights in this matter,
> Neither father nor lover.

Without the associations of earlier elegies, the emotion would outstrip the situation. As it stands, Roethke is mourning not only this student, whom he knew only slightly, but the deaths of us all.

"Old Lady's Winter Words" follows "Elegy for Jane." Here, Roethke takes on a fresh mask, an extreme one, and one that he would revive later to great effect in his "Meditations of an Old Woman." This bitter dramatic monologue explores the problem of old age (and ontological anxiety) as the persona clings to the past, comparing herself to "the half-dead," the aged who hug their last secrets. She yearns for a glimpse beyond the grave: "O for some minstrel of what's to be" (*CP*, p. 103). She wants God, or at least a sign, "a gleam, / Gracious and bland, / On a bright stone." But she struggles to recall her youth in vain, "The doors swinging open, / The smells, the moment of hay." She comes to realize now, "The good day has gone." And she meditates on the death of her spirit and her body, using concrete analogues from her daily life:

> I have listened close
> For the thin sound in the windy chimney,
> The fall of the last ash
> From the dying ember.
> I've become a sentry of small seeds,
> Poking alone in my garden.

As in the "Elegy for Jane," Roethke associates the old woman with the earth; she has broken down into seeds and now guards her own fragments. Will the seeds regenerate? No answer is forthcoming, so, like Yeats's old man in *The Tower*, a fury overcomes her: "If I were a young man, / I could roll in the dust of a fine rage." The poet establishes a strict correspondence between inner and outer weathers in the final lines. Nature is barren and it is wintertime; a cindery snow adheres to the rubble. The old woman wishes to rid herself of her body: "My dust longs for the invisible." Staying alive itself has become a chore, and despair settles in:

> I fall, more and more,
> Into my own silences.
> In the cold air,
> The spirit
> Hardens.

The tone of this poem, stoic and passionate at the same time, is one of Roethke's most delicate achievements, yet critics have largely ignored it. Only Malkoff comments, saying of the conclusion, "these lines are not entirely without comfort. Not in content, for the emptiness of the poem's vision holds no solace; but rather in the verse's tough, unsentimental tone."[10]

The poem reminds us of Robert Frost's "An Old Man's Winter Words" from *Mountain Interval* (1916). This precursor captures a similar state of mind and tone, using winter imagery to suggest a corresponding spiritual season. Roethke's old woman says:

> I'm reminded to stay alive
> By the dry rasp of the recurring inane,
> The fine soot sifting through my south windows.

Whereas Frost says of his old man:

> All out-of-doors looked darkly in at him
> Through the thin frost, almost in separate stars,
> That gathers on the pane in empty rooms.
> What kept his eyes from giving back the gaze
> Was the lamp tilted near them in his hand.

Both figures are sustained, though barely, by the external world which will not let them simply fall back into their own dark silence forever.

Roethke's magisterial sequence, "Four for Sir John Davies," is the penultimate poem in *The Waking*. Again, Roethke announces a brand new style: the end-stopped, highly formalized and rhetorical iambic pentameter in which so much of his later verse is composed. Roethke acknowledges his two great debts at the outset, taking on the masks of Davies and Yeats. (Yeats, to be accurate, rarely end-stopped his lines quite so drastically.) The epigraph from Davies that began this chapter directs us to Roethke's major source here, the Elizabethan "plain style" associated with such poets as Goodge, Gascoigne, Greville, Ralegh, and Davies. These were all poets Roethke taught in his creative writing course, offering their fine lyrics as models for imitation.

Both Yeats and Roethke shared the Platonic conception of the universe, which insisted upon that split between soul and body that follows by necessity from the antimaterialistic view of things. Their common interest in mysticism arises from the desire to participate in the eternal while still living in the temporal realm. Both poets believed in the power of art to "redeem the time" by creating that "artifice of eternity" which lifts man out of nature—a version of the Romantic quest for paradise. Finally, both poets wrote autobiographical verse for the most part, speaking of private passions in a public way.

The Davies sequence consists of four separate poems, each of which divides into four six-line stanzas, all maintaining a strict rhyme scheme (*ababcc*). This formality contrasts rather profoundly with the free verse of the "Lost Son" period, but it is a mistake to think that Roethke, by changing his style so radically, altered his vision. He is still creating, modifying, and extending his personal mythos; the same symbols are active; the imagery remains consistent with his earlier work. Indeed, the organic approach to style still obtains, for Roethke's new theme, the universal dance (taken from Davies), demands the formal pattern, with its repetition and rhyme, in imitation of dancing.

Davies, in *Orchestra*, bids his readers learn the dance for themselves and be in harmony with the heavenly patterns:

> Since all the world's great fortunes and affaires
> Forward and backward rapt and whirled are,
> According to the musicke of the spheares:
> And Chaunce her selfe, her nimble feete upbeares
> On a round slippery wheele that rowleth ay,
> And turnes all states with her impetuous sway.[11]

Roethke launches off from here, asking a question, then making an assertion of his own:

> Is that dance slowing in the mind of man
> That made him think the universe could hum?
> The great wheel turns its axle when it can;
> I need a place to sing, and dancing-room,
> And I have made a promise to my ears
> I'll sing and whistle romping with the bears.
> (*CP*, p. 105)

Roethke implies that something has happened since Davies's time to disturb the easy harmony of the universe. Man no longer hears celestial music; yet the poet *needs* to dance, and this need leads to the promise to "sing and whistle dancing with the bears." Bears recur in Roethke's poetry from this point on, symbolizing the spontaneous sense of play, that magical zone where the mask can become real, where the game is taken seriously. Bears in this context also refer to the celestial bears: Ursa Major and Ursa Minor. Roethke finally links the bears with Yeats! "Yes, I was dancing-mad, and how / That came to be the bears and Yeats would know."

"The Partner" follows "The Dance" and introduces once more the Jungian anima or feminine principle. Eros comes into play here, and the mystical associations of erotic love. The poet asks "What is desire? / The impulse to make someone else complete?" Then he affirms, "That woman would set sodden straw on fire." This is no vaguely defined, primordial

image of Woman: "She kissed me close, and then did something else. /
My marrow beat as wildly as my pulse." The concluding stanza widens
the context of this love:

> This joy outleaps the dog. Who cares? Who cares?
> I gave her kisses back, and woke a ghost.
> O what lewd music crept into our ears!
> The body and the soul know how to play
> In that dark world where gods have lost their way.

The poet, as the last couplet suggests, gains illumination in the realm of
sexual play. This idea permeates mystical literature, of course. One
thinks immediately of the Song of Solomon, of Spenser's *Ode to Heavenly
Beauty*, or of Milton's Adam, who justifies earthly love as a means of
ascending to heavenly love: "To love thou blam'st me not, for love thou
say'st / Leads up to heav'n, is both the way and guide." As Underhill has
explained:

> It was natural and inevitable that the imagery of human love and
> marriage should have seemed to the mystic the best of all images of
> his own 'fulfillment of life'; his soul's surrender, first to the call,
> finally to the embrace of Perfect Love. It lay ready to his hand: it
> was understood by all men: and, moreover, it most certainly does
> offer, upon lower levels, a strangely exact parallel to the sequence of
> states in which man's spiritual consciousness unfolds itself, and
> which form the consummation of the mystic life.[12]

The underlying mystical nature of the eros described in "The Partners" comes to the surface in "The Wraith" as the poet contemplates the
symbolical aspect of the love act:

> Incomprehensible gaiety and dread
> Attended what we did. Behind, before,
> Lay all the lonely pastures of the dead;
> The spirit and the flesh cried out for more.
> We two, together, on a darkening day
> Took arms against our own obscurity.

Eros is an affirmation of being against non-being, "the lonely pastures
of the dead" which lie at either end of life. The two lovers "take arms"
against the threat of non-being; it is a brilliant pun as well. This is the
private passion given public expression that recalls the later Yeats. A key
line in "The Wraith" soon follows: "The flesh can make the spirit
visible." This realization serves to reconcile the Platonic body-spirit

schism. Not surprisingly, Roethke had been reading at this time the theologian Paul Tillich's *The Courage To Be*, in which Tillich defines courage as self-affirmation *in spite of* non-being. His vision of eros embodies a kind of mutual self-affirmation, as when Roethke's partners "Took arms against their own obscurity." These lovers take arms literally and figuratively to ward off threatening ghosts.

Tillich exercised a subtle, but profound, influence on the later Roethke, who drew on *The Courage To Be* for ideas and corroboration of his own instincts. Tillich's basic existentialism supports Roethke's conclusion to the Davies sequence, "The Vigil," where the central motif is that of Dante's ascent through purgatory. The point here is that Dante believed in this vision of ascent. The first stanza ends with a question and an answer:

> Did Beatrice deny what Dante saw?
> All lovers live by longing, and endure:
> Summon a vision and declare it pure.

The coincidence, that Roethke's wife was also Beatrice, allows the poet to ground the sequence in myth and autobiography at the same time. The advice to "Summon a vision and declare it pure" parallels Tillich, who urges creativity as one sure way of overcoming the threat of nonbeing: "Spiritual self-affirmation occurs in every moment in which man lives creatively in various spheres of meaning."[13] This self-affirmation extends beyond the artist, says Tillich, to whomever participates spontaneously in response to a creative vision: "Everyone who lives creatively in meanings affirms himself as a participant in these meanings." Ontological anxiety is the result of noncreativity, which is nonparticipation in the lively dance of the universe summoned by Davies and affirmed by Roethke. The last lines of the sequence document the rewards of joining in the dance, culminating in the possibility of mystical union: "Who rise from flesh to spirit know the fall: / The word outleaps the world, and light is all." For a poet, especially, the gnostic leap from logos into pure light, from word to otherworld, has a particular richness of meaning.

"The Waking" serves as an epilogue to "Four for Sir John Davies," although it is a separate poem in its own right, as well as the title poem for the book. Blessing has written with special sensitivity about this poem: "a poem celebrating the 'always' that falls away whenever we near it and one which finds its only steadiness in the 'shaking' by which the world advances."[14] The poem is a villanelle, a highly wrought form, and one dependent upon two brilliant refrain lines. It is carefully contrived around these lines, which must come together as a final couplet *and* bring the poem to a conclusion! Each stanza, in turn, takes the refrain lines and slightly alters or extends their meaning. Indeed, the form itself dictates a tentative approach toward experience, for each refrain line, end stopped and seemingly final in its expression, is abruptly given a new color by its successive contexts. The reader engages in the *process* of art with the poet, testing each line as one tests a proposition, inching gradually toward some resolution, which is never really final. The poem's subject, in effect, is the Romantic dialectic, the movement toward synthesis which, in turn, gives one another thesis to begin with once more. Hegel's triadic way of reasoning acknowledges the ineluctable nature of truth. The *process* takes precedence over the result, as in "The Waking." Roethke's final stanza summarizes the poem's content and opens the way for new work, for the poet must always move toward that "always" which is near:

> This shaking keeps me steady. I should know.
> What falls away is always. And is near.
> I wake to sleep, and take my waking slow.
> I learn by going where I have to go.
> (*CP*, p. 108)

Here, Roethke embraces many of his key paradoxes: one must learn by going (the reverse of what is usual); one must wake to sleep (the gradual awakening of the spirit); movement steadies the uncertain man; and things must not be taken for what they seem (Plato's paradox), for what falls away, i.e., the physical world, is always at hand in the ideal world of spiritual reality that lies behind and sustains it.

In *Words for the Wind*, published in 1958, Roethke preserved his favorite poems and adds some new ones. There are five sections: "Lighter Pieces and Poems for Children," "Love Poems," "Voices and Creatures," "The Dying Man," and "Meditations of an Old Woman." There are no real departures in this volume, merely extensions and elaborations. I shall treat them briefly.

The lighter pieces are weakest; Roethke was by reputation a witty man, an amusing colleague and friend, but his poems for children and his light verse generally are dull. "Reply to a Lady Editor" seems to me his only successful venture in this realm. The second section, the love poems written to his wife, contains this poet's least interesting work in this genre; the Woman addressed or conjured in these poems tends more toward the Jungian archetype than toward Beatrice O'Connell. And this damages the poetry as love poetry.

The woman encountered in "The Dream," for instance, is a wraith. "She came toward me in the flowing air, / A shape of change, encircled by its fire" (*CP*, p. 119). Of course, the title does not lead one to expect more than a ghost, but the loss of "that anguish of concreteness" can be felt. Roethke seems to forget his own maxim: "The flesh can make the spirit visible" (CP, p. 106). The same problem weakens the other poems in this section: "All the Earth, All the Air," "She," "The Voice," "The Other," and "The Swan" are prone to abstraction; the poet loses that grip on the particulars of reality that invigorates his best writing.

The two most engaging poems in the book are, nonetheless, love poems; "Words for the Wind" and "I Knew a Woman" both transport the image of Woman into fresh areas of experience, the first one being a celebration of marital love, the second having a seriocomic tone with few parallels elsewhere in Roethke's work. Both were written shortly after the poet's marriage, and they reveal his luminous sense of participation in the dance, "Celebrating the marriage," as Wallace Stevens said, "Of flesh and air."[15]

"Words for the Wind" happens to have been Roethke's favorite poem. "For those who are interested in such matters," he wrote in an anthology called *Poet's Choice*, "the poem is an epithalamion to a bride seventeen years younger. W. H. Auden had given us his house, in Forio, Ischia, for several months. . . . I was able to move outside myself—for me sometimes a violent dislocation—and express a joy in another, in others: I mean Beatrice O'Connell, and the Italian people, their world, their Mediterranean."[16] The poem is a paean to the beloved, written in a strong three-beat line reminiscent of Yeats; part of its success derives from the regular meter working against slant rhymes (odd/glad, down/own, beak/back). The first stanza sets the spirited tone, which never lets up:

> Love, love, a lily's my care,
> She's sweeter than a tree.
> Loving, I use the air
> Most lovingly: I breathe;
> Mad in the wind I wear
> Myself as I should be,
> All's even with the odd,
> My brother the vine is glad.
> (CP, p. 123)

Familiar themes crop up: the dancing which keeps the poet steady in the universe ("Motion can keep me still"); the way the spirit reveals itself in the shape of the beloved ("The wind's white with her name"); and the fact that the spirit stays after the material world has gone ("What falls away will fall; / All things bring me to love"). The last stanza contains Roethke's summary statement about love:

I kiss her moving mouth,
Her swart hilarious skin;
She breaks my breath in half;
She frolicks like a beast;
And I dance round and round,
A fond and foolish man,
And see and suffer myself
In another being, at last.

Roethke's readings in modern existential theology included the work of Martin Buber, author of *I and Thou*; he conceived of his relationship with Beatrice in these holy terms. The lover of "Words for the Wind" has an I-Thou affection for his wife, affirming his own being in the presence of another's. Buber explains:

Every *real relation* with a being or life in the world is exclusive. Its Thou is freed, steps forth, is single, and confronts you. It fills the heavens. This does not mean that nothing else exists; but all else lives in *its* light. As long as the presence of the relation continues, its cosmic range is inviolable.[17]

This passage is a perfect gloss to "Words for the Wind," for the poet-lover, a further extension of the lost son, learns to live in the light of another, to "see and suffer" himself "in another being, at last."

"I Knew a Woman" combines innuendo and wit in a way unique to this poem. It begins with a mask: the innocent lover who cannot but praise his love extravagantly: "Of her choice virtues only gods should speak, / Or English poets who grew up on Greek" (*CP*, p. 127). The next two stanzas develop a series of witty or "metaphysical" conceits; for instance, he compares two lovers to a sickle and rake (punning on rake) in the act of mowing (which has sexual connotations):

She was the sickle; I, poor I, the rake,
Coming behind her for her pretty sake
(But what prodigious mowing we did make).

This particular conceit alludes to Marvell's "The Mower's Song," and Roethke, like Marvell, "brings new life to the convention-ridden pastoral love lyric through the injection into his poem of the intellectualized sensuality of metaphysical wit."[18] In a similar vein, Roethke picks up metaphors from Ben Jonson in the next stanza, continuing the verbal play until the last, more serious, stanza in which the larger meaning of eros falls under scrutiny:

Let seed be grass, and grass turn into hay:
I'm martyr to a motion not my own;
What's freedom for? To know eternity.
I swear she cast a shadow white as stone.
But who would count eternity in days?
These old bones live to learn her wanton ways:
(I measure time by how a body sways).

The poet demands a great deal from his readers here, shifting ruthlessly from concrete particulars to abstract statements, making huge leaps of intuition. As in "The Waking," the subject is the dynamic quality of experience, the *process* of reality, man's "martyrdom" to natural cycles. The word "martyr" must be read ironically, for though a martyr dies, he is reborn to greater glory; likewise, the lover gives up himself to his beloved's "motion," gives up his "freedom," and learns what eternity means. Like mystics, in fact, lovers seem to participate in the eternal while still being in the temporal. The great success of this poem derives from the opening levity which distracts the reader *away* from the serious content until he is swept into the rhythm so completely that he becomes, in effect, a "martyr to a motion" not his own.

The desire to transcend the flesh dominates most of the love poems in *Words for the Wind*: an intimation of the mysticism to come in *The Far Field*. Indeed, in "The Sententious Man" Roethke scorns those lovers who refuse to go beyond the material world, remarking: "True lechers love the flesh, and that is all" (*CP*, p. 131). The truest lovers hear the cry of the spirit behind the flesh:

I stay alive, both in and out of time,
By listening to the spirit's smallest cry;
In the long night, I rest within her name—

As if a lion knelt to kiss a rose,
Astonished into passionate repose.

The identification of the beloved with a rose and the lover with a lion is traditional. The lion is "in his strength and wholeness . . . the only creature potentially able to attain Perfection."[19] The rose represents the highest form of spiritual reality. The same poem, a short one, hauls into its sphere a number of other classic mystical symbols, such as the alchemical "philosopher's stone": "I know the motion of the deepest stone. / Each one's himself, yet each one's everyone." The philosopher's stone, in hermetic lore, cannot be found; it must be *made*, like a poem. All things are contained within it, as Boehme explained:

In this stone there lies hidden, whatsoever God and the Eternity, also heaven, the stars and elements contain and are able to do. There never was from eternity anything better or more precious than this, and it is offered by God and bestowed upon man; every one may have it . . . it is in a simple form, and hath the power of the whole Deity in it.[20]

Still, "The Sententious Man" fails as a poem, for in spite of its procession of mystical symbols, it has no center, no deep image at its source. It lacks the organic unity found in most of Roethke's better poems. Whereas "I Knew a Woman" blends a comic with a serious note, this poem is either heavy-handed ("Is pain a promise? I was schooled in pain") or forcedly comic ("I'm tired of brooding on my neighbor's soul; / My friends become more Christian, year by year"). The title does not redeem the poem: it should be called "The Sententious Poet."

"The Pure Fury" fails in the same way and shows Roethke's inability to write *about* ideas:

The pure admire the pure, and live alone;
I love a woman with an empty face.
Parmenides put Nothingness in place;
She tries to think, and it flies loose again.
How slow the changes of a golden mean:
Great Boehme rooted all in Yes and No;
At times my darling squeaks in pure Plato.

Apart from the appalling contortion of the last rhyme and the unsuccessful mixture of general and particular statements, Roethke has merely borrowed some ideas from *The Courage to Be*:

Non-being is one of the most difficult and most discussed concepts. Parmenides tried to remove it as a concept. But in order to do so he had to sacrifice life. Democritos re-established it and identified it with empty space, in order to make movement thinkable. Plato used the concept of non-being because without it the contrast of existence with pure essences is beyond understanding. It is implied in Aristotle's distinction between matter and form. . . . Jacob Boehme, the Protestant mystic and philosopher of life, made the classical statement that all things are rooted in a Yes and a No.[21]

When Shakespeare turned North's translation of Plutarch's *Lives* into poetry, as he did in *Antony and Cleopatra*, he transformed the general descriptions of his original into terse, image-laden verse. Roethke has scarcely altered Tillich, except to butcher his abstractions into serviceable pentameters.

"The Renewal" contains some philosophical material, but this time the poet makes a poem of his ideas. He resurrects the "Lost Son" imagery to good effect; the self-as-tree returns: "I teach my sighs to lengthen into songs, / Yet, like a tree, endure the shift of things" (*CP*, p. 135). The ghost of Otto Roethke blows in with the wind: "The night wind rises. Does my father live?" But this time the son remains unshaken by such threats. "Love alters all," and the poet-protagonist feels secure in this new steadiness. "The Renewal" becomes, ultimately, a meditation on the power of love to freshen the sense of self—to affirm being in spite of non-being. The question arises, "Will the self, lost, be found again?" And the last stanza confirms what we might expect: love brings on a renewal of the self through mystic illumination of that self: "Illumination brought to such a pitch," says the poet, "I find that love, and I am everywhere." The mystic always gives up selfhood in the mundane sense of that term; he now finds himself, the *self*, everywhere, a kind of collective *consciousness*.

The section entitled "Voices and Creatures" finds the poet plagued by many of the old guilts; the ghosts return as "grey sheep" at the beginning of "The Exorcism":

> The grey sheep came. I ran,
> My body half in flame.
> (Father of flowers, who
> Dares face the thing he is?)
>
> As if pure being woke,
> The dust rose and spoke;
> A shape cried from a cloud,
> Cried to my flesh out loud.
> (*CP*, p. 147)

The "Father of flowers" is Otto, and he calls from a cloud as before. The second part of this poem is livelier:

> In a dark wood I saw—
> I saw my several selves
> Come running from the leaves,
> Lewd, tiny, careless lives
> That scuttled under stones,
> Or broke, but would not go.

This is the same "bug-riddled foliage" where the lost son hunted. In short, this poem is a later footnote to that central work, "The Lost Son."

"The Song" recalls "the small voice of a child, / Close, yet far away"

(*CP*, p. 146). As usual, the past will not let go. The poet's old selves, imperfect and fragmented, come running back to him, as in "The Exorcism." And so the speaker in "The Small" complains, "The dead will not lie still" (*CP*, p. 148). The guilt called up by these ghosts provokes a morbid speculation in "Elegy" (ostensibly written for Dylan Thomas):

> Should every creature be as I have been,
> There would be reason for essential sin;
> I have myself an inner weight of woe
> That God himself can scarcely bear.
> (*CP*, p. 144)

Perhaps the most vivid poem in this section is "A Walk in Late Summer," with its visionary last stanza:

> A late rose ravages the casual eye,
> A blaze of being on a central stem.
> It lies upon us to undo the lie
> Of living merely in the realm of time.
> Existence moves toward a certain end—
> A thing all earthly lovers understand.
> That dove's elaborate way of coming near
> Reminds me I am dying with the year.
> (*CP*, p. 149)

The language, though tending toward abstraction, is redeemed by the ingenious word play (the quibble on "lie" and the ambiguity of "Existence moves toward a certain end"). A singular intensity unites the whole. The poet links the mystical rose with the end of existence and the task for lovers: to unmake time.

The three animal poems that complete "Voices and Creatures" show Roethke's continuing obsession with the lower ranges of the phylogenetic scale. In "Snake," "Slug," and "The Siskins," the poet wishes to become like the creatures under contemplation. After describing the snake, for instance, he says:

> I longed to be that thing,
> The pure, sensuous form.
>
> And I may be, some time.
> (*CP*, p. 150)

In "Slug" he says, "I'm sure I've been a toad, one time or another" (*CP*, p. 151). And in "The Siskins" he merely leans forward, rapt in meditation, as the tiny birds skip over the flowers as "Light as seed blowing off thistles!" (*CP*, p. 152). This typically Romantic desire to identify with the natural world is ubiquitous in Roethke, and these animal poems remind us, especially, of Keats or of D. H. Lawrence, whose "Snake" may have been the inspiration for Roethke's poem of the same title. In these animal poems, the poet returns to the concrete world of *The Lost Son*, which gives this work a vitality missing in the philosophical poems. Instead of making general statements, Roethke (like Lawrence) embodies aspects of his own personality in the animals he writes about. These poems, slight as they are, point toward the fine sequences which bring *Words for the Wind* to a conclusion.

"The Dying Man (In Memoriam: W. B. Yeats)" is Roethke's homage to the master. As before, the lesson of the mask is practiced, especially in the opening section, "His Words," where the great Irishman speaks for himself:

> "My soul's hung out to dry,
> Like a fresh-salted skin;
> I doubt I'll use it again.
>
> "What's done is yet to come;
> The flesh deserts the bone,
> But a kiss widens the rose;
> I know, as the dying know,
> Eternity is Now.
>
> "A man sees, as he dies,
> Death's possibilities;
> My heart sways with the world.
> I am that final thing,
> A man learning to sing."
> (*CP*, p. 153)

The soul, we are told, has been cured in the sun and may be of no further use, yet "What's done is yet to come." The logic of this seems tenuous, only becoming intelligible with the proverbial aid of "Eternity is Now." Time, seen from the mystical viewpoint, is not linear but circular. At the center of the great wheel lies the hub, Eliot's "still point of the turning world," signified by the rose. The pressures of imminent death bring this paradox into focus; as in *East Coker*, the poet discovers his beginning in his end.

In "What Now?"—the second section—the poet asks, "What's beating at the gate?" He wants to know what lies beyond physical life now, as the voices of Roethke and Yeats come together in a single mask:

I burned the flesh away,
In love, in lively May.
I turn my look upon
Another shape than hers
Now, as the casement blurs.

Vision of the physical world blurs, which allows the speaker to transfer his attention from the beloved to God. But in the third section, "The Wall," an old ghost materializes: Papa. "A ghost comes out of the unconscious mind / To grope my sill. . . . " Using symbol clusters encountered earlier, Roethke associates the ghost of father with a wall, something which obscures, divides, or encloses. He also associates the wall with the mystical Dark Night of the Soul, and he calls himself "A spirit raging at the visible," a line glossed by a phrase from the Davies sequence: "The visible obscures." Reality, in the Platonic sense, lies behind the material world, behind the wall, behind the visible reflections of truth which prevent us from encountering the real thing, that Ultimate Truth which Roethke names "a dazzling dark behind the sun."

"The Exulting" recalls the ecstasy passages of the "Lost Son" sequence. The poet declares: "I love the world; I want more than the world / Or after-image of the inner eye." He had worked out this concept in an earlier notebook, saying that "The eye, of course, is not enough. But the outer eye serves the inner eye, that's the point."[22] As usual, illumination occurs in connection with *positive* images of the father, and this poem is no exception. The idea here is that each son *becomes* his father as he supplants him, which is a spin-off of the oedipal myth.

"They Sing, They Sing" takes the lost son one step further in his journey; we encounter the apotheosis of Woman and a return to the dance, which, as a metaphor, is almost interchangeable with singing. The new woman-image includes vestiges of mother, moon, and earth goddesses:

All women loved dance in a dying light—
The moon's my mother: how I love the moon!
Out of her place she comes, a dolphin one,
Then settles back to shade and the long night.
A beast cries out as if its flesh were torn,
And that cry takes me back where I was born.

This Woman resembles Robert Graves's White Goddess, who combines the triple qualities of mother, bride, and killer-hag,[23] or the traditional Greek goddess of three aspects: Artemis (the night-huntress), Hecate (moon), and Persephone (Queen of Hades). Roethke owned *The White*

Goddess and knew it well; his later work often invokes the symbol of the
moon when alluding to the feminine principle, especially as it suggests
his Muse. The woman in the above stanza is partly mother, tied to the
dolphin image taken from Yeats, although the beast who cries out has
associations with the beloved of "Words for the Wind" ("She frolicks
like a beast").

The inspired last stanza of "They Sing, They Sing" (which brings
"The Dying Man" to a close) sums up Roethke's thoroughly Romantic
belief in the necessity of the quest for self-affirmation in spite of the non-
being which threatens from without:

> The edges of the summit still appall
> When we brood on the dead or the beloved;
> Nor can imagination do it all
> In this last place of light: he dares to live
> Who stops being a bird, yet beats his wings
> Against the immense immeasurable emptiness of things.

The lengthening of the ultimate line to an alexandrine gives extra weight
to the final image. As Tillich said, "Emptiness and loss of meaning are
expressions of the threat of non-being to the spiritual life. This threat is
implied in man's finitude and actualized by man's estrangement. It can
be described in terms of doubt, its creative and its destructive function
in man's spiritual life. Man is able to ask because he is separated *from*,
while participating *in*, what he is asking about."[24] One must *dare* to beat
one's wings against the emptiness, accepting doubt as a condition of life.
As Tillich continues, "One takes the risk of going astray and the anxiety
of this risk upon oneself." So one avoids the extreme situation "until it
becomes unavoidable and the despair of truth becomes complete." This
unavoidable task for the modern writer is always the affirmation of being
in spite of non-being. Roethke accepts this responsibility and, in doing
so, places himself beside his older contemporary Wallace Stevens, who
concludes the "Notes Toward a Supreme Fiction" with a great affirmation: "I have not but I am and as I am, I am."[25] This stance should not be
mistaken for the self-absorption of Blake's Ulro; it is the self-affirmation
of the man-as-artist, beholding what he has created, including his *self*,
and declaring its purity. As Roethke would come to say in a very late
poem, "The Abyss," "Being, not doing, is my first joy" (*CP*, p. 222).

The last part of *Words for the Wind* contains the five sections of the
"Meditations of an Old Woman." They resemble in form and manner
the poems of *Praise to the End!*—although Roethke exchanges the mask
of the lost son for that of an old woman, for whom the poet's mother,
Helen Roethke, provided the model. The familiar motif of the journey

recurs: the literal journey is a ride on a bus, but the movement toward death is explicit. Like all Roethke's journeys, regression plays a part in the poem's direction. The heroine achieves partial illuminations, like the lost son, but she slips back toward that final apocalypse in death.

The "First Meditation" establishes the free verse rhythms which distinguish this sequence from the rest in the book. The concrete texture of reality which marked the "Lost Son" poems is recaptured to great advantage:

> On love's worst ugly day,
> The weeds hiss at the edge of the field,
> The small winds make their chilly indictments.
> Elsewhere, in houses, even pails can be sad;
> While stones loosen on the obscure hillside,
> And a tree tilts from its roots,
> Toppling down an embankment.
> (CP, p. 157)

Nature responds to the old woman's feelings, mirroring them. The external world reflects the internal: the Emersonian assumption. Yet there is no joy here; the old woman must journey toward the condition of unity, the moment of illumination. For now, "The spirit moves, but not always upward."

Blessing, whose study focuses on the "dynamic" quality of Roethke's verse, sees "Meditations" as the poet's attempt to "develop more fully the possibilities inherent in the use of a dramatic persona."[26] Roethke, having put on the mask of Yeats in "The Dying Man" now dons an antithetical persona, one that allows the imagination free play. The psychic delvings of the "Lost Son" sequence were fine preparation for this new journey, in which the old woman regresses and recalls younger days around the familiar greenhouse. She says, " . . . I seem to go backward, / Backward in time." She remembers:

> Two song sparrows, one within a greenhouse,
> Shuttling its throat while perched on a wind-vent,
> And another, outside, in the bright day,
> With a wind from the west and the trees all in motion.

Meditative poetry always begins in the memory, often symbolized by the wind. The two sparrows here, one inside the glass enclosure and the other outside, represent the Romantic dichotomy of interior and exterior realms. "One sang, then the other," as if they were echoing worlds. But the journey looks to be tortuous, proceeding much as

> . . . a salmon, tired, moving up a shallow stream,
> Nudges into a back-eddy, a sandy inlet,
> Bumping against sticks and bottom-stones, then swinging
> Around, back into the tiny maincurrent, the rush of brownish-
>   white water,
> Still swimming forward.

The "First Meditation" ends with the speaker's remembrance of chance insights, the occasional epiphanies she found at the end of a long day, "A flame, intense, visible." The open field served her well, too, as a place where illuminations often occurred. She concludes, "In such times, lacking a god, / I am still happy."

"I'm Here" follows, beginning in the memory and moving forward toward the present. Like the old woman of "Old Lady's Winter Words" she recalls a green time:

> I was queen of the vale—
> For a short while,
> Living all my heart's summer alone,
> Ward of my spirit,
> Running through high grasses,
> My thighs brushing against flower-crowns.
> (*CP*, p. 161)

But she acknowledges the deficiencies of adolescence, a time of waiting: "A longing for another place and time, / Another condition." She sees how every age group envies another, how one is rarely satisfied by the present except in those isolated epiphanies for which, she complains, she was often unprepared. One instance comes to mind; she was walking down a path once and caught her dress on a rose brier; bending over to untangle herself, "The scent of the half-opened buds came up over me. / I thought I was going to smother." One recalls the line from "A Walk in Late Summer"—"A late rose ravages the casual eye" (*CP*, p. 149). In both cases the speakers were unready for illumination and were either ravaged or smothered by the sensual experience which, if properly attended to, might have led them upward to spirituality.

A tentative resolution is reached in "Her Becoming," the third poem in the sequence. The old woman has "learned to sit quietly" and meditate. Roethke always respected the art of meditation, as his notebooks show. He wrote:

> Everything will be found to hinge finally on the idea of meditation.
> This idea has suffered a steady decline in the Occident, along with

the transcendent view of life in general . . . yet it is not certain that religion itself can survive unless men retain some sense of wisdom which may be won by sitting in quiet meditation.[27]

So the old woman proceeds, contemplating the details of nature, turning the images over quietly in her mind, learning that "There are times when reality comes closer: / In a field, in the actual air" (CP, p. 166). The symbol of the open field persists, and the clue-symbols of stones and wind are present. The last lines point to a state of equilibrium and self-assurance if not self-transcendence:

My shadow steadies in a shifting stream;
I live in air; the long light is my home;
I dare caress the stones, the field my friend;
A light wind rises: I become the wind.

The penultimate "Fourth Meditation" finds the heroine outside of herself again; she speculates on the meaning of her life, starting with a confession:

I was always one for being alone,
Seeking my own way, eternal purpose;
At the edge of the field waiting for the pure moment;
Standing, silent, on sandy beaches or walking along green
    embankments.
(CP, p. 168)

Yet her disposition to wait for the "pure moment" only just survives the unexpected demands of her past: "The dead make more impossible demands from their silence." She cannot escape from history, from the coil of memory wound up in her unconscious mind. This realization precedes the image of a lark rising songless from a stone: an aberration. Something is amiss. The familiar questioning section follows as the heroine turns the meditation inward:

What is it to be a woman?
To be contained, to be a vessel?
To prefer a window to a door?
A pool to a river?
To become lost in a love,
Yet remain only half aware of the intransient glory?
To be a mouth, a meal of meat?
To gaze at a face with the fixed eyes of a spaniel?

The self-definition begins abstractly, with geometrical shapes, yet descends into bitter specifics, " a meal of meat." The old woman feels contempt for herself, for no doubt she once fit these definitions. She goes on to scorn these conventional roles of women in society, the "match-makers, arrangers of picnics" who populate suburbia. She inquires, "What do their lives mean, / And the lives of their children?" Answers are not forthcoming, but one expects the usual voices of the dead to help out (as they helped out in the "Lost Son" poems when the hero was in trouble): "Near the graves of the great dead, / Even the stones speak."

"What Can I Tell My Bones?" completes the sequence and *Words for the Wind*. It takes up where the "Fourth Meditation" ends—on the note of uncertainty:

> Beginner,
> Perpetual beginner,
> The soul knows not what to believe.
> (*CP*, p. 171)

She asks, "Before the moon draws back, / Dare I blaze like a tree?" The question of self-affirmation is at hand, and the answer demanded is Yes. But the old woman, still, does not possess Boehme's resounding courage to affirm. She reports her internal divisions:

> The self says, I am;
> The heart says, I am less;
> The spirit says, you are nothing.

Tillich's advice to incorporate doubt within the context of faith could be useful to her; she declares "I am" but feels unsure of her belief in a supporting spiritual world. One recalls that she confessed to "lacking a god." But raw *need* draws her closer to faith than one would have expected at the outset of "Meditations:"

> I rock in my own dark,
> Thinking, God has need of me.
> The dead love the unborn.

This realization leads to various illuminations in the final section where she discovers the healing power of love, declaring:

> I'm released from the dreary dance of opposites.
> The wind rocks with my wish; the rain shields me;
> I live in light's extreme; I stretch in all directions;
> Sometimes I think I'm several.

This old crone recalls the "natural man" of Wallace Stevens's "Esthétique du Mal" who explores the physical world carefully and observes

the horizon's limits, all the while participating in a full life of the imagination, saying that

> . . . out of what one sees and hears and out
> Of what one feels, who could have thought to make
> So many selves, so many sensuous worlds,
> As if the air, the mid-day air, was swarming
> With the metaphysical changes that occur,
> Merely in living as and where we live.[28]

Released from what Milton called "the hateful siege of contraries," the
old woman experiences a final illumination, achieves the condition of
joy which brings most of Roethke's meditative sequences to conclusion:

> The sun! The sun! And all we can become!
> And the time ripe for running to the moon!
> In the long fields, I leave my father's eye;
> And shake the secrets from my deepest bones;
> My spirit rises with the rising wind.

"What came to me vaguely is now clear," she asserts, and calls this illumination "Unprayed-for, / And final." This remains one of Roethke's
most resolute endings.

The most obvious criticism of "Meditations" is that the voice of the
persona is more Roethke's than his mother's. In most of the stanzas, it
would be difficult to distinguish the old woman's psychic rumblings
from that of the lost son. The preoccupations are familiar, and are
Roethke's own. Where differences occur, they seem rather superficial.
Still, "Meditations" is one of Roethke's most interesting poems from
this period; the mask of Yeats is momentarily dropped, and that "anguish of concreteness" can once again be detected. The style often looks
forward to the Whitmanesque expansiveness of *The Far Field*; indeed,
Roethke himself wrote to critic Ralph J. Mills, Jr.: "I came to some of
Eliot's and Yeats's ancestors long before I came to them; in fact, for a
long time, I rejected both of them. . . . So what in the looser line may
seem in the first old lady poem to be close to Eliot may actually be out
of Whitman, who influenced Eliot *plenty*, technically . . . " (*SL*, p. 230).
One feels the growing presence of Whitman throughout "Meditations,"
in the bird imagery, in the catalogues, in the flexible long lines. The voice
behind the persona is clearly Roethke, Roethke-as-Whitman.

As a selection, *Words for the Wind* preserves the best poems from *Open
House*, *The Lost Son*, *Praise to the End!* and *The Waking*; new poems are
added, the love poems, the Davies and Yeats sequences, and "Meditations of an Old Woman." One finds in its pages a dazzling array of

personae, although the poet's own voice is never completely lost. The new poems extend and elaborate the basic myth of the lost son, incorporating the lesson of the mask, taking the poet on that long journey out of the self. The "dreary dance of opposites" becomes, in these new poems especially, the "universal round" of Sir John Davies, the dance of love that releases the hero from self-absorption. Love's proper exercise leads to self-transcendence, renewal, and the affirmation of being in spite of non-being. These are the lost son's final insights, the celebration of which provides the subject material for his last volume, *The Far Field*.

CHAPTER TWELVE

THE WAY OF ILLUMINATION

Illumination equals adjustment of outer life and inner life: equilibrium.

> Roethke, "Teaching Notes"

Self is the bridge. When man crosses that bridge, if blind, he shall see; if sick, he shall be well; if unhappy, he shall be happy. When he crosses that bridge, though it be night, it shall be day; for heaven is shining always.

> Chandogya-Upanishad 8, 4

The self must be a bridge, not a pit.

> Roethke, "Notebooks" (1945)

The publication of *Words for the Wind* put Roethke in the front rank of contemporary poets. Awards were showered on him: critics were, by and large, generous. Students flocked to Washington to study under him, and he received many invitations to read at colleges around the country. Yet the periodic bouts of mental instability which had plagued him earlier returned; as was suggested earlier, the problem seemed to worsen in direct proportion to his public success. On top of this, his physical health began to fail. In his letters, he complains of aches and pains, of sleeplessness, and of general irritability. Nonetheless, from 1959 until his death in 1963 he managed to publish sixty-one poems; many of them, in fact, were written in the Halcyon House Sanatorium itself. For this poet, writing poetry was a necessary and inevitable activity.

One of the fascinating aspects of Roethke's last years is his awareness of approaching death. In his last book, mortality threatens him more than ever before; "*The Far Field*," says Frederick

J. Hoffman, "demonstrates the extent to which Roethke had defined death to himself before the summer of 1963."[1] The effort to atone with God (and Otto) takes on a new insistence in his work; it is as if the poet knew of his death several years in advance. These poems fall into the tradition of the *ars moriendi*: they are, in effect, preparations for the final moments.

Not long before dying, Roethke wrote in his teaching notes: "Death is a fruit which each life bears; we must bring forth the death that is ours."[2] We may read these last poems as an effort to "bring forth" this death, which in Roethke's terms is more an apocalypse than a surrender. The mystical Way of Illumination begun in *Words for the Wind* now becomes central; the lost son moves out into the open field and readies himself for a final illumination. But unlike many traditional mystics, who seek release from the physical world into the realm of pure spirit, Roethke comes to what Hoffman calls "a peculiarly American 'stance,' the Emersonian confidence in *seeing* the spirit in matter . . . in a sense, in *creating* matter (or forming it) through the power of the transcending will."[3] Thus, as we read in *Nature*:

> He [the poet] unfixes the land and sea, makes them revolve around the axis of his primary thought, and disposes them anew. Possessed himself by a heroic passion, he uses matter as symbols of it. The sensual man conforms thoughts to things; the poet conforms things to his thoughts.[4]

Indeed, the apocalypse that Roethke conjures in *The Far Field* has its closest ancestor in *Sea-Drift* in which Whitman receives "The word final, superior to all" offered up by the sea: "Death, death, death, death, death."[5]

The Far Field is made up of four sections: "North American Sequence," "Love Poems," "Mixed Sequence," and "Sequence, Sometimes Metaphysical." Especially in the first section, there is a fresh expansiveness, hinted at earlier, but now in full strength. For the most part, the mask of Whitman replaces Yeats, allowing the poet freedom to catalogue as many "things" as he pleases. The open-ended meter permits Roethke's incredible verbal energy to spill over; after the tight forms of *Words for the Wind*, *The Far Field* breathes easily. The meditative genre dominates this last book as the poet perfects the techniques of "The Dying Man" and "Meditations of an Old Woman." Yet there is no real departure in subject matter; the myth of the lost son, with its personal symbology, is once again rehearsed. It is also extended. The long journey out of the self is, Roethke would have us believe, accomplished. The mystical ascent from flesh to spirit begun in the Davies sequence—up Purgatorial Hill—

reaches a conclusion in this last volume, which is Roethke's *Paradiso*. The final shape of Roethke's career remains uncannily perfect.

"North American Sequence" records a poet's attempt to transcend the sensual world, but not by denying it. In lines which recall many of the greenhouse poems, "The Longing" surveys

> A kingdom of stinks and sighs,
> Fetor of cockroaches, dead fish, petroleum,
> Worse than castoreum of mink or weasels,
> Saliva dripping from warm microphones,
> Agony of crucifixion on barstools.
>
> (*CP*, p. 187)

As Mills says, "The poet is at the nadir, sunk in a world of the senses, tormented by a hypersensitive awareness of physical and moral decay."[6] The poet wants to know "How to transcend this emptiness?" The meaning of the title becomes clear toward the end of the poem; he says, "I would with the fish, the blackening salmon, and the mad lemmings, / The children dancing, the flowers widening." And, still later "I long for the imperishable quiet at the heart of form." This is the poet's ultimate goal, the direction of his meditations. Nevertheless, in this first poem, the longings appear contradictory; nature partakes of no recognizable form; Roethke sees, instead, the Heraclitean flux.

Hugh B. Staples sees "The Longing" as an overture to the "North American Sequence":

> In a manner that suggests counter point in music, the principle of alternation controls the elaborate pattern of contrasting elements in the poem: body and soul, the sense of self and the release from subjectivity, earth and water, past and present, motion and stasis. . . . As in the *Four Quartets*, this dialectic operates within the individual poems as well as in the sequence as a whole, but each poem has its own dominant theme and mood, and presents a contrast to the poem on either side of it. The sequence, then, can be regarded as a tone poem consisting of an overture ("The Longing"), in which the major themes appear, followed by four movements in which the tensions and oppositions of the whole sequence are summarized and move toward a resolution.[7]

The allusion to Eliot is important, for in "The Longing" Roethke confronts his precursor directly, asking if "Old men should be explorers?" The themes that Staples singles out are also the focus of the *Quartets*, of course. Eliot's final vision of the mystical rose, the symbol in which all paradoxes find resolution, parallels Roethke's concluding poem, "The Rose."

In "Meditation at Oyster River" Roethke begins the quest for Illumination of the Self, which Underhill divides into three phases:

1. A joyous apprehension of the Absolute: still distinct from the self.
2. Clarity of vision: the phenomenal world becomes extremely visible and particular: heightening of perception generally: a sense of the true significance of the physical world as an external thing.
3. A strong sense of the transcendental self—psychic energy increases.[8]

Clarity of vision marks the opening section of the "Meditation at Oyster River":

Over the low, barnacled, elephant-colored rocks,
Come the first tide-ripples, moving, almost without sound, toward me,
Running along the narrow furrows of the shore, the rows of dead clam shells;
Then a runnel behind me, creeping closer,
Alive with tiny striped fish, and young crabs climbing in and out of the water.
(CP, p. 190)

The mask of Whitman is much in evidence; the seaside imagery consciously echoes such poems as "Out of the Cradle Endlessly Rocking," "As I Ebb'd with the Ocean of Life," or "On the Beach at Night," all of which represent stages of Whitman's own mystical journey. The catalogues of natural details suggest that heightening of perception which Underhill mentions. It is part of the prelude to the discovery of the "transcendental self" or the "self-beyond-self," the self which Roethke said "persists like a dying star."

The poet, in his meditation, seeks out the "pure moment" (which recalls Wordsworth's "spots of time"), the point of intersection of the timeless with time (Eliot's preoccupation in "The Dry Salvages"), the point of equilibrium which prepares the way for final illumination:

In this hour,
In this first heaven of knowing,
The flesh takes on the pure poise of the spirit,

Acquires, for a time, the sandpiper's insouciance,
The hummingbird's surety, the kingfisher's cunning.

The poem ends with an illumination not unlike that of "A Field of Light" from *The Lost Son* as the poet declares: "I rock with the motion of morning." In effect, identification has taken place. The inner and outer realms come into Emersonian alignment.

"Journey to the Interior" is a key poem in the "North American Sequence"; it recalls the earlier descents into infernal regions and becomes, as it were, a temporary detour in the long journey out of the self. As Roethke puts it,

In the long journey out of the self,
There are many detours, washed-out interrupted raw places
Where the shale slides dangerously
And the back wheels hang almost over the edge
At the sudden veering, the moment of turning.
(*CP*, p. 193)

The metaphorical nature of the journey is given immediate prominence, but the details rapidly make the car trip across the American West the poem's literal setting; Roethke evokes the local spirit of the Teton Mountains and the grassy plains with a rich panoply of images. In the final section the poet has a minor illumination, the sense of his "body thinking" (a wonderful version of Eliot's "felt thought"); he reports, "I have known the heart of the sun." And this knowledge must now be repossessed.

At the beginning of "The Long Waters," which follows, the poet disparages the physical "world of the dog," the lowest rung on the mystical ladder. He admits to a certain "foolishness with God" and an inordinate desire for "the peaks, the black ravines, the rolling mists"—all the extremes of experience (*CP*, p. 196). Invoking Blake's nurse Mnetha, Mother of Har, Roethke looks for that balance in nature provided by the anima, the feminine principle. The advice offered by the salt in *The Lost Son*—"Look by the sea"—is once again followed; the poet returns to the water's edge:

To a rich desolation of wind and water,
To a landlocked bay, where the salt water is freshened
By small streams running down under fallen fir trees.

The seaside stirs up memories of a place "Where impulse no longer dictates, nor the darkening shadow," the paradise before the fall into creation. Roethke's symbols of redemption—wind and stone—recur as, in the last stanza, he pictures a childhood idyll:

I see in the advancing and retreating waters
The shape that came from my sleep, weeping:
The eternal one, the child, the swaying vine branch,
The numinous ring around the opening flower,
The friend that runs before me on the windy headlands,
Neither voice nor vision.

He concludes, not by rejecting the physical world completely, but by absorbing it in Whitmanesque fashion: "I embrace the world." The progress we have seen from revulsion at the world to a vigorous acceptance opens the way for the title poem.

"The Far Field" gathers in summary fashion many of the smaller illuminations gained by the lost son thus far. It tells us nothing new about Roethke, nor does it widen his mythos; rather, like Yeats's "Circus Animals' Desertion," the poem enumerates old themes. It is the work of a poet bringing his career to a focus. Its subject is the self-beyond-self, the self which persists eternally, illumined by years of meditation. As before, the journey motif sets the poem in motion, and, as in the "Journey to the Interior," a car trip lends a note of realism to what might easily be a wholly metaphorical venture. We learn quickly that the journey is not taking place now; the poem is a *dream* of journeys. It is a record of the soul's progress from flesh to spirit, likened to

... driving alone, without luggage, out a long peninsula,
The road lined with snow-laden second growth,
A fine dry snow ticking the windshield,
Alternate snow and sleet, no on-coming traffic,
And no lights behind, in the blurred side-mirror.
(CP, p. 199)

This lonely passage through a stormy night by car is the contemporary counterpart to the more traditional image of the ship at sea in a great storm (as in Hopkins's "Wreck of the Deutschland"). The sense of human frailty against the violent strength of natural forces has always been a good subject for poetry (one recalls Roethke's own previous poem on this theme, "Big Wind"). The terror of being stalled in a snowdrift is unrelieved at the end of the first section.

Switching the scene to the open field near the greenhouse, and simultaneously dipping into memory, the poet revisits a familiar Roethkean landscape where, "at the field's end,"

Not too far away from the ever-changing flower-dump,
Among the tin cans, tires, rusted pipes, broken machinery,—
One learned of the eternal.

He recollects his childhood through the next long section of the poem, resurrecting the sensitive young boy who suffers for the animals and fishes; but there is some distance now in the voice that says:

> My grief was not excessive.
> For to come upon warblers in early May
> Was to forget time and death.

These are traditional Romantic sentiments, yet Roethke's lyricism gives them new life. The portrait of a young boy follows, one who lies down in the silt of a slowly moving stream and puts his fingers into an empty shell, thinking, "Once I was something like this, mindless, / Or perhaps with another mind, less peculiar." A believer in reincarnation, the boy straddles a wet log with his skinny knees and thinks:

> I'll return again,
> As a snake or a raucous bird,
> Or, with luck, as a lion.

Sullivan finds the tone of this passage hard to assess, calling it serious and nostalgic.[9] But far from indulging in sentimental longing for a previous state, the poet remains strangely detached, alluding to this time when he "learned not to fear infinity." She does, however, notice the underlying playfulness which is characteristic of Roethke at his best, and this is perhaps the most illusive quality in his work.

In the third section Roethke isolates and develops the associations of death and water that conclude the previous section; it is a meditation on death. The recollected past gives way to the present as the adult persona appears to be literally and figuratively in midstream. "I feel a weightless change," he says, "a moving forward / As of water quickening before a narrowing channel / Before the banks converge." The tree (self) now "retreats into its own shadow," which suggests that the speaker, in meditation, is tunneling inward. One remembers the ghostly voice from "The Lost Son": "Dark hollows said, lee to the wind." The speaker in "The Far Field" moves into an eddy, taking shelter from the force of the current. Again alluding to Eliot's *Quartets*, he says: "I have come to a still, but not a deep center, / A point outside the glittering current." Here is another of Roethke's irresolute resolutions. Yet there is paradoxically a sense of renewal in mortality:

> I am renewed by death, thought of my death,
> The dry scent of a dying garden in September,
> The wind fanning the ash of a low fire.
> What I love is near at hand,
> Always, in earth and air.

The sense of death as a passage provokes this optimism. Roethke savors that taste of the eternal that he finds in the temporal dimension, those little clues which go everywhere around us largely undetected. He catalogues them, much in the same way as did Whitman or, again, Eliot, in passages like the following:

> To be conscious is not to be in time
> But only in time can the moment in the rose-garden,
> The moment in the arbour where the rain beat,
> The moment in the draughty church at smokefall
> Be remembered.[10]

In the fourth and final section we are given an image of the protean self that survives time and circumstances:

> The lost self changes,
> Turning toward the sea,
> A sea-shape turning around,—
> An old man with his feet before the fire,
> In robes of green, in garments of adieu.

"The garb is symbolic," Blessing argues, "for the green of the robes suggests perpetual renewal, while the 'garments of adieu' hint at a ceaseless falling away."[11] This is the third stage of illumination, where a strong sense of the transcendental self is attended by an increase in psychic energy. Roethke goes on to describe "the final man" who emerges from this contemplation:

> His spirit moves like a monumental wind
> That gentles on a sunny blue plateau.
> He is the end of things, the final man.

Critics all point to Stevens's "Asides on the Oboe" as the source of Roethke's formulation:

> In the end, however naked, tall, there is still
> The impossible possible philosophers' man,
> The man who has had the time to think enough,
> The central man, the human globe, responsive
> As a mirror with a voice, the man of glass,
> Who in a million diamonds sums us up.[12]

Yet Emerson's notion of the "true man" who stands at the center of his culture and speaks with authority underlies both Stevens and Roethke; "The Poet," Emerson wrote in his journal, "should install himself and shove all usurpers from their chairs by electrifying mankind with the right tone, long wished for, never heard. The true centre thus appearing, all false centres are suddenly superseded, and grass grows in the Capitol."[13]

The poem's last stanza essentially expounds its first line: "All finite things reveal infinitude"—the main theme of the poem. It moves toward the beautiful summary lines:

> The pure serene of memory in one man,—
> A ripple widening from a single stone
> Winding around the waters of the world.

One thinks immediately of the notebook entry: "All the present has fallen: I am only what I remember." As the sum of the conscious and unconscious minds, the memory contains within its sphere the entire universe. And each man stands at the center of this universe sending out his imagination like the stone whose ripples widen around the world. Fully attuned to the harmonies of nature, this "final man" is also similar to Wallace Stevens's Nomad Exquisite who creates the world around her:

> As the immense dew of Florida
> Brings forth
> The big-finned palm
> And green vine angering for life,
>
> .   .   .   .   .   .
>
> So, in me, come flinging
> Forms, flames, and the flakes of flames.[14]

In Roethke's art the memory becomes, finally, a stage whereon the poem of the mind is enacted.

"The Rose," which brings "North American Sequence" to its conclusion, embodies Roethke's most complete presentation of the mystical Way of Illumination. Like Dante, Yeats, and Eliot before him, Roethke places the rose at the summit of his vision, suggesting that he has at last attained that "imperishable quiet at the heart of form" wished for in "The Longing." Three stages of illumination can be clearly discerned: awareness of the Absolute, heightened perception, awakening of the transcendental self. The poem opens with an emphasis on the physical place where this illumination happens; the poet says:

> There are those to whom place is unimportant,
> But this place, where sea and fresh water meet,
> Is important.
>
> (CP, p. 202)

Here the eternal and temporal realms intersect, and a whelm of images follows—a Whitmanesque catalogue of American birds. Special significance is allotted the kingfisher, whose wings flash in the sun (reminiscent of Hopkins's kingfishers catching fire). The meditator asks himself:

> Was it here I wore a crown of birds for a moment
> While on a far point of the rocks
> The light heightened,
> And below, in a mist out of nowhere,
> The first rain gathered?

The succession of images increases the poet's awareness of the eternal presence, the Absolute.

The second section takes us back to the greenhouse and the rose symbol as the poet explores memory once again. Meditation always takes one into the past, as we have seen. Now, standing by the sea, the speaker sees a "rose in the seawind." This rose stays in one place even as the wind blows over it: a still point of the turning world. This vision triggers the crucial memories of a childhood paradise. Roethke says:

> And I think of roses, roses,
> White and red, in the wide six-hundred-foot greenhouses,
> And my father standing astride the cement benches,
> Lifting me high over the four-foot stems, the Mrs. Russells, and his
>   own elaborate hybrids,
> And how those flowerheads seemed to flow toward me, to beckon
>   me, only a child, out of myself.

So he asks the central question: "What need for heaven, then / With that man, and those roses?" *There* was his earthly paradise, where Otto was God. Nothing more was needed. Through the use of memory—memory brought to new life via meditation—the lost Eden of childhood is restored; the "paradise within" promised to Adam by the Archangel Michael is realized.

The third section of the poem, in the usual manner of the meditative genre, provides a series of concrete details for contemplation. The Michigan landscape is recalled, its birds, flora and fauna, its various weathers. And Whitman presides over these stanzas like an attendent spirit; the flexible, long lines echo the master throughout. The poet says: "Beautiful my desire, and the place of my desire." He refuses to feel guilty about his desires; rather, he blesses their presence. This is a positive restatement of Blake's wonderful Proverb of Hell: "He who desires but acts not, breeds pestilence."[15]

The fourth and final section of the meditation brings the speaker back into the present; the Pacific Northwest seacoast replaces the Midwest landscape. The Absolute, embodied in the mystical rose, which is a literal rose swaying in the sea-wind, reveals itself. The poet's self, *not* merging with the Absolute (which would entail the final stage of union), gives way to the transcendent self. The poet says:

> Near this rose, in this grove of sun-parched, wind-warped madronas,
> Among the half-dead trees, I came upon the true ease of myself,
> As if another man appeared out of the depths of my being,
> And I stood outside myself,
> Beyond becoming and perishing,
> A something wholly other.

This is ecstasy in its root sense of being "beside oneself."

A summary image of the rose, "this rose in the seawind, / Rooted in stone, keeping the whole of light" completes the poem. We inevitably recall the final image of the *Four Quartets*:

> And all shall be well and
> All manner of thing shall be well
> When the tongues of flame are in-folded
> Into the crowned knot of fire
> And the fire and the rose are one.[16]

Both Roethke and Eliot attempt to "redeem the time," to discover the timeless moment *in time*, for—as Blake says—"Eternity is in love with the productions of time."[17] Roethke and Eliot rely on the same symbols: the kingfisher, the fire, and the rose; but Roethke eschews the Christian aspects of this symbolism. Whereas Eliot's symbols remain emblematic, Roethke's continually refer back to the literal level; his rose is a *rose for real*. Also, he does not share Eliot's concern for history; his personal history remains primary. Eliot, in this way, is anti-Romantic and consciously so.

As noted, Roethke's mysticism in general owes a great deal to Neo-Platonism, and his sea-rose bears close resemblance to the Plotinian One, the focus of all creation. Plotinus says:

> The One does not aspire to us, to move around us; we aspire to it, to move around it. . . . We are always around The One. If we were not, we would dissolve and cease to exist. Yet our gaze does not remain fixed upon The One. When we look at it, we then attain the end of our desires and find rest. Then it is that, all discord past, we dance an inspired dance around it.[18]

By substituting the word "rose" for "The One" in the above passage, a fair paraphrase of the last part of Roethke's meditative poem would be accomplished. "The Rose" as a whole must be praised for its sureness of rhythm, its clarity, and its concision; it is Roethke's finest poem in this vein. Of course, we are expecting the poet to do the impossible here, to describe the ineffable. But given the intractable nature of his subject, Roethke manages to convey something of his personal ecstasy. "The poem speaks for itself," says Staples, "and the skill with which all its elements are blended into one total impression of peace and harmony demands applause rather than explanation."[19]

The brief sequence of "Love Poems" which follows looks meager beside the "North American Sequence," with its vast spaces and detailed imagery. Nonetheless, a few poems stand out for their wit and passion. "Light Listened," for example, recalls the energetic word-play of "I Knew a Woman":

> O what could be more nice
> Than her ways with a man?
> She kissed me more than twice
> Once we were left alone.
> Who'd look when he could feel?
> She'd more sides than a seal.
> (*CP*, p. 212)

Yet one could justifiably complain about most of the late love poems. Roethke often falls again into the trap of abstraction, forgetting the lessons of his apprenticeship. Now some of his verbal ploys have become mannerisms; for instance, "A green thing loves the green / And loves the living ground" in this poem echoes a number of similar lines in earlier poems. "Her Words," "The Apparition," "Her Reticence," "Her Time," and "Song" are uninteresting, mannered, and less vivid than their counterparts in *Words for the Wind*. But one lyric, "Wish for a Young Wife," is of surpassing grace. Here Roethke identifies his beloved with a reptile, a creature of instinct. The age difference, which the title suggests, adds to the poignant sense of impending death highlighted by the last two lines:

> My lizard, my lively writher,
> May your limbs never wither,
> May the eyes in your face
> Survive the green ice
> Of envy's mean gaze;

> May you live out your life
> Without hate, without grief,
> And your hair ever blaze,
> In the sun, in the sun,
> When I am undone,
> When I am no one.
> (*CP*, p. 217)

The intensities of this poem—produced by the careful manipulations of vowel sounds and consonants, the breathless tone, the taut lyric structure, and the fierce emotion held in tight check—are all characteristic of Roethke in top form.

The same randomness from which the cycle of "Love Poems" suffers, especially by contrast with "North American Sequence," also plagues the "Mixed Sequence." The title, of course, prepares us for a miscellany, which is what we get. Familiar topics recur: the greenhouse, the father-florist, the need for a balancing feminine principle, the pure moment of mystical perception. Perhaps the most compelling of these poems is "The Abyss," which returns to many techniques first used in *Praise to the End!* The poem's subject is, again, the mystic's progress through the various stages described by Underhill. It opens with the speaker in the middle of a spiritual crisis of an unspecified nature; Roethke employs the traditional symbol of the stairwell (found in mystical poems from those of St. John of the Cross to Eliot):

> Is the stair here?
> Where's the stair?
> "The stair's right there,
> But it goes nowhere."
>
> And the abyss? the abyss?
> "The abyss you can't miss:
> It's right where you are—
> A step down the stair."
> (*CP*, p. 219)

This idea, the ever-presence of non-being, has been encountered before. But the abyss normally hides behind the bright objects that dazzle and mislead us into thinking everything is well. The first section ends with the wind slowing—the calm alerting us to an approaching storm.

As he encounters "that anguish of concreteness" again, the poet calls out:

Be with me, Whitman, maker of catalogues:
For the world invades me again,
And once more the tongues begin babbling.
And the terrible hunger for objects quails me:
The sill trembles.

He takes the caterpillar (a variant of his ubiquitous worm) for his chief symbol of mortality: "For I have moved closer to death, lived with death." He dissociates himself from the eagle or kingfisher of "North American Sequence," preferring now to consort with "a mole winding through earth" or a "night-fishing otter." He courts the dark side of the universe, believing that self-affirmation demands a confrontation with non-being. This is the stage Underhill often calls Purgation, which involves a "deliberate recourse to painful experiences and difficult tasks."[20] The effort recalls the lost son's earlier descents into infernal regions of the unconscious mind.

The third section shows the poet in temporary withdrawal from the objects for which he hungered previously. Echoing Eliot, he says, "Too much reality can be a dazzle, a surfeit." And he returns for imagery to the greenhouse, remembering an open door "in a florist's storeroom" and the subsequent "rush of smells." He laments the "terrible violence of creation" which, like Blake, he identifies with the fall of man. But he goes on to argue that meditation can restore the calm and clarity of pure consciousness; he approaches the Oriental concept of the empty mind, the mind "linked back" to its source, which is the ultimate goal of yoga and religion in general (re-ligio). This illumination, however, is temporary, and the world of objects invades once again.

So, in the fourth section, the poet re-enters the everyday world, asking "How can I dream except beyond this life?" as if to apologize for the withdrawal of the previous section. The texture of Roethke's language here resembles that of "The Lost Son," and this section parallels "The Return":

I envy the tendrils, their eyeless seeking,
The child's hand reaching into the coiled smilax,
And I obey the wind at my back
Bringing me home from the twilight fishing.

The rhythms and diction of this fine section are well tried. In a summary passage the poet says:

I rock between dark and dark,
My soul nearly my own,
My dead selves singing.

This warrants attention. For the two darks are one: the eternal emptiness at either side of life. The image is close to Underhill's description of the Dark Night of the Soul, the sense of Divine Absence. But there is a strange calm here, different from the sheer terror one associates with this stage (Hopkins's "Terrible Sonnets" come to mind). Roethke's meditator rocks through temporal existence now, almost in possession of his soul again after a lifetime's yearning. The speaker then receives supernatural aid as the shade advises: " 'Adore and draw near. / Who knows this— / Knows all.' "

The final section celebrates the renewal of self in a typical illumination passage, although the borrowings from Buddhism here inject a fresh note; the poet declares:

The Lord God has taken my heaviness away;
I have merged, like the bird, with the bright air,
And my thought flies to the place by the bo-tree.

Being, not doing, is my first joy.

It was under the bo tree that the Buddha gained permanent enlightenment, and Roethke clearly exaggerates his own experience by comparison. Nonetheless, his language is exalted and moving. The final rhythms suggest the influence of the King James Bible and one almost reads "hath taken" for "has taken." The concluding aphorism points to the abiding influence of Kenneth Burke; one has come to expect the final illumination to take proverbial form. As William Heyen has written of "The Abyss": "In this poem Roethke dramatizes, for an age that has lost its faith, an individual's hard and dark mystic way to God, whose essence he best perceives when he descends into and experiences the true nature of the Divine Abyss."[21]

A number of poems in "Mixed Sequence" re-create the greenhouse Eden. "Elegy," for instance, records the death of Roethke's Aunt Tilly who, like Mnetha, Mother of Har, was an attendent nurse-spirit. She "sat with the dead when the relatives left" and "tended the infirm, the mad, the epileptic" (CP, p. 223). Completely selfless, " . . . yet she died in agony, / Her tongue, at the last, thick, black as an ox's." In spite of a number of vivid lines, the poem lacks the unity of tone and well-wrought shape of Roethke's best work. And the passion that modified his "Elegy for Jane" is conspicuously absent here. Similarly, "Otto" is less vigorous than earlier poems that deal directly with Roethke's father; nevertheless, it gives evidence of this poet's abiding obsession with Papa. The portrait of Otto Roethke is largely anecdotal; we see the pig-headed man who

would never suffer fools gladly, who would chase poachers off his prop-
erty with a shotgun, and yet who could build a "house for flowers!"
(*CP*, p. 224). The poem ends with a moving remembrance of the lost
paradise; the reservoir of memory is suddenly tapped, and the poet is
nearly overwhelmed by nostalgia. The final couplet reveals the poet's
sense of inexorable separation from his greenhouse Eden:

> In my mind's eye I see those fields of glass,
> As I looked out at them from the high house,
> Riding beneath the moon, hid from the moon,
> Then slowly breaking whiter in the dawn;
> When George the watchman's lantern dropped from sight
> The long pipes knocked: it was the end of night.
> I'd stand upon my bed, a sleepless child
> Watching the waking of my father's world.—
> O world so far away! O my lost world!

The quest for a childhood paradise continues in "The Chums" with a
recollection of boyhood friends; some are now in prison, some are dead,
and none will have read his books. The poem has a chilly undercurrent,
for Roethke recalls that when he slipped on the ice they saw he "fell
more than twice" and didn't help (*CP*, p. 225). Yet he is "grateful for
that."

"The Lizard" brings the poet back into the present; he sits on a Mediterranean terrace, contemplating the odd creature who, like the poet,
has eaten too well. The poem is unexceptional. Its counterpart, "The
Meadow Mouse," a meditation on the capricious nature of evil, is better.
The last stanza calls up a view of the universe as startling and impersonal
(and cruel *because* of this impersonality) as Frost's "Design." Roethke
says:

> I think of the nestling fallen into the deep grass,
> The turtle gasping in the dusty rubble of the highway,
> The paralytic stunned in the tub, and the water rising,—
> All things innocent, hapless, forsaken.
> (*CP*, p. 227)

Three lyrics of mixed quality follow. "Heard in a Violent Ward" is
Roethke's effort to install himself, by association, in the exalted company
of Blake, Christopher Smart, and John Clare. "The Geranium," which
follows, offers a sentimental portrait of the artist as a "sensitive man."
The subject recalls the greenhouse poems, but by comparison this poem
is sloppy and self-conscious, bordering on self-parody. The poem's tone

is uncertain, as if the poet does not quite know how to present himself. The poem ends heavy-handedly, as the speaker claims to have fired his poor maid because she threw out a beloved geranium!

Most of the poems which follow, bringing "Mixed Sequence" to an end, exhibit what Keats called Negative Capability; the poet identifies with something outside of himself, losing himself completely in the object under contemplation, and thereby finding himself as well. The Emersonian doctrine of correspondences is a version of this technique of going beyond solipsistic self-consciousness. The longing for identification is, according to Stevens, the motive for metaphor; he says, "You like it under the trees in autumn, / Because everything is half dead."[22] In Roethke's "The Storm (*Forio d'Ischia*)" the lovers creep into bed with a storm whistling around their cottage; but the storm seems as much a part of them as something external:

> We lie closer on the gritty pillow,
> Breathing heavily, hoping—
> For the great last leap of the wave over the breakwater,
> The flat boom on the beach of the towering sea-well,
> The sudden shudder as the jutting sea-cliff collapses,
> And the hurricane drives the dead straw into the living pine-tree.
> (*CP*, p. 231)

The storm is terrifying, yet it seems a source of energy, a "violence without" which commands a necessary "violence within."

"The Thing" and "The Pike" follow, continuing the examination of violence in the natural world. In the former, a flock of large birds annihilates a smaller bird, "the thing." At first, they simply trailed it behind them:

> Then the first bird
> Struck;
> Then another, another,
> Until there was nothing left,
> Not even feathers from so far away.
> (*CP*, p. 232)

The poet draws an analogy between the birds who destroy the weaker one and some picnickers who eat veal and "little larks arranged on a long platter." The instances of violence (if one may call the picnic such) are presented without comment by the poet, starkly. He makes no value judgment. Likewise, in "The Pike" Roethke examines another dark aspect of nature, focusing on the fish which strikes from "beyond the end of a mossy log," disturbing the stillness of a pond (*CP*, p. 233). One could easily interpret this poem, like "The Lizard" and "The Thing" before it, as psychic allegory, reading the pond as memory that is disturbed by the fish as father. This dimension is present in a peripheral way. But Roethke seems more intent to work in the symbolist mode of Lawrence's *Birds, Beasts, and Flowers*. One thinks of poems like "Fish" and "Snake," where Lawrence refuses to be allegorical, concentrating on the animal under his aim, fixing it with an image. He presents the thing itself, drawing the reader into the object's magnetic field. The style of Roethke's poems, with their loose lines and sensuous imagery, recalls Lawrence specifically. As La Belle says, "Roethke borrows and yet modifies some of Lawrence's most characteristic technical devices."[23]

Of the last few poems in the sequence, "The Manifestation" and "The Moment" stand out as summary poems. In the former, the poet reflects:

Many arrivals make us live: the tree becoming
Green, a bird tipping the topmost bough,
A seed pushing itself beyond itself,
The mole making its way through darkest ground,
The worm, intrepid scholar of the soil.
(*CP*, p. 235)

That is, there are many points of illumination on the long journey out of the self. Roethke invokes a series of familiar metaphors for the protean self in this short lyric: tree, bird, plant (seed), and worm. In each case the organism strains to go beyond itself. Roethke then asks, adopting the tone of a professor: "Do these analogies perplex?" He offers four more examples, all of them images of motion within a larger context of rest, to make his point that the self is permanent, the transcendent self, and it must be viewed against the wider background of eternity. He concludes: "What does what it should do needs nothing more," repeating the Scotian doctrine of Gerard Manley Hopkins—namely, that each created thing should strive to accomplish whatever its limitations permit. In the metaphysics of Duns Scotus, creation is seen as *process* or becoming. In this view, the individual self never arrives at a condition of static being; rather, being involves constant evolution or becoming, the "seed pushing itself beyond itself." This does not contradict the final aphorism of "The Abyss," for being *is* becoming, which is opposed to mere "doing." One "does" the same things over and over. But being is a process, a continual widening of contexts, the ripples "winding around the waters of the world." And this process leads, as always, to the condition of joy proclaimed in the last poem in "Mixed Sequence," "The Moment": "What else to say? / We end in joy" (*CP*, p. 238).

This condition of joy prepares us for the decisive final "Sequence, Sometimes Metaphysical," where Roethke completes that long journey out of self by joining that universal dance alluded to in "Four for Sir John Davies." Mills has said that the poems of this sequence are, "because of their formal manner, condensed in the presentation of experience."[24] The poems focus on the moment of cosmic awareness for the most part, relentless in their inward drive. The mask of Whitman falls to the side; Blake, Yeats, and earlier mystical poets hover over this sequence. Unlike the other poems of *The Far Field*, these lyrics are spare, never descriptive; the poet wants nothing to attenuate the vision. Each poem is an act of attention, a revelation. The poet strips away the appearances to behold the reality that underlies the physical world.

The first poem in the sequence, "In a Dark Time," serves as a mystical prolegomenon to what follows. Critics have lavished attention on the poem; indeed, it was the subject of a symposium by John Crowe Ransom, Babette Deutsch, Kunitz, and Roethke himself.[25] The Yeatsean cadences, the dazzling imagery and underlying passion of the poem are impressive; yet its quality as a *poem* seems debatable. As an account of a mystical experience, it is certainly fascinating.

The poem moves from the Dark Night of the Soul to the final union with the Godhead. Underhill's description of the Dark Night parallels Roethke's:

> The "mystic death" or Dark Night is therefore an aspect or incident of the self's self-loss in the Abyss of the Divine Life; of that mergence and union of the soul with the Absolute which is the whole object of the mystical evolution of man. It is the last painful break with the life of illusion, the tearing away of the self from that World of Becoming in which all its natural affections and desires are rooted, to which all its intellect and senses correspond; and the thrusting of it into that world of Being where at first, weak and blinded, it can but find a wilderness, a "dark." No transmutation without fire, say the alchemists: No cross, no crown, says the Christian. All the great experts of the spiritual life agree—whatever be their creed, their symbols, their explanation—in describing this stress, tribulation, and loneliness, as an essential part of the way from the Many to the One.[26]

Thus, Roethke explains that, "In a dark time, the eye begins to see" (*CP*, p. 239). He meets his shadow in the shade, hears his echo in the familiar dark woods, this time an "echoing wood." By announcing himself "A lord of nature" who nonetheless weeps before a tree, Roethke hints at an ironic undertone of this poem which must be kept in mind lest we should value the surface of the poem too highly. The modern Romantic poet *needs* this saving edge of irony, however thin.

This seeming self-abasement gives way, in the next stanza, to a self-justification couched in Yeatsean rhetoric: "What's madness but nobility of soul / At odds with circumstance?" The persona goes on to proclaim the purity of his despair, but one wishes he had shown us his despair or made us despairing, as in "Elegy for Jane." The speaker has come to a crossroads, a "place among the rocks," a familiar Dantesque landscape, where one path leads to a cave (death), another up a winding path (Purgatorial Hill). The abyss presents itself.

The third stanza sets forth the Emersonian doctrine of correspondences and argues that self-loss is essential to a mystic aspiring to union with the Absolute. The "unnatural" luminosity of the Dark Night pervades the stanza:

> A steady storm of correspondences!
> A night flowing with birds, a ragged moon,
> And in broad day the midnight come again!
> A man goes far to find out what he is—
> Death of the self in a long, tearless night,
> All natural shapes blazing unnatural light.

And this leads, in the last stanza, to union. First, the soul is compared to "some heat-maddened summer fly" that buzzes at a window. The glass must be removed before the mystic can find the freedom of true reality. And the personal self must be relinquished. "The self, then," says Underhill, "has got to learn to be its own center and circumference: to make that final surrender which is the price of final peace."[27] Making the last inquiry into self ("Which I is *I*"), the poet-mystic ends his quest:

> A fallen man, I climb out of my fear.
> The mind enters itself, and God the mind,
> And one is One, free in the tearing wind.

"Fallen," of course, has to be read ironically. The fall is from flesh *to* spirit, hence, out of fear. The odd notion of the mind entering itself and God entering the mind is taken from Richard of St. Victor; it suggests the dissolution of all boundaries between self and soul, between soul and God. All contrarieties are resolved, and a new, somewhat terrifying freedom is gained. There is no guarantee that the condition of union will continue. The mystic, like anyone else, has to live in the temporal sphere while participating in the eternal one—until his final release in death.

The poem contains Roethke's most diagrammatic account of the mystic progress of the soul. Yet the bare fact remains that it is less believable than some earlier poems, such as "The Rose." It reads like a versification of Underhill's paradigm; abstractions obtrude everywhere. And the final stanza is embarrassingly self-conscious. One simply cannot equate Roethke with St. Theresa, Richard of St. Victor, or any other classical mystic. Like most other mystical poets, he attained illuminations, *intimations* of immortality; nothing more. With the possible exceptions of St. John of the Cross and Dante, poets rarely even try to portray the final union in their verse. Attempts to express this union in the language of poetry, as in Blake's Prophetic Books, often end in failure.

The remaining poems of "Sequence, Sometimes Metaphysical" expand or qualify particular sections of "In a Dark Time." The experience of terror which precedes the final union is the subject, for example, of "In Evening Air." The poet prays: "Make me, O Lord, a last, a simple thing / Time cannot overwhelm" (*CP*, p. 240). The poem is set at nightfall, around a campfire, and flames flicker off a wall (reminiscent of Plato's metaphor of the cave) which represents the veil between time and eternity, body and spirit. The poet reflects at the end: "How slowly dark comes down on what we do." In "The Sequel," which serves as an epilogue of sorts to "In a Dark Time," the poet wonders, perhaps justifiably, "Was I too glib about eternal things?" (*CP*, p. 241). Indeed, he was. Although the poem contains a number of irritating abstractions, it seems an honest effort by the poet to interpret his mystical impulses. The claims to transcendental vision are absent; the theme of lovers in their dance returns:

> We danced, we danced, under a dancing moon;
> And on the coming of the outrageous dawn,
> We danced together, we danced on and on.

Roethke slips back into the sensual world; the Absolute does not satisfy a living man permanently. The poem, in fact, records a failure of mystical penetration.

And "The Motion" confirms this failure. The poet cannot desert the call of his flesh; he needs earthly love, the base from which all lovers mount the Platonic scale: "By lust alone we keep the mind alive, / And grieve into the certainty of love" (*CP*, p. 243). This sentiment recalls the honeymoon lover of "Words for the Wind" who wrote:

> What time's my heart? I care.
> I cherish what I have
> Had of the temporal:
> I am no longer young

But the winds and water are;
What falls away will fall;
All things bring me to love.

So, in "The Motion," Roethke inquires, "Who but the loved know love's a faring-forth?" He appeals, like Wordsworth and Emerson before him, to the child's special vision, demanding, "O who would take the vision from the child?" Rhetorical questions abound, and one feels the lack of concrete imagery here, especially by contrast with the "North American Sequence" and its welter of objects. But the great Romantic themes continue in slightly altered form.

One never really expects a coherent philosophical system to emerge from any poet's work; every poem is a closed system in itself, a home-made world with private borders and necessary connections. But Roethke seems to have felt some guilt over his inconsistencies; in "Infirmity" he admits: "In purest song one plays the constant fool / As changes shimmer in the inner eye" (CP, p. 244). However, he justifies himself admirably: "I love myself: that's my one constancy." Self-love, perhaps, provides that singular passion which unifies his work as a whole. From here, the poet moves into a sordid portrait of his weakening body, as though the strengthening of his spirit required a diminishing of his flesh. With the fluid draining from a swollen knee and a shoulder pumped full of cortisone, the poet compares himself to an aged tree rotting from the inside out. Still, in the midst of physical decay, he takes comfort in the eternal presence: "The deep eye sees the shimmer on the stone; / The eternal seeks, and finds, the temporal." "Infirmity," like "The Sequel," rings truer than the more purely mystical lyrics; now the poet acknowledges the grave difficulties which accompany the Way of Illumination: "Eternity's not easily come by." Yet, he can observe at the last, "How body from spirit slowly does unwind / Until we are pure spirit in the end." A brief epilogue follows in "The Decision," where the same theme is summarized: "Running from God's the longest race of all" (CP, p. 245).

The abiding problem of relapse from mystical illumination back into a lower state of consciousness absorbs the poet in "The Marrow." He asks, "What's the worst portion in this mortal life?" and answers, humorously, "A pensive mistress, and a yelping wife" (CP, p. 246). The pure moment of union is certainly not sustained! But the poet refuses to give up the ascent; as he states: "Brooding on God, I may become a man." This brooding falls within the great tradition of religious meditation that underlies so much of Western poetry. Mystics are rare, but the end of meditation is not necessarily union with God. Its lesser, but nonetheless real, purpose is to kindle the affections, to awaken the sense of a Divine Presence. Meditation is that essential exercise which, constantly practiced, establishes a sense of self in relation to God. Thus, the final stage of any formal meditation is that of the colloquy or conversation with God. Hence, Roethke addresses the Absolute in "The Marrow": "Godhead above my God, are you still there?" And, later, "Lord, hear me out, and hear me out this day: / From me to Thee's a long and terrible way." As Malkoff and Sullivan have said, the notion of the Godhead above God occurs in Tillich's *Courage to Be* and that was probably Roethke's source for this idea, essentially a rhetorical device employed by theologians to account for the anthropomorphic aspects of the Christian God. It is a further abstraction from God, resembling the One of Plotinus.

The last poems of "Sequence, Sometimes Metaphysical" tell of hope restored, of renewal and final illuminations. The movement in "I Waited" is from a barren landscape to a bright seaside where a sense of gladness follows a long vigil. As in Eliot, the wind symbolizes the spirit; it presages rain, which is redemptive. In "The Tree, The Bird," which comes next, Roethke conjures once more the image of self-as-tree. The familiar voice calling from the cloud (God-Otto) is present. The bird has become a sign of the ascending spirit, as in the poetry of St. John of the Cross, Eliot, and others. The tree, rooted in the physical world, is prey to all motions of the wind. The bird is the soul arising out of the tree; it pierces the veil of heaven. (Roethke comes close to allegory in this metaphysical conceit.) A final illumination comes in the last lines: "Thus I endure this last pure stretch of joy, / The dire dimension of a final thing" (*CP*, p. 248).

Similarly, in "The Restored" the poet's soul enters the shape of a bird. But this time the bird has lost use of a wing; disaster seems at hand until, miraculously, the wing is restored:

> That delicate thing
> Grew back a new wing.
>
> And danced, at high noon,
> On a hot, dusty stone,
> In the still point of light
> Of my last midnight.
> (*CP*, p. 249)

"The Right Thing" is a villanelle, and it recalls "The Waking," Roethke's earlier triumph in this form. In the earlier poem, he had said:

Light takes the Tree; but who can tell us how?
The lowly worm climbs up the winding stair;
I wake to sleep, and take my waking slow.

That is, illumination often takes us by surprise. The tree represents the permanent self; the worm is the temporal and sensual self, struggling to mount the stair of time and get *beyond* time. But the process is acknowledged to be painful and slow. The poet recapitulates this theme in "The Right Thing," exuding a newfound confidence in the ultimate success of his spiritual journey:

Let others probe the mystery if they can.
Time-harried prisoners of *Shall* and *Will*—
The right thing happens to the happy man.
(*CP*, p. 250)

Roethke lays claim here to the Unity of Being which Yeats took for his goal. "God bless the roots!" says Roethke, "Body and soul are one!" Yet one cringes at this assertive tone. The earlier villanelle, which proceeds by an intricate series of highly concrete images and symbols, excels "The Right Thing" in every respect.

Fortunately, the last sequence and *The Far Field* itself end with Roethke's intense and moving lyric, "Once More, the Round." "What's greater, Pebble or Pond?" he asks (*CP*, p. 251). But pebble and pond partake of the same substance, as all things relate to the One, the ground of being. The poem celebrates Roethke's spiritual rebirth, his ongoing participation in the cosmic dance. Here dancer and dance are one; the "hateful contraries" are resolved: "And everything comes to One, / And we dance on, dance on, dance on." The poem contains all of Roethke's favorite symbols of the protean self: bird, tree (leaf), fish, and snail. It is fitting that the dance of love should bring his work to a close. As Underhill observed:

Man, once conscious of Reality, cannot evade it. For a time his separated spirit, his disordered loves, may wilfully frustrate the scheme of things: but he must be conquered in the end. Then the mystic process unfolds inexorably: Love triumphs: the "purpose of the world" fulfills itself in the individual life.[28]

The Far Field, which Roethke never brought into final shape before his death on 1 August 1963, remains an imperfect collection; yet many of its poems can be counted among his best, especially the Whitman-esque meditations of "North American Sequence." These last poems extend and refine the mythos of the lost son, taking the poet-hero beyond the dangerous clutch of self-absorption via the Way of Illumination. The long journey out of the self, begun in *Words for the Wind*, was at once tortuous and delightful; for, in spite of the terrors which seem necessarily to attend the Romantic on his quest for unity of being, Roethke's final message is ever: "All things bring me to love." American Romantic literature would be much the poorer without this posthumous volume.

PART FOUR

CONCLUSION

*To have paced out the whole circumference of modern consciousness,
to have explored every one of its recesses—this is my ambition, my
torture, and my bliss.*

> Nietzsche, copied by Roethke into his "Notebooks"
> *(24 January 1963)*

Roethke copied this epigraph into his notebook
in the last year of his life, perhaps identifying
his own task with Nietzsche's. Certainly the desire to explore consciousness in its entirety is
fundamentally a Romantic impulse. It would be
foolish to say that Roethke achieved as much as
this; yet he did search dim regions of the subjective mind with uncommon persistence. He
found in the recesses of memory those images
which perhaps could liberate him from the ruin
of his own past. His world view was deeply Romantic, following from Blake and Wordsworth
on one side, from Emerson and Whitman on
the other. Like his great contemporary, Wallace
Stevens, he was writing "the poem of the mind
in the act of finding / What will suffice." But
unlike Stevens, he was willing to settle for
nothing less than mystical union with the Divine Presence. In this ambition, he seems closer
to Emerson, who wanted his ideal poet to claim
everything:

> Every spirit builds itself a house; and be-
> yond its house, a world; and beyond its
> world, a heaven. Know then that the world
> exists for you. For you is the phenomenon
> perfect. What we are, that only can we see.
> All that Adam had, all that Caesar could,
> you have and can do. Adam called his
> house, heaven and earth; Caesar called his
> house, Rome; you perhaps call yours, a

cobbler's trade; a hundred acres of ploughed land; or a scholar's garret. Yet . . . your dominion is as great as theirs, though without fine names. Build, therefore, your own world. As soon as you conform your life to the pure idea in your mind, that will unfold its great proportions. A correspondent revolution in things will attend the influx of the spirit.[1]

Roethke built his own world, shaping his life to the pure idea in his mind. The contours of his private world can be studied in the *Collected Poems*, and this study provides a map of his wonderful, idiosyncratic planet.

Roethke's specific connections were Romantic, especially with the American visionary side. More so than any other contemporary poet, he carried on an exhaustive dialogue with his precursors. For this reason we have looked closely at the apprentice years to see how his early attitudes about originality and imitation were formed. There will always be critics ready to dismiss Roethke with a backhanded swipe: "He's an imitator." The response to this is, simply, that he *is*; but he uses imitation as a technique for liberating his own strongly original voice. "In a time when the romantic notion of the inspired poet still has considerable credence," he wrote, "true 'imitation' takes a certain courage. One dares to stand up to a great style, to compete with papa" (*SP*, pp. 69–70). Roethke has this courage, competes, and—sometimes—wins.

In all, *The Lost Son* remains the central volume, this poet's most durable achievement, and the key to his work. This is not to dismiss the love lyrics of his middle period or the best of his later meditative sequences, which deepen and extend the autobiographical mythos at the core of all his best writing, the quest for the greenhouse Eden. The cycles of death and rebirth are crucial here, providing the contrarieties that generate creative energy. The long poem sequences, Roethke's favorite medium, make constant use of this pattern; the poet's most basic movement is from desolation and fear to consolation and joy. In this, Roethke becomes a meditative poet par excellence.

It looks clear now that Roethke has earned a permanent place in the literature of American Romanticism. Finally, it is Roethke's fierce honesty with himself that illumines his best work; when he succeeds, it is because he has managed to speak directly about his most personal and, often, disturbing experiences. When he fails, it is because of self-deception or affectation. That he came to understand this truth about himself is evident in a moving fragment taken from one of his last, unpublished notebooks:

Teach me, sweet love, a way of being plain!
My virtues are but vices in disguise.
The little light I had was Henry Vaughan's.
I hunted fire in ice: the soul's unease,
In the loose rubble, the least glistening stone,
And what I found was but one riddled bone:
I move, unseeing, toward an absolute
So bright within it darkens all I am.[2]

NOTES

CHAPTER ONE

1. Some of the best essays in this area are collected in Harold Bloom's anthology, *Romanticism and Consciousness* (New York: Norton, 1970), and in *Romanticism: Vistas, Instances, Continuities*, ed. David Thorburn and Geoffrey Hartman (Ithaca: Cornell University Press, 1973).

2. *The Complete Works of Ralph Waldo Emerson* (Boston: Houghton Mifflin, 1903), p. 329.

3. Hyatt H. Waggoner, in *American Poets from the Puritans to the Present* (Boston: Houghton Mifflin, 1968), demonstrates the Emersonian influence on American poetry as a whole.

4. James McIntosh, *Thoreau as Romantic Naturalist: His Shifting Stance Toward Nature* (Ithaca: Cornell University Press, 1974), p. 29.

5. René Wellek, *Concepts of Criticism* (New Haven: Yale University Press, 1963), p. 160.

6. Louis L. Martz, "A Greenhouse Eden," in *Theodore Roethke: Essays on the Poetry*, ed. Arnold Stein (Seattle: University of Washington Press, 1965), pp. 14–35.

7. Denis Donoghue, "Roethke's Broken Music" in *Theodore Roethke: Essays on the Poetry*, p. 136.

8. *The Collected Poems of Theodore Roethke* (New York: Doubleday, 1966), p. 150. All subsequent quotations are taken from this edition and are cited as *CP* with page number in the text.

9. *The Collected Poems of Wallace Stevens* (New York: Knopf, 1954), p. 325.

10. Ralph J. Mills, Jr., ed., *On the Poet and His Craft: Selected Prose of Theodore Roethke* (Seattle: University of Washington Press, 1965), p. 11; hereafter cited in the text as *SP*.

11. Norman O. Brown, *Life Against Death: The Psychoanalytical Meaning of History* (Middletown: Wesleyan University Press, 1959), pp. 85–86.

12. All unpublished journal entries are taken from the Theodore Roethke Papers in possession of the University of Washington Libraries and are cited as Roethke Papers followed by box and file numbers and the date of the entry, where known; the entries quoted are Roethke Papers, 34–41, 8 January 1944 and July 1945.

13. Roethke Papers, 34–41, 8 January 1944.

14. Rosemary Sullivan, *Theodore Roethke: The Garden Master* (Seattle: University of Washington Press, 1975).

15. Roethke Papers, 35–66, 13 August 1945.

16. Ralph Waldo Emerson, *Selected Prose and Poetry*, ed. Reginald L. Cook, 2d ed. (San Francisco: Rinehart Press, 1969), p. 129. Subsequent quotations are hereafter referred to in these notes as Emerson, *Selected Prose and Poetry*.

17. Richard Allen Blessing, *Theodore Roethke's Dynamic Vision* (Bloomington: Indiana University Press, 1974), p. 68.

18. Karl Malkoff, *Theodore Roethke: An Introduction to the Poetry* (New York: Columbia University Press, 1966), pp. 63–109.

19. Harold Bloom, "The Internalization of Quest Romance" in *Romanticism and Consciousness*, p. 6.

20. Emerson, *Selected Prose and Poetry*, p. 5.
21. Ibid., p. 37.
22. Charles J. Smith, "The Contrarieties: Wordsworth's Dualist Imagery," *PMLA* 69 (1954): 1181.
23. M. H. Abrams, *Natural Supernaturalism* (London: Oxford University Press, 1971), p. 284.
24. William Wordsworth, *The Prelude* (1805), ed. E. de Selincourt (London: Oxford University Press, 1933), p. 39.
25. *The Complete Poetry and Prose of Walt Whitman*, 2 vols. (New York: Pellegrini and Cudahy, 1945), 1: 80.
26. Abrams, *Natural Supernaturalism*, p. 431.
27. Whitman, *Complete Poetry and Prose*, 1: 88.
28. Emerson, *Selected Prose and Poetry*, pp. 37–38.
29. F. W. J. Schelling, Introduction to *Ideen zu einer Philosophie der Natur*, translated and quoted by McIntosh, *Thoreau as Romantic Naturalist*, p. 51.

CHAPTER TWO

1. Roethke Papers, 32–1, 30 November 1930.
2. Allan Seager, *The Glass House: The Life of Theodore Roethke* (New York: McGraw-Hill, 1968), pp. 15–18.
3. Roethke Papers, "Annotated Books Collection."
4. Ralph J. Mills, Jr., ed., *Selected Letters of Theodore Roethke* (Seattle: University of Washington Press, 1968), p. 230. Hereafter cited in the text as *SL*.
5. Seager, *The Glass House*, p. 76.
6. Roethke Papers, 8–9, 1935.
7. Blessing, *Theodore Roethke's Dynamic Vision*, p. 5.
8. Ruth Limmer, ed., *What the Woman Lived: Selected Letters of Louise Bogan* (New York: Harcourt, Brace, Jovanovich, 1973), pp. 102–3.
9. Roethke Papers, 3–17, "Incoming Letters," 3 March 1936.
10. Limmer, *What the Woman Lived*, p. 169.
11. Roethke Papers, 3–18, "Incoming Letters," 3 August 1937.
12. Ibid., 3–19, "Incoming Letters," 28 June 1939.
13. Limmer, *What the Woman Lived*, pp. 56–57.
14. Stanley Kunitz, *A Kind of Order, A Kind of Folly* (Boston: Atlantic-Little, Brown, 1975), p. 78.
15. Roethke Papers, 8–33, "Incoming Letters," 31 January 1936.
16. Roethke Papers, 8–33, "Incoming Letters," 30 October 1935.
17. Jenijoy La Belle, "Martyr to a Motion Not His Own: Theodore Roethke's Love Poems," *Ball State University Forum* 16 (Spring 1975): 71.
18. Roethke Papers, 8–33, "Incoming Letters," November 1935.

CHAPTER THREE

1. M. H. Abrams, *The Mirror and the Lamp: Romantic Theory and the Critical Tradition* (New York: Oxford University Press, 1953).
2. Frank Kermode, *Romantic Image* (London: Fontana, 1971), p. 18.
3. Roethke Papers, 35–60, July 1945.
4. Ibid., 34–51, 1944.

5. Ibid., 34–62, 16 December 1946; 34–54, 1944; 34–49, 3 August 1944; 34–63, 26 July 1945.

6. John Keble, review of John Lockhart's *Life of Scott* (1838) in *Occasional Papers* (Oxford: Oxford University Press, 1877); quoted by Abrams in *The Mirror and the Lamp*, p. 145.

7. C. K. Ogden and I. A. Richards, *The Meaning of Meaning*, 3d. ed. (London: Kegan Paul, 1930), p. 149; I. A. Richards, *Principles of Literary Criticism*, 5th ed. (London: Kegan Paul, 1934), pp. 267, 273.

8. Roethke Papers, 72–20, "Teaching Notes"; 36–17, October 1947; 36–56, 31 March 1945; 34–34, 1943; 36–98, December 1947.

9. Ibid., 36–89, January-October 1946.

10. Preface to the *Lyrical Ballads, Wordsworth's Literary Criticism*, ed. N. C. Smith (London: H. Milford, 1905), pp. 21–22.

11. Roethke Papers, 55–18, "Teaching Notes," 6 September 1944; 62–2, "Teaching Notes."

12. Emerson, *Selected Prose and Poetry*, p. 130.

13. Kermode, *Romantic Image*, pp. 13, 60.

14. Roethke Papers, 65–19, "Teaching Notes."

15. Samuel Taylor Coleridge, *Biographia Literaria*, ed. George Watson (London: J. M. Dent, 1956), pp. 173–74.

16. Emerson, *Selected Prose and Poetry*, p. 136.

17. J. G. Herder, "On the Knowing and Feeling of the Human Soul" (1778); quoted by Abrams in *The Mirror and the Lamp*, p. 204.

18. Roethke Papers, 35–68, 23 October 1946; 72–19, "Teaching Notes"; 34–44, 1944; 36–88, 23 October 1946; 34–49, 1944.

19. T. S. Eliot, *Selected Essays* (London: Faber, 1932), p. 287.

20. Quotations taken from the verses preceding the Prospectus in its original place at the end of *Home at Grasmere*. Quoted by Abrams, *Natural Supernaturalism*, p. 21.

21. Whitman, *Complete Poetry and Prose*, p. 50.

22. Emerson, *Selected Prose and Poetry*, p. 137.

CHAPTER FOUR

1. Blessing, *Theodore Roethke's Dynamic Vision*, p. 40.

2. Malkoff, *Theodore Roethke: An Introduction to the Poetry*, pp. 32–33.

3. See Jenijoy La Belle, *The Echoing Wood of Theodore Roethke* (Princeton: Princeton University Press, 1976).

4. Yvor Winters, "The Poems of Theodore Roethke," *Kenyon Review* 3 (Autumn 1941): 515; quoted by Malkoff, *Theodore Roethke: An Introduction to the Poetry*, p. 35.

5. Manuscript from The Theodore Roethke Manuscripts Collection of the Pennsylvania State University Library.

6. La Belle, *The Echoing Wood*, pp. 13–16.

7. Sullivan, *Theodore Roethke: The Garden Master*, pp. 18–19.

8. A. O. Lovejoy, *The Reason, the Understanding, and Time* (Baltimore: Johns Hopkins University Press, 1961), pp. 137–38.

9. Roethke Papers, 32–4, July 1934.

10. Ibid., 34–38, 1943; 34–38, 1943; 34–53, 19 January 1945; 34–56, 31 March 1945; 34–65, 12 August 1945.

11. Ibid., 34–34, 1943.

12. Ibid., 34–39, 3 August 1944.

13. Ibid., 35–66, 13 August 1945.

14. Review of *Open House* in *Browse*, a publication of the College Bookstore of Penn State College, 8 March 1941, being an early version of a review to appear a month later in *Saturday Review*, 30 April 1941, p. 30.
15. Roethke Papers, 34–54, 3 March 1945.

CHAPTER FIVE

1. Kenneth Burke, *The Philosophy of Literary Form* (Baton Rouge: Louisiana State University Press, 1941), p. 63.
2. Wallace Stevens, *The Necessary Angel* (New York: Knopf, 1951), p. 118.
3. Geoffrey Hartman, *The Unmediated Vision* (New York: Harcourt, Brace and World, 1966), pp. 156, 155, 161.
4. Wallace Stevens, *Collected Poems*, p. 239.
5. Roethke Papers, 36–97, October 1947; 34–49, 3 August 1944.

CHAPTER SIX

1. See Abrams, *The Mirror and the Lamp*, chapter 8.
2. Coleridge, *Biographia Literaria*, pp. 173–74, 177.
3. Emerson, *Selected Prose and Poetry*, p. 127.
4. Roethke Papers, 34–42, 1942.
5. Kenneth Burke, *Counter-Statement* (1931; reprint ed., Berkeley: University of California Press, 1968); *Permanence and Change: An Anatomy of Purpose* (1935; reprint ed., New York: Library of the Liberal Arts, 1968); *Attitudes Toward History* (1937; reprint ed., Boston: Beacon Press, 1961).
6. Burke, *The Philosophy of Literary Form*, pp. 1, 3, 12.
7. Abrams, *Mirror and the Lamp*, pp. 138–48.
8. Burke, *The Philosophy of Literary Form*, p. 26.
9. Ibid., p. 36.
10. Burke, *Permanence and Change*, p. 151, n. 1.
11. Roethke Papers, 34–36, 3 April 1943.
12. William Wordsworth, *Poetical Works*, ed. Thomas Hutchinson (London: Oxford University Press, 1936), p. 460.
13. Brown, *Life Against Death*, p. 86.
14. *The Basic Writings of Sigmund Freud*, ed. A. A. Brill (New York: Modern Library, 1938), pp. 492, 493, 497.
15. Burke, *The Philosophy of Literary Form*, p. 258.
16. Lionel Trilling, *The Liberal Imagination* (Garden City: Doubleday, 1953), p. 61.
17. Quoted by Trilling, *The Liberal Imagination*, p. 44.
18. Freud, *The Basic Writings*, p. 722.
19. Quoted by Trilling, *The Liberal Imagination*, p. 53.
20. Burke, *The Philosophy of Literary Form*, p. 268.
21. Roethke Papers, 34–41, 8 January 1944; 35–65, 12 August 1945.
22. Burke, *The Philosophy of Literary Form*, pp. 269, 270.
23. Ibid., pp. 273, 278, 285.
24. Ibid., pp. 38–39.
25. Roethke Papers, 34–34, 2 February 1943.
26. Ibid., 34–46, 2 April 1943.
27. Ibid., 34–38, 25 December 1943.
28. Ibid., 34–39, 5 January 1944.

29. Ibid., 34–41, 8 January 1944.
30. Ibid., 34–45, 14 February 1944.
31. Ibid., 34–51, 1944.
32. Ibid., 34–52, 4 January 1945.
33. Ibid., 34–53, 19 January 1945.
34. Ibid., 35–54, 3 March 1945.
35. Ibid., 35–55, 4 March 1945.
36. Ibid., 35–56, 31 March 1945.
37. Ibid., 35–59, July 1945.
38. Ibid., 35–60, July 1945.
39. Ibid., 35–61, July 1945.
40. Ibid., 35–62, 25 July 1945.
41. Ibid., 35–63, 26 July 1945.
42. Ibid., 35–65, 12 August 1945.
43. Ibid., 35–66, 13 August 1945.
44. Ibid., 35–67, 20 November 1945.
45. Ibid., 35–68, 25 November 1945.
46. Ibid., 36–69, 1945.
47. Ibid., 36–70, 1945.
48. Sigmund Freud, *Beyond the Pleasure Principle*, trans. J. Strachey (London: Hogarth, 1950), p. 50.
49. Emerson, *Selected Prose and Poetry*, pp. 35–36.

CHAPTER SEVEN

1. Kenneth Burke, "The Vegetal Radicalism of Theodore Roethke," *Sewanee Review* 58 (Winter 1950): 52
2. Martz "A Greenhouse Eden" in *Theodore Roethke: Essays on the Poetry*, p. 27.
3. Roethke Papers, 35–59, July 1945.
4. Burke, "Vegetal Radicalism," p. 70.
5. *American Mercury* 56 (1943): 366.
6. Roethke Papers, 23–49, 1944.
7. Roethke Papers, 22–68. Roethke sent this poem to Katherine Stokes on 6 February 1944.
8. John D. Boyd, "Texture and Form in Theodore Roethke's Greenhouse Sequence," *Modern Language Quarterly* 32 (September 1972): 424.
9. Blessing, *Theodore Roethke's Dynamic Vision*, p. 70.
10. Quoted by Malkoff, *Theodore Roethke: An Introduction to the Poetry*, p. 49.
11. Sullivan, *Theodore Roethke: The Garden Master*, p. 27.
12. Roethke Papers, 34–32, 8 January 1944.
13. Malkoff, *Theodore Roethke: An Introduction to the Poetry*, p. 53.
14. Ibid.
15. La Belle, *The Echoing Wood*, p. 28.
16. Wordsworth, *Poetical Words*, p. 147.
17. Màlkoff, *Theodore Roethke: An Introduction to the Poetry*, p. 53.
18. Blessing, *Theodore Roethke's Dynamic Vision*, p. 79.
19. La Belle, *The Echoing Wood*, pp. 29–30.
20. Emerson, *Selected Prose and Poetry*, pp. 38, 6.

CHAPTER EIGHT

1. Roethke Papers, 36–9, 7 October 1947.
2. Mircea Eliade, *Myth and Reality* (London: Allen and Unwin, 1964), p. 79.
3. *The Basic Writings of C. G. Jung*, ed. V. S. de Laszlo (New York: Modern Library, 1959), pp. 116, 284, 287.
4. T. S. Eliot, *Collected Poems* (London: Faber, 1963), p. 63.
5. Thomas Mann, "Freud and the Future," *Life and Letters Today* 15, no. 5 (Autumn 1936): 89.
6. Joseph Campbell, *Hero with a Thousand Faces* (New York: World Publishing Company, 1970), p. 246.
7. Ibid., p. 383.
8. Mircea Eliade, *Rites and Symbols of Initiation* (New York: Harper and Row, 1965), pp. 3, 9.
9. Ibid., p. 9.
10. Roethke Papers, 34–50, 1944.
11. Mircea Eliade, *Myths, Rites, Symbols*, ed. W. C. Beane and W. G. Doty, 2 vols. (New York: Harper and Row, 1976), 2: 409–10.
12. La Belle, *The Echoing Wood*, pp. 90–91.
13. Eliade, *Myth and Reality*, pp. 80, 81.
14. Ibid., pp. 85–86.
15. Eliot, *Collected Poems*, p. 79.
16. Emerson, *Selected Prose and Poetry*, p. 6.
17. Roethke Papers, 3–35, "Incoming Letters," 3 October 1945.
18. Sullivan, *Theodore Roethke: The Garden Master*, p. 48.
19. Roethke Papers, 3–35, "Incoming Letters."
20. W. K. Wimsatt, *The Verbal Icon* (University Press of Kentucky, 1954), p. 115.
21. Emerson, *Selected Prose and Poetry*, p. 5.
22. Roethke Papers, 34–36, 1943.
23. Emerson, *Selected Prose and Poetry*, p. 36.
24. Sullivan, *Theodore Roethke: The Garden Master*, p. 50.
25. Burke, "Vegetal Radicalism," p. 95.
26. Martz, "A Greenhouse Eden" in *Theodore Roethke: Essays on the Poetry*, p. 35.

CHAPTER NINE

1. James Joyce, *Portrait of the Artist as a Young Man* (London: Jonathan Cape, 1958), p. 7.
2. Ralph J. Mills, Jr., *Theodore Roethke* (Minneapolis: University of Minnesota Press, 1963), p. 18.
3. La Belle, *The Echoing Wood*, p. 56.
4. Malkoff, *Theodore Roethke: An Introduction to the Poetry*, pp. 80–81.
5. Roy Harvey Pearce, "The Power of Sympathy," in *Theodore Roethke: Essays on the Poetry*, p. 183.
6. William Wordsworth, *The Prelude* (1805), ed. E. de Selincourt (London: Oxford University Press, 1960), chap. I, lines 344–50.
7. La Belle, *The Echoing Wood*, p. 46.
8. See Wimsatt, *The Verbal Icon*, esp. "The Structure of Romantic Nature Imagery."
9. Malkoff, *Theodore Roethke*, p. 99.
10. Wordsworth, *The Prelude* (1805), chap. VI, lines 566–72.
11. Sullivan, *Theodore Roethke: The Garden Master*, p. 75.

12. Emerson, *Selected Prose and Poetry*, p. 130.
13. Harry Levin, *James Joyce* (London: Faber, 1960), p. 162.

CHAPTER TEN

1. William Blake, *Complete Writings*, ed. Geoffrey Keynes (London: Oxford University Press, 1966), p. 623.
2. Richard Ellmann, *Yeats: The Man and the Masks* (London: Faber, 1961), pp. 175–76.
3. Joseph Campbell, *The Masks of God: Primitive Mythology* (New York: Viking, 1969), p. 21.
4. Emerson, *Selected Prose and Poetry*, p. 140.
5. Mills, "In the Way of Becoming: Theodore Roethke's Last Poems," in *Theodore Roethke: Essays on the Poetry*, p. 135.

CHAPTER ELEVEN

1. Robert Heilman, "Theodore Roethke: Personal Notes," *Shenandoah* 16 (October 1964): 62.
2. Roethke Papers, 72–20, "Teaching Notes."
3. Ibid., 35–84, "Teaching Notes," 6 April 1946.
4. Evelyn Underhill, *Mysticism* (London: Methuen, 1911), pp. 206–10.
5. See Emerson's essay on Plato, *Selected Prose and Poetry*, p. 187.
6. Roethke Papers, 34–36, 3 April 1943.
7. *The Confessions of Jacob Boehme*, ed. and trans. W. Scott Palmer (London: Methuen, 1920), pp. 27–28.
8. Malkoff, *Theodore Roethke: An Introduction to the Poetry*, pp. 102–3.
9. Roethke Papers, 72–26. Quoted by Roethke from C. G. Jung, *Contributions to Analytic Psychology* (London, 1928), p. 246.
10. Malkoff, *Theodore Roethke: An Introduction to the Poetry*, p. 114.
11. Sir John Davies, *Orchestra or a Poem of Dauncing* (1586) (Middlesex, England: The Stanton Press, 1922), p. 30.
12. Underhill, *Mysticism*, pp. 162–63.
13. Paul Tillich, *The Courage to Be* (London: Collins, 1952), p. 54. Malkoff and Sullivan consider Tillich's influence on Roethke at some length in their respective studies.
14. Blessing, *Theodore Roethke's Dynamic Vision*, p. 223.
15. Stevens, *Collected Poems*, p. 83.
16. Theodore Roethke, in *Poet's Choice*, ed. Paul Engle and Joseph Langland (New York: Dell, 1962), p. 99.
17. Martin Buber, *I and Thou*, trans. R. G. Smith (Edinburgh: T & T Clark, 1970), p. 78.
18. La Belle, *The Echoing Wood*, p. 121.
19. Underhill, *Mysticism*, p. 175.
20. Boehme, "The Threefold Ways of Man," quoted by Underhill, *Mysticism*, pp. 171–72.
21. Tillich, *The Courage to Be*, pp. 141–42. Cited by Malkoff, *Theodore Roethke: An Introduction to the Poetry*, p. 131.
22. Roethke Papers, 36–88, 23 October 1946.
23. See Robert Graves, *The White Goddess* (London: Faber, 1946).
24. Tillich, *The Courage to Be*, pp. 55–56.
25. Stevens, *Collected Poems*, p. 405.
26. Blessing, *Theodore Roethke's Dynamic Vision*, p. 118.

27. Roethke Papers, 36–63, 26 July 1945.
28. Stevens, *Collected Poems*, p. 326.

CHAPTER TWELVE

1. Frederick J. Hoffman, "The Poetic Shape of Death," in *Theodore Roethke: Essays on the Poetry*, p. 109.
2. Roethke Papers, 72–23, "Teaching Notes."
3. Hoffman, "The Poetic Shape of Death," in *Theodore Roethke: Essays on the Poetry*, p. 111.
4. Emerson, *Selected Prose and Poetry*, pp. 25–26.
5. Whitman, *The Complete Poetry and Prose*, pp. 242–43.
6. Mills, "In the Way of Becoming," in *Theodore Roethke: Essays on the Poetry*, p. 120.
7. Hugh B. Staples, "The Rose in the Sea-Wind: A Reading of Theodore Roethke's 'North American Sequence,'" *American Literature* 36, no. 2 (May 1964): 192–93.
8. Underhill, *Mysticism*, pp. 288–89.
9. Sullivan, *Theodore Roethke: The Garden Master*, p. 160.
10. Eliot, *Collected Poems*, p. 192.
11. Blessing, *Theodore Roethke's Dynamic Vision*, p. 153.
12. Stevens, *Collected Poems*, p. 250.
13. Emerson, Journal entry for 27 June 1846, quoted in Harold Bloom, *The Ringers in the Tower* (Chicago: University of Chicago Press, 1971), p. 218.
14. Stevens, *Collected Poems*, p. 95.
15. Blake, *Complete Writings*, p. 151.
16. Eliot, *Colleted Poems*, p. 223.
17. Blake, *Complete Writings*, p. 151.
18. *The Essential Plotinus*, trans. Elmer O'Brian (New York: New American Library, 1964), p. 84. From *Ennead* VI: 9 (9).
19. Staples, "The Rose in the Sea-Wind," p. 202.
20. Underhill, *Mysticism*, p. 205.
21. William Heyen, "The Divine Abyss: Theodore Roethke's Mysticism," *Texas Studies in Language and Literature* 11, no. 2 (Summer 1969): 1068.
22. Stevens, *Collected Poems*, p. 288.
23. La Belle, *The Echoing Wood*, p. 147.
24. Mills, "In the Way of Becoming," in *Theodore Roethke: Essays on the Poetry*, p. 128.
25. See Anthony Ostroff, "The Poet and His Critics," *New World Writing* 19 (1961): 189–219.
26. Underhill, *Mysticism*, p. 480.
27. Ibid., p. 475.
28. Ibid., p. 162.

CONCLUSION

1. Emerson, *Selected Prose and Poetry*, p. 38.
2. Roethke Papers, 42–210, 1962.

INDEX

Library of Congress Cataloging in Publication Data
Parini, Jay.
Theodore Roethke, an American romantic.
Includes index.
1. Roethke, Theodore, 1908–1963—Criticism and
interpretation. 2. Romanticism—United States.
I. Title.
PS3535.039Z76   811'.5'4   79–4022
ISBN 0–87023–270–3